THE AMERICAS IN A CHANGING WORLD

THE AMERICAS IN A CHANGING WORLD

A REPORT OF THE COMMISSION ON UNITED STATES-LATIN AMERICAN RELATIONS

with a Preface by Sol M. Linowitz

Selected papers by KALMAN H. SILVERT, STANLEY HOFFMANN, RIORDAN ROETT, JORGE I. DOMINGUEZ, ROBERT G. COX, DAVID RONFELDT, C. FRED BERGSTEN, ROGER HANSEN

NYT

QUADRANGLE / *The New York Times Book Company*

Library of Congress Cataloging in Publication Data

Commission on United States-Latin American Relations.
The Americas in a changing world.

Includes bibliographical references and index.
1. United States—Foreign relations—Latin America.
2. Latin America—Foreign relations—United States.
I. Silvert, Kalman H. II. Title.
JX1428.L38C65 1975   327.73'08   74-26014
ISBN 0-8129-0561-X

Contents

THE
AMERICAS IN
A CHANGING
WORLD

A REPORT OF THE COMMISSION ON UNITED STATES-LATIN AMERICAN RELATIONS

Julien Engel
Richard Fagen
Roger Hansen
Stanley Hoffmann
Ann Hollick
Robert Hormats
Roger Leeds
Theodore Moran

Henry Raymont
Riordan Roett
David Ronfeldt
Thomas Skidmore
Philip Trezise
Franklin Tugwell
Bryce Wood

Preface

When I was asked to assume the Chairmanship of this Commission, I had reservations about undertaking a new study of United States-Latin American relations. I knew that over the years, there had been a steady stream of studies setting forth proposals for U.S. relations with the countries of the hemisphere. Too often, those reports merely gathered dust on crowded shelves, disappointing those who hoped their recommendations might be translated into actions.

Not surprisingly, many of my colleagues also raised the question of why a new commission was needed at this time to study and report on United States-Latin American relations.

We came to the same conclusion: that the fundamental changes which have taken place in the world, within Latin America, and in the United States in recent years make timely—and indeed urgent—a reordering of relationships in this hemisphere. It was our conviction that these developments demanded a fresh assessment of the state of those relationships and of the premises upon which past U.S. policies have been based. They also called for new efforts to alter specific U.S. policies to reflect the changing realities of the 1970s.

In undertaking this project, we were encouraged by signs of

growing recognition in Washington and other hemisphere capitals that constructive regional relations are important to all of us. The meetings of Foreign Ministers in Mexico City, Washington, and Atlanta earlier this year opened a frank new dialogue between the United States and its Latin American neighbors. Settlements were achieved on long-standing bilateral disputes between the U.S. and Mexico, and between the U.S. and Peru. There was progress in negotiations toward a new Panama Canal treaty. These and other promising signs convinced us last May, when the Commission was established, that the time was opportune for a new study.

The Commission, twenty-three members in all, is an independent bipartisan group of private citizens from different sectors of U.S. society. Many have had extensive experience in Latin American affairs. Several have served in high governmental positions involving foreign policy. All have a deep and abiding interest in improving hemispheric relations.

The report that follows summarizes our findings and submits our recommendations after five months study, discussion, and sometimes heated debate. The report does not pretend to be all-inclusive. Instead it suggests an overall U.S. approach in the hemisphere, and attempts to give meaning to that approach by making specific recommendations for action on those issues deemed most important and troublesome.

Our recommendations are addressed to the people and government of the United States; we have not presumed to prescribe to Latin America. It is our hope that the report will stimulate discussion and consideration within the executive and legislative branches of the U.S. government, but also among citizens' groups, the media, scholars and businessmen throughout the nation. Broad popular support will be essential to bring about the kinds of policy changes we recommend.

The Commission drew upon a wide spectrum of informed U.S. and Latin American opinion as well as the varied individual experiences of its members in the course of our study. It would be impossible to express here our thanks to each of the individuals who have contributed to the Commission's work, but we owe a debt of gratitude to the many scholars, diplomats, officials of international agencies, journalists, businessmen, and others who gave the Commission the benefit of their expertise and advice. I also want to express, on behalf of the Commission, our appreciation to the Center for Inter-American Relations for its stimulus and sponsorship of this project, and to the Ford Foundation, the Rockefeller Brothers Fund, and the Clark Foundation for their financial support. Our appreciation also to The Arkville Erpf Fund for their contribution for the Spanish translation and to the International Nickel Company for their contribution for the Portuguese translation.

Finally, all of us on the Commission would be remiss if we did not extend our sincere appreciation to the Commission's Executive Director, Arnold Nachmanoff, and Associate Director, Ann Kieswetter, for their tireless efforts and many useful contributions. In addition, we would like to thank Abraham Lowenthal, Special Consultant, Gregory Treverton, Rapporteur, Ann Harrington, Research Assistant, and Deborah Witonski, Secretary, for their invaluable support of the Commission's work.

One final personal note. We, in the United States, too often see our neighbors to the South as a source of problems. I believe we would do well to consider how much the Latin American nations can contribute to solving the problems that beset all of us in this interdependent world. There are great talents, diverse resources, and a rich heritage of common ideals in this hemisphere. The United States and the nations of Latin America complement each other and need each other.

Luis Quintanilla, a distinguished Mexican writer and diplomat, referring to the Western Hemisphere, once wrote:

> Not only do geographical closeness and similar historical backgrounds bring us together, but we share in common an idea about the organization of society and of the world. In other words, to face the fact of America is to glance at any map. From pole to pole, from ocean to ocean, we are all in the same boat, we were created to live together.

A unique opportunity exists today for the United States and its neighbors to work together in shaping a world in which our common interests will be served and our common ideals advanced. It is my hope that this report will be a helpful step in that direction.

Sol M. Linowitz

Washington, D.C., October 29, 1974

Contents of the Report

9

I. *A Changed United States Approach to Latin America*

The United States should change its basic approach to Latin America and the Caribbean.

Dramatic transformations within Latin America and the Caribbean, major developments in the wider international arena, and significant changes in the terms on which this hemisphere relates to the rest of the world, all have undermined the assumptions which governed U.S. policy in the Americas from the Monroe Doctrine through the Good Neighbor policy to the Alliance for Progress and its successor, the Mature Partnership. We strongly believe that the policies which the United States has inherited from the past—including many of their most basic assumptions and goals—are inappropriate and irrelevant to the changed realities of the present and the trends of the future.

Consider a few examples of how dramatically Latin America* and the United States, and their relations with the world have changed in hardly more than a decade:

—Ten years ago, almost any form of cooperative action among Western Hemisphere nations required U.S. initiative and leadership; today, the effective functioning of the Andean Pact and other bodies indicates that Latin American countries are fully capable of cooperating in their own interest, without and, at times, against the United States.

—A decade ago, the United States was deeply involved militarily, economically, politically in many areas of the world and was about to embark upon a long and tragic war in Indochina; today, U.S. involvement in that war is over; the U.S. military presence overseas has been sharply reduced; economic and military assistance programs have been lessened; a "low profile" adopted.

—Ten years ago, the Cuban missile crisis was a recent memory and the Cold War was in full swing; today, relations have been opened with China; Soviet-U.S. trade is expanding dramatically; a process of detente is underway.

—Ten years ago, Latin American governments were, by and large, diplomatically quiescent and generally content to follow the lead of the

---

* In the interest of brevity, the term "Latin America" is used hereafter to include South America, Central America, the Caribbean and Mexico.

11

U.S. in the United Nations and other international bodies; today, the Latin American countries are moving out on their own in the world scene; Brazil aspires to a leading role in world affairs; and an active *intra*-Latin American pattern of diplomatic and economic interaction has replaced the situation in which all lines converged on Washington.

—Ten years ago, the dominant item on the agenda of U.S.-Latin American relations was U.S. concern about preventing the export of communism to Latin America; today, the dominant concerns of Latin American countries revolve around national development and access to the U.S. market for their exports.

—During the past decade economic dynamism rather than stagnation has been the norm for the region. In the early 1960s the region's gross domestic product was growing at an annual rate of 5.5 per cent (in constant 1970 dollars); since then the rate has been rising rapidly, reaching 6.9 per cent in 1972. Per capita product also rose from $420 in the first half of the 1960s to close to $600 in the second half. Growth in the manufacturing sector averaged 6.5 per cent during 1960–1961; by 1972, it reached 9.2 per cent.

In sum, Latin America has changed; the relations between Latin America and the rest of the world have changed; the relations between Latin America and the United States have changed; the role of the United States in world affairs has changed.

These changing realities suggest that the United States should adopt a new approach toward Latin America and the Caribbean, respectful of the sovereignty of the countries of the region, and tolerant of a wide range of political and economic forms. It should be concerned less with security in the narrowly military sense than with shared interests and values that would be advanced by mutually satisfactory political and economic relations, and free of the paternalism conveyed by the rhetoric of "special relationships" while remaining sensitive to the unique qualities of inter-American relations. Above all, it should be set in a consistent pattern of global economic policies genuinely structured to make more stable and equitable the terms of exchange between the most industrialized and advanced countries and the rest of the nations of the world, including those—many of them in Latin America—which are rapidly expanding their participation in the world economy.

This Commission realizes that a basic change in the U.S. approach to Latin America will not be easy to accomplish. Old assumptions and habits are difficult to discard. Lack of sustained official and general public interest in Latin America by the United States makes it hard to impress on our country's citizens, or even on its officials, how much has been happening in the Americas. But unchanging policies in the face of rapidly changing conditions is a sure recipe for trouble. Without such change, serious long-term problems could develop, to say nothing of short-term disasters.

The following pages expand on the reasons the Commission believes a new approach to Latin America is necessary and the steps it thinks the United States should take to bring its policies into line with the needs of the 1970s.

II. *The New Context of U.S.-Latin American Relations*

The international landscape is today dominated by three central features:

1. The Cold War no longer overwhelms all other issues for the United States, as it tended to do for 20 to 25 years after World War II.

2. Economic and related technological problems have assumed new significance, with growing awareness of both the regional and the global interdependence of nations.

3. The nation-state, nevertheless, remains the dominant political structure of the present era, although there is an increased recognition that national behavior must be made mutually compatible with that of other nations.

Each of these trends suggests the need for a new United States approach to Latin America. Any new U.S. policy must, of course, reflect national interests, but such interests will be served by collaborating with Latin America in a way that reconciles national goals of each nation with regional and global systems of interdependence.

A. THE GLOBAL CONTEXT

The global picture is changing. While the strategic political and military balance between the nuclear superpowers will continue to be a central theme in the foreseeable future, competition between the United States and the Soviet Union is changing as the two nations become increasingly burdened by the costs of nuclear competition and as they ponder the risks of nuclear confrontation.

The relative power of other nations has increased. These nations, including some in Latin America, are playing increasingly effective roles on the international scene. A freer play of forces and interests is developing in international relations.

These global shifts have had some basic effects on U.S. foreign policy. Technological advances in weaponry have reduced the need for overseas bases and alliances. The United States (and hopefully the Soviet Union) is increasingly sensitive to the need to keep local and regional conflicts outside the context of the superpower relationship, and to seek relative influence rather than the kind of absolute control which might precipitate nuclear confrontation. Revolutions in other countries and intra-regional conflicts no longer are seen automatically as battlefields of the Cold War.

The impact of the oil crisis of 1973, and the specters of commodity shortages and pervasive global inflation demonstrate the extent of interdependence among nations and the fragility of the international economic order. These concerns have begun to dominate foreign policy as governments try to protect the political, social, and economic well-being of their citizens. At the same time, actors beyond direct control of governments—multinational corporations, special interest groups, international agencies—are impinging on national societies to a greater extent.

It is now clear that no single nation, not even one as strong and wealthy as the United States, can attain complete economic and political security in today's complex, unsettled, and interdependent world situation. Nor can any group of nations control the processes and institutions which regulate international commerce and finance. Moreover, no nation can escape into self-sufficient isolation.

What is needed is greater cooperation among all nations, large and small. New approaches need to be developed to increase world food production, to assure a proper distribution of foodstuffs, and to reduce population pressures. New international approaches to control the use of the ocean and its resources must be evolved. The international monetary system must be revised to cope with such new realities as flexible exchange rates and massive transfers of oil revenues. Commodity practices and the transfer of technology all need to be studied and new formulas set up to govern these activities. Access to markets for manufactured goods are among the priorities of the more advanced developing nations, while large concessional aid and humanitarian relief is needed by the less advantaged nations.

U.S. relations with Latin America have taken on new significance in this changing global environment. The countries of the region will play an increasingly important role in confronting these global problems in the years ahead.

B. THE LATIN AMERICAN CONTEXT

As the Commission surveys the present state of Latin America, the most striking situation in the post-World War II period is the extent to which growth is evidenced everywhere in the area. Over the past decade, Latin America has experienced the fastest population growth—currently at an annual rate of 2.8 per cent—of any region in the world. If this trend continues, its current population of 300,000,000 persons will double in 25 years; that is, there will be two Latin Americans for every resident of the United States. This explosion of people has occurred simultaneously with sustained economic expansion, shown in these situations:

—Annual economic growth has, as a whole, exceeded 6 per cent a year since 1968—more than the hopeful planners of the Alliance for Progress had dared project. The economic performance of certain countries has been spectacular, with Brazil as a good case. Its manufacturing exports have been climbing recently at an annual rate of 85 per cent and have multiplied 20-fold since 1964.

—Foreign exchange bottlenecks which plagued Latin American economies for much of the past two decades have now largely disappeared for all but a few resource-poor countries with swollen oil bills and little to sell abroad. For most, foreign-exchange reserves have been accumulating because of high resource prices, expanded production, and a wide diversification of manufactured and raw agricultural exports.

—With the exception of the Caribbean countries (excluding Cuba), economic growth has reduced Latin American "dependence" on the United States. Of the total foreign trade of Latin American nations, 12.3 per cent was within the region itself in 1970–1972, as contrasted with only 8.2 per cent 10 years earlier. Somewhat over a third of the region's total trade is with the countries of Western Europe, Canada, and Japan. In the meantime, the U.S. share of the Latin American market has dropped from 38.5 per cent in 1960–1962 to about 32.8 per cent in 1970–1972.

—The relative importance of U.S. private investment in most of Latin America has also declined in recent years, and the type of investment has changed. Traditional massive investments in natural resources and public utilities have declined sharply, with U.S. money going more and more to manufacturing, distribution, and service industries. Moreover, European and Japanese competitors are playing a larger and more potent role.

It needs to be noted, however, that all countries in Latin America, and to some extent this applies especially to the most rapidly growing ones, suffer from very unequal distributions of wealth, income, and economic opportunity. Disparities are growing rather than diminishing. Political repression is sometimes used to maintain the hold of governments whose income policies do little to ameliorate the lot of the poorer classes in society.

In addition, the least developed economies are faced with an inability to keep up with rising world prices and ever more pressing internal demands. All Latin American nations feel themselves in need of improved access to rapidly changing technologies, and seek to protect themselves more effectively against the possibility that powerful multinational corporations will pursue interests deemed contrary to those of their host countries.

Whatever the weaknesses and problems, however, the overall economic situations of at least half the Latin American countries encourage a mood of optimism and self-confidence. Brazil is well on the way to becoming a major industrial power. Mexico has grown impressively and the recent oil discoveries make its prospects look even brighter. The countries of the Andean Common Market—Bolivia, Chile, Colombia, Ecuador, Peru, Venezuela—though buffeted by political currents, are strengthening their economic ties and beginning to gain advantages from the formation of an enlarged market area and from newly discovered resources. Venezuela, oil-rich and endowed with vast natural resources, is looking about the region and even beyond for ways to invest its earnings and exert its influence.

In addition to an improved economic picture, a second reason for Latin America's greater assertiveness is the emergence throughout the region of much more powerful national governments. The role and force of the state has grown sharply in Latin America during the past two decades: governments tax more, spend more, regulate more, prohibit more and influence more than Latin American regimes used to. Technocrats, civilian and military, have become a dominant influence in Latin American politics. Although the specific forms of government vary widely in today's Latin America, there is a trend toward various types of bureaucratic authoritarianism. Elite groups which in the past fostered close relations with the United States have been displaced in many countries by new nationalistic groups resentful of U.S. hegemony.

Despite the trend toward governmental authoritarianism, major new constituencies have entered the political and social process. Literacy has expanded significantly almost everywhere. University enrollments are exploding in most countries. The demand for newspapers, books, and journals is at unprecedented levels. And Latin America's intellectuals, particularly in the social sciences, are gaining a world audience for their theories and works. These crucial social trends are making possible mass political movements in Latin America.

Given these new political, social, and economic situations, the countries of Latin America and the Caribbean have entered much more prominently than ever on the world scene as independent actors. Most of the major countries have projected their diplomacy outside the hemisphere in ways that were unthinkable a decade ago. Many countries have generated close ties with the countries of Europe, East and West, and with Asian capitals. A few governments have taken important roles in various international arenas in some of which there is the potential for conflict with the United States. Perhaps more importantly, within the region the Latin American states have begun to collaborate diplomatically in international collective bargaining.

What needs to be recognized is that the majority of Latin American and Caribbean states are preparing themselves to fulfill a global international role, and not only an intra-hemispheric one.

One point should by now be clear about Latin America: the region includes many units and sub-groups, each with different traits and diverse relations with the United States. Some of the major countries share characteristics and interests associated more with the nations of North America, Europe and Japan than with the countries of the Third or Fourth World. These nations are highly urbanized, literate and industrialized societies, often with per capita incomes which compare favorably with some European nations. Other countries are still locked into the vicious cycle of desperate poverty. They remain dependent in part on the policies followed by their more advanced neighbors, whose economic and political decisions affect them sharply. Many of the countries are at intermediate levels of economic and social development. Some countries are expanding the participation of their citizens in the making of national decisions; others have been closing off participation in various ways. Some countries in the region are still very closely linked to the United States by long-standing patterns of economic and political interaction, or by the more recent intermingling of populations which results from sustained migration; others are increasingly oriented toward extra-hemispheric involvements and exchanges.

Despite this variety, however, the countries of Latin America and the Caribbean share an interest in beneficial relations with the United States. None of these countries has as great an impact on the United States as it has on them. But taken together these nations comprise an area of substantial importance to the United States and one that is increasingly effective in autonomously defining its interests.

C. THE UNITED STATES CONTEXT

If, as has been suggested, Latin America is changing and evolving, so is the United States. It no longer dominates world economic and military affairs as it once did. In some measure, this reflects changes at home, but it also results from changes abroad, not only in Latin America, but elsewhere. In addition to the Soviet Union and China,

Japan has emerged as a major industrial power, and a more cohesive Western Europe has become a major actor in world politics and economics. Finally, many Third World nations are now exercising an influence undreamed of a few years ago. This pattern of changing relationships and power structures can be expected to continue.

The experiences of the United States over the past decade, both at home and abroad, have contributed to the realization in this country that it is neither appropriate nor feasible for the United States to be policeman or tutor everywhere in the world. A "lower profile" has been adopted, and a new concept of the role and power of the United States in world affairs—one founded on a more realistic assessment of national interests—now characterizes U.S. foreign policy. The United States no longer exercises a veto power over the initiatives of its allies. The greater complications of mutuality, collaborative diplomacy, and flexible economic relationships will play a greater part in shaping future U.S. practices abroad.

Over the past 25 years, U.S. primacy in Western affairs has been achieved at high cost—contributing to inflation, a war orientation in industrial development, political discord, and extensive secrecy in government. It is no small wonder then, given an atmosphere of primary concern for national security, that relations with the less powerful nations, and Latin America particularly, were shaped largely by that concern. The Alliance for Progress was in some measure an attempt to accommodate security considerations with concern for the domestic welfare of Latin American nations. The Alliance was a reflection of both generous intention and Cold War considerations.

Of late, the United States has faced a variety of challenges: unemployment, racial conflict, the long war in Vietnam, and a major crisis of governmental leadership—all of which have seriously tested the coherence of the United States as a nation. This testing is likely to continue amidst the developing energy crisis, commodity shortages, and inflation now facing the world. All of this is bound to affect U.S. ways of thinking about the international community. What is most needed at this point is an international policy that will not further strain the nation, but rather contribute to solving some of these problems. Significantly, the process of nation-building in the Latin American countries also depends on the same sort of international policy. Thus, a commonality of interest exists between the United States and Latin America at this juncture. The shared experience of working to solve problems which the United States and Latin America face can only serve to strengthen ties between the peoples of North and South America.

III. *Toward a New Framework for United States Policy*

In suggesting that the United States alter its basic approach to Latin America, the Commission proposes no over-arching new program, with a list of proposals to be ratified in hemispheric meetings and presented to Congress for funding. To do so would excite expectations which might not be fulfilled. Rather the Commission seeks a new framework for U.S. actions toward Latin America, one which can provide guidelines for dealing with specific political, economic, and cultural issues.

This policy framework has to reflect the facts that:

—Latin American countries are and will remain extremely diverse in their ideologies, political systems, economic systems, and levels of development.

—Latin American countries are playing and will continue to play increasingly active and independent roles in international organizations and other arenas of world politics.

—Non-hemispheric states will play increasingly important roles in Latin American affairs.

—The principal issues of U.S. policy toward Latin America will increasingly be issues which are not peculiar to U.S.-Latin American relations but rather involve global economic and political relationships.

Given these changed conditions, the Commission urges that new U.S. policies in specific areas of U.S.-Latin American relations reflect the following broad principles.

A. U.S.-LATIN AMERICAN COOPERATION IN THE GLOBAL ARENA

The United States should no longer assume, as it often has, an easy or permanent mutuality of interest between ourselves and the countries of Latin America and the Caribbean. Common interests do indeed exist, but they need to be nurtured. At the same time conflicts and points of tension cannot be ignored.

In taking a more active role in global politics, the Latin American countries have at their disposal significant material resources, rapidly growing economies, increasingly integrated national societies, and a tradition of diplomatic skill. In addition, they can capitalize upon their historically close relations with the United States. Yet their identification, and the very real convergence of their interests with many of the countries of the Third World are also assets. The Latin American countries will thus be increasingly able to exercise leadership in international arenas which could in specific cases be either helpful or harmful to the United States. In pursuing this more active role, they obviously will act in their own self-interest.

For its part, the United States should act so that Latin American countries may find it in their interest to work with the United States in international bodies and to support a position compatible with that of the United States or, at least, not to take the lead in promoting opposition to the United States. The United States should, therefore, do what it can to adjust its policies in international arenas to take account of Latin American interests, and to attempt through a process of reciprocal support and mutual adjustment to develop effective working relations with the Latin American countries.

B. SENSITIVITY OF GENERAL POLICIES TO LATIN AMERICAN INTERESTS

The issues of primary importance in U.S.-Latin American relations are, in many respects, the main issues of general concern to industrialized and less-industrialized nations. These include such problems as the terms and conditions of private investment, trade and tariff preferences, commodity supplies and prices, the oceans, human rights, and the transfer of technology. In these areas, the United States cannot, by and large, have one policy for Latin America and another policy for the rest of the world. These problems are global, and they require global policies and global solutions. They are also, nonetheless, particularly critical problems in U.S.-Latin American relations.

Policy measures which are drawn up in general terms may in

practice have especially deleterious effects on Latin American countries. U.S. policy-makers should be sensitive to this danger and should avoid adopting general policies which, although not consciously designed to do so, impose particular burdens upon Latin American societies. The challenge here is to formulate policies which recognize the historic ties between the United States and Latin America and yet restructure those ties in terms of the increasingly complex global network of relations among industrialized and developing countries.

C. THE ELIMINATION OF PATERNALISTIC AND DISCRIMINATORY POLICIES

In the past, the disparities in size and power between the United States and Latin American countries have led the United States to adopt "special" policies towards Latin America in an effort to affect the behavior of Latin American governments. Other legislative policies, although phrased in general terms, have been in fact directed primarily at Latin American countries. Some of these policies—such as restrictions on military sales—have been meant to be beneficial; others—such as automatic sanctions in cases of expropriation—have been designed to be retaliatory. Whatever the intention, in the changed circumstances of today, such policies can only be viewed as paternalistic and discriminatory.

Consequently, Congress and the Executive Branch should, at a minimum, repeal policies which apply special restrictions or penalties to Latin America or which seek to impose on Latin American countries a U.S. conception of what is good for them.

D. RESPECT FOR HUMAN RIGHTS

Respect for human rights has been and should continue to be a prime concern of the United States. All nations in the hemisphere not only share common ideals of freedom, but also subscribe to the Universal Declaration of Human Rights. This internationally accepted code of conduct specifically condemns genocide, other atrocities, and infringements of the basic rights of citizens. Such actions, when sanctioned by governments in Latin America or elsewhere, generally lead to discord and instability. Therefore, while recognizing and respecting diversity and national autonomy in the hemisphere, this Commission holds that it is clearly in the interests of the United States, acting within internationally prescribed legal bounds, to make clear its opposition to such acts of injustice because they are wrong and because they are destructive of the mutual trust and civility which are essential to the effective functioning of both national societies and the international system.

E. COOPERATIVE ECONOMIC RELATIONSHIPS

In the past, broad U.S. policies toward Latin America, such as the Alliance for Progress, often reflected concern over possible threats to U.S. security from Latin America. At present and for the foreseeable future, Latin America poses no such threat. Military security, therefore, need not be the overriding goal and ordering principle for U.S. policy in Latin America. Economic issues instead will be the critical ones during the coming years.

Consequently, U.S. policy should give highest priority to working out mutually beneficial economic relationships between the United States and Latin America concerning investment, trade, the transfer of technology, and, particularly, U.S. access on fair terms to Latin American primary commodities and Latin American access on fair terms to U.S. markets for manufactured goods and commodities.

To implement these basic principles, the United States must alter many specific policies which no longer serve useful purposes. These suggestions are discussed in the following sections. In some cases, the Commission suggests departures from current trends; in other areas, it expresses its support for new initiatives—some of which are already underway. The range of issues is wide: from political matters, such as Cuba and the Panama Canal; to economic issues, including threatened or applied coercive sanctions in economic disputes, as well as the critical question of human rights in the nations of the hemisphere, north and south.

The Commission believes these specific policy recommendations taken together would represent a start toward creating a more constructive U.S. approach toward Latin America. But these recommendations for modification of existing policies are not in themselves sufficient. Building a reasonable basis for cooperation with the countries of Latin America requires more: it requires translating the new approach into positive new initiatives on matters of concern to the hemisphere, and to the world as a whole. The United States must act in ways consistent with both the changed nature of inter-American relations and with the requirements of global interdependence.

IV. *Political Relations*

A. NON-INTERVENTION, POLITICAL DIVERSITY AND HUMAN RIGHTS

The time has passed when the United States could justify, even to its own citizenry, the practice of intervention in Latin America. Unilateral U.S. military intervention, such as occurred in the Dominican Republic in 1965, must not be repeated. Covert U.S. involvement in the domestic politics of Latin America, such as occurred more recently in Chile, is indefensible and should be ended. U.S. national interests are not served by such activities for they are inconsistent with a mutually respectful world order in which governments are responsible for their own actions and policies. Overt or covert intervention by other nations does not necessarily justify employment of such self-defeating practices by the United States.

Verbal commitments to stop interventionist practices are necessary but not sufficient. International pledges through treaties and multilateral declarations are also helpful but are unlikely to add much to national commitments. Further safeguards against inappropriate governmental activities should be built into U.S. governmental machinery. Strengthened Congressional participation in the foreign policy-making and review processes may help to assure that all agencies of the U.S. government adhere to expressed national policy.

Recommendation:

1. The United States should refrain from unilateral military interventions in Latin America, and covert U.S. interventions in the internal affairs of Latin American countries should be ended. The President and the Congress

should ensure that all agencies of the U.S. government fully respect the sovereignty of the countries of Latin America.

Latin American nations will continue in the coming years to possess widely varying political and economic systems. Although such diversity in the hemisphere may sometimes directly affect U.S. interests, these tendencies clearly reflect the desire of nations of the hemisphere, north and south, to determine their own futures.

While the United States must reject both overt intervention and more subtle attempts to impose its own political preferences elsewhere, the United States should not be ambiguous about its own commitment to democratic institutions and liberties. But this does not mean that the U.S. government should withhold diplomatic recognition, use force, or apply economic sanctions on the basis of ideological affinities. It does mean that the tone of our relations and the broad range of our activities with countries should reflect the basic U.S. belief in the ideals of democratic society. The United States cannot afford to be reticent about its commitment to fundamental human values.

The United States should be clear, especially, about the obligations of all nations to protect the essential human rights set forth in the Universal Declaration of Human Rights. Those rights have been systematically and repeatedly violated in Latin America—as well as elsewhere in the world.

The Commission has been particularly saddened by the recurring reports from responsible sources—including church authorities, bar associations and other private groups—of arbitrary arrests, torture and the disappearance of political prisoners, secret trials and secret imprisonments in Latin American countries of varying political colorations.

The Commission cannot judge the accuracy of individual reports, nor can it know the extent to which the various actions described represented official government policy as opposed to the excesses of ineffectively restrained police and security forces. However, the Commission condemns such activities. These shocking departures from established international norms are matters for deep concern, particularly in a hemisphere whose nations share the heritage of simultaneous birth in the spirit of revolution against foreign tyranny and with common dedication to basic ideals of human freedom and respect for the rights of individuals.

Agencies, such as the Inter-American Commission on Human Rights, which aim to investigate reported violations, deserve full support. While internationally endorsed fact-finding and publicity cannot by themselves prevent the violation of human rights, they can surely make it more uncomfortable for governments to ignore established standards.

All governments, including that of the U.S., should take into consideration the findings of such international commissions and other evidences of systematic disregard for human rights in deciding on the substance and tone of bilateral and multilateral relations. Private and public expressions of disapproval of repressive practices are appropriate in specific cases. The doctrine of non-intervention does not bar the United States or other countries from reminding other member-states of the United Nations or Organization of American States (OAS) of their obligations with regard to human rights.

To the maximum extent possible, the U.S. government should try to assure that its programs do not aid or abet repressive regimes in carrying out inhumane activities. The Commission again stresses that ideolgical or political posturing or intervention should be avoided, but it is sure that consistent expressions of fundamental moral values are not wrong. Without them, the priorities attached to tangible interests may result in a slide toward moral blindness.

Finally, the United States should adopt—and should encourage other nations of the hemisphere to adopt—consistent and generous policies to welcome refugees who are victims of repressive activities. The right of political asylum was, until recently, universally respected in Latin America, but regrettably it is no longer. The United States should signal its intention to assist the afflicted within the limits of our national resources, whether the repression of which they are victims comes from the left or the right, from adversary regimes or allied governments. Expanding the U.S. emergency immigration program for political refugees would make that signal clear. The Commission does not believe, however, that there should be any sanctuary in the hemisphere for those who engage in hijackings or kidnappings.

Recommendations:

2. The United States should urge all states in the region to provide free access and essential guarantees to the Inter-American Commission on Human Rights. It should support efforts to strengthen the staff and enhance the prestige of the Commission, and should help assure that the Commission's reports are fully publicized and discussed in the OAS General Assembly.

3. The United States should press for the investigation of reported violations of human rights by appropriate international commissions, and it should take the findings of those groups into account in deciding on the substance and tone of its bilateral and multilateral relations.

4. As a demonstration of its determination to do what it can to alleviate the distress caused by political repression, the United States should expand its emergency immigration program for political refugees, whether those refugees flee oppression of the left or right.

B. CUBA

For almost fifteen years, United States policy has attempted to isolate Cuba politically and economically. The stated U.S. objectives have been to thwart Cuba's export of revolution to other Latin American countries and to reduce Cuba's military ties with the Soviet Union. In addition to these explicit goals, there was, no doubt, an ideological desire to minimize the potential success of the Castro government and thereby to limit the appeal of Cuba's revolution as a development model.

Despite significant changes in Cuban, hemispheric, and global conditions, the United States has continued (with decreasing effect) to try to keep Cuba isolated within the hemisphere. Even though the Cuban government consolidated its power and modified some of its policies, and U.S. relations with the Soviet Union and China moved from Cold War to accommodation, Washington's Cuban policy continued essentially unchanged.

The Commission does not believe a continuation of the policy of isolation with regard to Cuba meaningfully advances any current U.S. interests. Politically, the United States runs the risk of becoming the country which is isolated as one Latin American country after another renews relations with Cuba. Economically, the U.S. embargo is ineffective; it may serve as much to deny American manufacturers a chance to compete for exports as it does to deprive the Cuban regime of supplies.

And if the U.S. policy were more effective, it would be inconsistent with the aim of creating a peaceful structure of international cooperation which all nations, regardless of ideology, have an incentive to maintain.

The objective of U.S. policy should be to facilitate Cuba's participation in a constructive pattern of inter-American and international relations, and to reduce Cuba's incentive to promote violent subversion elsewhere in the hemisphere or to make military facilities available to the Soviet Union. While there can be no guarantee of success, the Commission believes these objectives are more likely to be achieved by encouraging hemispheric trade relations and other contacts with Cuba than by isolating the island.

Whatever the case in the early 1960s, Cuba's material support of subversive movements in other Latin American countries has diminished in recent years. Its residual activities appear to be largely rhetorical; they do not now threaten the security of the United States nor of the Latin American countries. Establishing mutually beneficial relations with the countries of the hemisphere should provide further incentives to Cuba to maintain proper relations.

Preventing the possible expansion or potential use of Soviet military facilities in Cuba is, of course, a legitimate concern of the United States, but this is primarily a function of U.S.-Soviet relations, not U.S.-Cuban relations. To the extent that Cuba has the ability to diminish the level of Russia's military involvement there, it has little incentive to seek such a reduction until its relations with the United States improve.

The United States has acknowledged elsewhere in the world that it should not define the limits of ideological diversity for other nations. That principle should now be applied to Cuba. Latin Americans can and will assess for themselves the merits and disadvantages of the Cuban approach; the United States need not try to do this for them.

The United States can and should continue to express its strong opposition to authoritarian practices, in Cuba and elsewhere, which violate the essential human rights of individuals. As the Commission's previous statement on human rights urged, it is crucial that the United States find effective means for making its views influential, including the mobilization of informed international opinion, which may affect national policies. The U.S. policy of "economic denial" has had no such positive results; on the contrary, the embargo indiscriminately and adversely affects the lives of innocent Cuban men, women, and children. Far from weakening the present regime, the embargo (and U.S. attempts to limit travel, contacts, and exchanges with Cubans) makes it easier for the Cuban government to justify and prolong its tight control over the intellectual and political activities of the Cuban people.

A further hope is that ending Cuba's isolation may contribute to an eventual reconciliation among the Cuban communities on the island and in the United States and other countries of the hemisphere.

Recommendation:

5. The United States should take the initiative in seeking a more normal relationship with Cuba. While emphasizing that progress toward improved relations requires positive action on both sides, the Commission urges that the United States act now to end the trade embargo.

This recommended U.S. initiative toward Cuba should be implemented in conjunction with the Latin American countries. At the earliest opportunity—presumably the forthcoming Meeting of Foreign Ministers of the Organization of American States—the United States should consult with other OAS members, indicating its willingness to support repeal of the measures against Cuba adopted at the Ninth Meeting of Consultation of Ministers of Foreign Affairs in July 1964. Assuming that the OAS resolutions are repealed, the U.S. government should then revoke Executive regulations restricting trade between the United States and Cuba and ought to act, within the President's discretionary authority, to suspend any legislative provisions which penalize third countries for trading with Cuba.

Regardless of progress or a Cuban response in other areas, the United States, taking into consideration its discussions with other OAS members, should move quickly to: (a) drop its restriction on travel to and from Cuba; (b) make evident its willingness to permit cultural, scientific, and educational exchanges on a non-official basis; and (c) make clear its willingness to improve cooperative arrangements with Cuba on practical matters of mutual concern, such as hijacking and weather watching, and to negotiate on such additional matters as may be indicated. Appropriate opportunities should be taken for dealing with Cuba informally within international organizations. The United States government should encourage and facilitate, not discourage, non-official cultural exchanges and other forms of contact.

If and when Cuba's response permits, the Commission believes the President should be prepared to take other Executive actions and to seek whatever legislative changes may be necessary to facilitate commercial and cultural relations with Cuba. We should also be prepared to consider renewal of bilateral diplomatic relations as well as other steps to facilitate Cuba's integration into a constructive pattern of inter-American relationships.

When both Cuba and the United States have taken conciliatory steps toward constructive relations, it should be possible to resolve outstanding issues, such as securing compensation for expropriated U.S. properties, agreeing on the status of the U.S. base at Guantanamo, and fostering reconciliation among separated elements of the Cuban community.

C. PANAMA AND THE PANAMA CANAL

The terms of the 1903 treaty between the United States and Panama are a constant source of friction between the two countries and increasingly have come to be viewed by other Latin Americans as symbolic of a distasteful bygone era in American diplomacy.

The treaty ceded perpetual control—"as if it were sovereign"—over five hundred square miles of Panamanian territory to the United States. It effectively made the Canal Zone a "state within a state," an American community administered by the U.S. government in the middle of Panama. In its present form, the Zone is viewed by Panamanians of all political persuasions as an undesired colonial enclave and an affront to Panama's national dignity.

In the ten-mile wide Zone, which bisects Panama, the United States maintains courts and police which enforce U.S. laws on Panamanians as well as North Americans. The United States, through a military governor, operates nearly all commercial enterprises in the Zone, controls large tracts of unused land and manages virtually all the deepwater port facilities in Panama as part of the maintenance and operation of the Canal. It maintains substantial military facilities in the Zone, including the U.S. Southern Command.

Given present day international realities, the Canal Zone is an anachronism. Panama is determined, by altering the 1903 treaty, to gain jurisdiction over its own territory and to obtain a greater share of the direct benefits from its most important national resource—its geography. The Commission believes that reaching an equitable new agreement with Panama regarding the Canal would serve U.S. interests not only in Panama but throughout Latin America by removing one of the last vestiges of Big Stick diplomacy.

Since 1964, the United States has recognized the desirability of establishing a relationship which both protects important U.S. interests and is consistent with Panamanian sovereignty in a hemisphere of independent nations. On February 7, 1974, Secretary of State Kissinger committed the United States to the prompt negotiation of a new Canal treaty based on a Statement of Principles agreed to with the Panamanian Foreign Minister.

The Commission believes those principles accommodate the basic interests of both nations. Under them, the United States could continue to use the land and facilities necessary to operate the Canal, while Panama would receive jurisdiction over its territory, a more equitable share of the benefits produced by the Canal, and growing participation in the operation and defense of the Canal. A new treaty, of fixed duration, also would permit the facility to be enlarged as needed.

Perpetual U.S. control of the Canal and total jurisdiction over the territory of the Canal Zone is not necessary either to keep the facility operating or to protect other United States interests.

On the contrary, maintaining the status quo could mean greater jeopardy to U.S. interests, not only in Panama but also throughout the hemisphere. It is possible to conceive of a time when the United States might ultimately be required to defend its position in Panama by the use of force in the midst of a hostile population and in the face of universal condemnation by the region and the world.

The lack of international sympathy for maintaining the status quo has been demonstrated in a variety of forums, including the United Nations and the Organization of American States.

The United States and Panama share positive interests in the Canal, and the negotiation of a new treaty offers an opportunity to solidify that commonality of interest. The Canal is important economically and strategically but less and less so as changes occur in patterns of world commerce and in the technologies of shipping and weaponry. The utility of the Canal in the future may well depend on expansion of its capacity, which can only be accomplished with Panama's cooperation.

The Commission realizes there are formidable obstacles to the negotiation and ratification by the Senate of a new treaty. The issue is an emotional one, often badly misunderstood in the United States; the U.S. government must do a better job than it has in the past of fostering a public awareness of the actual issues involved. And it must help Panamanian leaders to understand that confrontation tactics for domestic political purposes will not create a sympathetic understanding of Panama's position in the United States.

Recommendations:

6. We strongly support the signing and ratification of a new Panama Canal treaty based on the Statement of Principles accepted by both countries on February 6, 1974. Any arrangement should in fairness take into account the interests of U.S. citizens in the Canal Zone.

7. Consistent with the Statement of Principles and in the interests of efficiency and economy, the President should now take appropriate measures to reduce U.S. government personnel and operations which are not clearly essential to the Canal's operation and defense. In this connection the United States Armed Forces Southern Command should be transferred from the Canal Zone to the continental United States.

D. ARMS TRANSFERS AND MILITARY ASSISTANCE

Until the mid-1960s the United States was the predominant supplier of military equipment and training to Latin America; it provided the region over $2 billion in military assistance (or about 15 per cent of total aid to Latin America) in the period following World War II. This U.S. program initially was based on a view of the shared hemispheric need for security from the Soviet Union and its allies. Following the Cuban Revolution, the emphasis shifted to strengthening Latin American governments to deal with internal insurgencies.

The focus on internal subversion coincided with concern in the United States about needless diversion of resources from development. Beginning in the mid-1960s, the United States refused to sell modern weapons (including jet aircraft) to Latin American countries, and those restrictions as well as several others were embodied in Congressional legislation.*

Latin American governments, however, simply turned to European suppliers for equipment which was often more costly than that originally requested from the United States. Since 1967, 87 per cent of Latin American arms expenditures have been made outside the United States. The resulting situation satisfies no one: Latin American countries resent discriminatory United States restrictions, and some U.S. critics decry the decline in the U.S. share of the market, while others are disappointed that U.S. policy has failed to curb arms purchases.

The Commission has examined the case for the United States continuing to maintain a substantial military assistance program or military presence in Latin America. It has concluded that there are no significant internal security or extra-hemispheric military threats which warrant continuance of such programs. Nor should the United States attempt to regain a dominant position in the weapons market by actively promoting arms sales or by offering government credits on terms softer than a competitive, commercial basis. While the United States cannot unilaterally prevent sovereign nations from purchasing equipment they believe is required for their national defense, aggressively encouraging the purchase of U.S. arms by Latin American countries, as has occasionally been done in the past, cannot be justified. Doing so would counter no threat to U.S. security, nor would it provide the United States with significant economic benefits, for the

---

* Sec. 504a (Conte Amendment) and Sec. 620s (Combined Symington-Conte Amendment) of the Foreign Assistance Act of 1971; and Sec. 1 (Reuss Amendment), Sec. 4 (Conte Amendment), Sec. 33 (Fulbright Amendment), and Sec. 35 (Symington-like Provision) of the Foreign Military Sales Act for FY1972 (FMSA).

Latin Americans may in any case prefer to avoid excessive dependence on a single supplier. Even if it tried, the United States could not regain the dominant position in the Latin American arms market which would give it leverage over intraregional conflicts. More important, actively encouraging Latin American states to purchase U.S. equipment would run counter to regional and global U.S. aims of limiting spending of scarce resources for arms. It could, moreover, upset local balances of power, thus potentially involving the United States in exacerbating regional disputes.

The United States does have a legitimate interest in maintaining constructive relations with Latin American military leaders, many of whom play principal political roles in their countries; making conventional military equipment and training facilities available on a non-discriminatory commercial basis may be part of what is required to maintain those relations. Legislative restrictions on arms transfers to Latin America have been ineffective in preventing arms purchases and have resulted in deep resentment among Latin American military and political leaders, who have viewed such stipulations as paternalistic. The restrictions are inconsistent with the attempts this Commission supports to make policies toward Latin America mutually respectful. It is also inappropriate to discriminate against Latin America when total military expenditures consume a much lower percentage of the GNP of that region than of most other parts of the world.

The massive levels of conventional arms purchases throughout the world, however, deserve serious international attention. U.S. firms alone sold billions of dollars worth of equipment last year. The Commission believes the United States should take the initiative in bringing together major supplier and consumer nations in efforts to establish wherever feasible—on sub-regional, regional, or global levels—internationally agreed limitations on the sale and purchase of conventional armaments.

Although no Latin American nation presently possesses nuclear weapons, at least two countries, Argentina and Brazil, have the potential to develop such weapons. The proliferation of nuclear arms capabilities could have a dangerous impact on regional power balances. Therefore, the United States should assure that its nuclear assistance

REPORT OF THE COMMISSION / 35

agreements with Latin American countries include appropriate international safeguards. It should also seek ways to encourage adherence by all nuclear powers and all nations in the region to the 1967 Treaty for the Prohibition of Nuclear Weapons in Latin America (Treaty of Tlatelolco).

The United States also has an important interest in not associating or seeming to associate itself, through the maintenance of military programs, with security forces whose repressive activities may involve the United States, willingly or not, in activities inconsistent with U.S. commitments to human rights and freedoms. The United States cannot assure in other countries respect for the human rights it values, but it can desist from providing training or equipment which would assist security forces found to be engaged in violating such rights.

Recommendations:

8. The United States should encourage and, where appropriate, participate in efforts to develop sub-regional, regional and global conventional arms limitation agreements among supplier and consumer nations.

9. The United States should terminate grant military materiel assistance programs in Latin America. The recently abolished Agency for International Development (AID) public safety program in Latin America, which provided equipment and training to police forces, should not be revived.

10. The United States should not actively encourage the purchase of arms by Latin American countries. However, legislative restrictions on arms transfers that discriminate against Latin America ought to be repealed. Conventional military equipment should be available to Latin American countries on a competitive, commercial and non-discriminatory basis—the same as that governing sales to other friendly nations except those engaging in military hostilities or whose security forces are found by appropriate international processes to be systematically violating human rights.

11. U.S. Military Assistance Advisory Groups in Latin America should be phased out and replaced by small inter-service liaison offices or joint commission delegations (possibly as part of Military Attache Offices), whose primary responsibilities would involve coordination of professional exchanges and training, rather than sales promotion or advisory functions.

E. ECONOMIC SANCTIONS

The unilateral imposition of coercive economic sanctions is inappropriate in the changing context of hemispheric and global relations. The threat or use of U.S. economic power to influence the internal processes or policies of Latin American countries is inconsistent with our efforts to build a just and peaceful international order, one in which differences among nations are resolved by negotiation rather than confrontation. The coercive use of U.S. economic power is not only deeply resented by Latin Americans, but also is generally counterproductive. Automatic sanctions exacerbate confrontations with Latin American nationalisms, damaging both the climate for negotiating reasonable settlements of the problems the sanctions were supposed to address, and the prospects of achieving the kind of constructive relationships that our national interests require in an era of growing interdependence.

1. *Expropriation and Fisheries Disputes*

Private foreign investment has been and will continue to be important to the development of Latin American countries. However, the investment process is not static; adjustments are sometimes required on the part of investors and host countries. Too often, when disputes over such adjustments have arisen between a Latin American government and an individual company, the U.S. government has become embroiled in fruitless confrontations with Latin American governments. The threat and/or use (formal or informal) of economic sanctions*—such as the Hickenlooper and Gonzales Amendments which call for automatic aid cut-offs in unresolved expropriation disputes—have rarely been helpful to the investor, and almost always have ensured that bilateral relations would be poisoned, often to the detriment of other U.S. investors.

---

* Provided for in Sec. 620(e) (1) of the Foreign Assistance Act of 1961, as Amended, known as the Hickenlooper Amendment; and sec. 21 and 22 of the Inter-American Development Bank Act of 1972, known as the Gonzales Amendment. President Nixon's Policy Statement on Economic Assistance and Investment Security in Developing Nations issued January 19, 1972, also calls for similar economic sanctions.

The U.S. government cannot ignore the rights of its citizens under international law, but neither can it assume that U.S. corporate interests are homogenous nor that the national interest automatically coincides with the perceived interest of an individual firm. Coercive sanctions which escalate individual investment disputes into nationalistic confrontations between governments should be avoided. The resolution of investment disputes ought to be left primarily to host governments and companies, and where feasible, impartial dispute settlement procedures. However, where such processes fail or are unavailable and companies seek diplomatic recourse, our government should negotiate with flexibility and patience and not be forced— through automatic sanctions—into the position of staking its overall relations with other countries on the interests of individual investors.

Similarly, legislative amendments requiring automatic retaliatory sanctions* in disputes over fisheries have at times exacerbated nationalistic reactions and strained bilateral relations with Latin American coastal states. The Commission believes that international agreement on a new regime for the oceans is the best way to avoid future fisheries conflicts. However, pending negotiation of a new international agreement, the Commission supports efforts to minimize tensions between the United States and Latin American countries over fishing rights. A first step would be the elimination of the automatic sanctions cutting off economic aid and military sales in the event of seizure of U.S. fishing vessels in disputed waters. In these cases, as in cases of investment disputes, the threat of coercive sanctions is more likely to stiffen the host country's position rather than induce it to relax its demands.

Recommendation:

12. The United States should abandon the threat or application of unilateral measures of economic coercion in its relations with the countries of Latin America. Specifically, the Commission urges:

* Provided for in Sec. 5 of the Fisherman's Protective Act of 1967, as Amended; Sec. 3 of the Naval Ship Loan Extension Act of 1967; Sec. 620 (e) (1) of the Foreign Assistance Act of 1961, as Amended; and Sec. 3 (b) of the Foreign Military Sales Act, as Amended.

(a) Repeal of the Hickenlooper and Gonzales Amendments and revocation of the January 1972 Presidential policy statement on expropriation.

(b) Repeal of the amendments to the Foreign Assistance Act, Foreign Military Sales Act, and Ship Loan Act which provide for automatic economic sanctions in cases of fisheries disputes.*

(c) Rejection by the United States of economic pressures or policies of economic denial to affect the internal processes of Latin American countries. Such measures should be considered only pursuant to appropriate resolutions of the United Nations or the Organization of American States.

2. *The Inter-American Development Bank*

The U.S. role in the decision making of the Inter-American Development Bank (IDB) is a specific issue, related to the use of economic sanctions, which troubles Latin Americans. The United States, which holds 38 per cent of the votes (as opposed to 24 per cent in the World Bank), can effectively veto proposed actions by the IDB's Fund for Special Operations where a two-thirds majority is required for approval. The use of this voting power to serve parochial U.S. political objectives contradicts the ideals of partnership supported by the United States and hampers the effectiveness with which the Bank pursues its accepted objective of promoting the economic and social development of Latin America.

In addition, U.S. efforts to make IDB actions reflect U.S. policy goals can have a negative effect on potential contributors to the Bank. Such contributors may fear that through participation in the Bank they will be associated with U.S. foreign policy objectives they do not share. Yet, it is in the interest of the United States and Latin America that other developed countries and the more prosperous Latin American nations make substantial financial contributions to the Bank. As these other nations share this financial burden, it is only appropriate that they should also share the responsibility of overseeing the policies and management of the Bank.

---

* Mr. Heinz believes this Recommendation should be contingent upon agreements being reached regarding coastal states' rights and the historic rights of others regarding the utilization and conservation of migratory species.

The Commission believes it is not necessary for the United States to retain its unilateral veto power in the IDB Fund for Special Operations. This could be accomplished by modification of the Bank's charter to permit the contributions of other nations to be counted in such a way as to dilute the U.S. share of the total votes below one-third without, however, any reduction in the level of U.S. contributions to the Bank. Alternatively, the United States could propose an amendment of the charter which would eliminate the requirement for a two-thirds majority.

Over the short term, the important factor is how the United States uses its voting power in the IDB rather than any change in its share of the votes. In the Commission's view, the United States could improve hemispheric relations significantly by treating the Inter-American Development Bank like a truly multilateral development institution and not as an instrument to achieve short-term U.S. foreign policy objectives.

Recommendations:

13. The United States should propose a modification of the Inter-American Development Bank charter to encourage additional contributions by other nations in a manner which would permit dilution of the U.S. voting share below one-third, or alternatively, to eliminate the requirement for a two-thirds majority in the Fund for Special Operations. But such action must be accomplished in a manner which would not lower the level of U.S. contributions to the Bank.

14. The United States should assure that its actions in the Inter-American Development Bank and other multilateral development institutions accord with the broad purposes of those institutions and are not taken primarily to serve narrow U.S. political or economic interests.

F. THE ORGANIZATION OF AMERICAN STATES

The role of the OAS in inter-American relations is a subject of considerable debate. Founded in 1948 to provide an institutional structure for collective security in the region, the OAS today seeks to redefine its functions—indeed its utility—in the light of changing conditions.

Despite the criticisms and real shortcomings of the OAS, the Commission believes it plays a useful part in regional relations and has the potential to perform increasingly important functions of mutual benefit to the United States and the Latin American nations. The OAS provides a forum for inter-American consultation, particularly on matters which may ultimately be treated in global contexts. Whether policy decisions by regional leaders are taken within or outside the formal structure of the OAS, the institutional structure offers permanent mechanisms for staffing, implementing, and monitoring mutually agreed upon actions and programs. As noted earlier, the organization can help to promote greater respect for fundamental human rights by publicizing violations of such rights and discussing such cases at high political levels.

The OAS can play a particularly significant role in avoidance and mediation of intra-regional conflicts. The potential for such disputes could increase as Latin American nations interact more intensely and as these countries pursue their national interests in the international arena. The pressures of domestic politics may fan aggressive nationalisms, and regional power politics may also thrust Latin American nations into conflict with one another. All of us in the Americas share common interests in seeing that local conflicts do not broaden into the strategic arena, nor compel wasteful diversions of resources from nation-building to military purposes.

Consideration is now being given by the member governments to reforming the structure of the OAS in order to give it greater effectiveness in inter-American affairs. Structural change will not, however, assure a strengthened OAS unless the member states are agreed on and committed to its purposes and determined to work together in furtherance of its objectives. The United States should be guided by the views of the Latin American States as to what role they expect the OAS to play in dealing with hemispheric matters.

Recommendations:

15. The United States should encourage the strengthening of the OAS conciliation and peacekeeping capacities.

16. With respect to the future role of the OAS—including its structure,

leadership and location—, the United States should be guided primarily by Latin American initiatives and wishes.

V. *Cultural Relations*

Many of the tensions and difficulties in U.S. relations with Latin America stem from real disparities in power and interests. Those disparities can narrow only gradually, and problems will no doubt persist in inter-American relations for some time. Yet, clearly, differences are magnified by poor communications and lack of understanding on both sides. Educational institutions, the media, and the general public in the United States pay insufficient attention to Latin America, and many of our political leaders have scant knowledge of the area.

Lack of understanding of Latin America in the United States exacerbates the tendency in the government to downplay Latin American considerations. "Latin American" policy often is made in contexts that have little to do with the region. That situation is likely to continue because of the underlying realities of foreign policy. Yet, better understanding of Latin America is bound to have favorable effects upon the quality and degree of attention accorded to Latin America by the United States.

Political, economic and military relations among states ordinarily deal with concrete problems. But underlying these problems are intangible relationships that are general rather than particular, emotional rather than rational, and not necessarily related to current issues. These relationships are based upon deep-seated assumptions that one country maintains about another. Such a reading of a national or continental personality proceeds from the degree to which a foreign culture is understood. Language and customs, manners and attitudes, politics and public functions, as much as sports or advertising, are among many observable cultural symptoms which project a national identity.

Cultural exchanges between North and South America provide an avenue for improving understanding, but in their present form they are too scattered, limited, and elitist. If they are to reach wider levels of the population, and if they are to lead to an improved mutual understanding, valuable contacts established by individuals must be broadened, guided, and financed.

Nothing could be more opposed to the expansion and the deepening of such contacts than the present travel restrictions that inhibit free access among many nations of the hemisphere. Existing restrictions on entry into the United States do not apply only to Latin Americans, but they are a particular irritant in United States-Latin American relations. Leading Latin American intellectuals have suffered inconvenience and embarrassment at the hands of U.S. consular and immigration officials rigidly implementing the law. To the extent that such regulations are based upon purely political grounds, these vestiges of the Cold War should be removed and every effort made to facilitate legitimate movement of persons.

But beyond such remedies, an effective cultural exchange program under present conditions can only be achieved through cooperative efforts between government and private cultural enterprise. Government sponsorship is needed to coordinate and provide funds for the execution of significant private cultural programs. The National Endowments for the Arts and the Humanities, charged with cultural responsibility within the United States, may serve as a suitable model for an international cultural exchange agency. A first step might be creation of a multinational board, financed by an allocation from the earnings of the Inter-American Development Bank, providing for exchanges between Latin America and the United States.

Such an entity could consider increases and improvements in exchange programs on various levels. It could also encourage formation of an hemispheric news exchange to combat paucity of information that presently marks United States coverage of Latin America and that also separates individual states within the region. A policy board could consider the establishment of specialized libraries of books, films and records, the organization and use of national archives, and the subsidization of translations of significant current and past classics. It might also call upon the richness of museums, to make available the benefits of the hemisphere's artistic and archeological wealth for all peoples, as well as to afford opportunities for artists and intellectuals to meet in inter-American conferences designed for mutual professional and creative enrichment.

Recommendations:

17. U.S. immigration legislation should be reviewed systematically with the aim of eliminating restrictions barring travel and migration on purely political grounds. The Commission urges that the President promptly seek Congressional approval for amendments designed to eliminate these restrictions. In the meantime, we urge the President to instruct all relevant U.S. agencies to interpret and apply existing legislation in the light of changed circumstances and priorities.

18. The United States should propose establishment of an Inter-American Endowment for Cultural Exchange, with funding from a percentage of the earnings of the Inter-American Development Bank. The mandate of such an entity should be broadly defined and its functioning should remain free from the pressures of government agencies in any of the participating countries. Its sole purpose should be to utilize the talents and capacities of institutions and individuals toward a better and broader understanding among the nations of the Americas.

19. The U.S. government should provide increased support for Latin American Area Studies at all levels of the educational system.

VI. *Economic Relations*

The United States and the nations of Latin America share a vital interest in helping to resolve the serious economic problems facing the world today. A new set of rules is required to govern the exchange of goods and services among nations so that all countries—developed and developing   can realistically expect to benefit. We believe actions in this hemisphere can contribute significantly to that goal. Rather than recommending a "special relationship" based on a spirit of favoritism or exclusion, we recommend a special effort to act in the region in ways that build toward, and support more efficient and equitable global arrangements.

The Commission recognizes that solutions to many of the economic problems and dilemmas of the present day will not be forthcoming unless there are concerted world efforts to solve them. The issues are complex and cannot be resolved solely within a hemispheric context. This Commission has not attempted to prescribe universal solutions; what it has tried to do is suggest some ways in which the United States may work cooperatively with the other nations of the Americas to advance their common interests.

Three sets of issues dominate the agenda of inter-American economic relationships: access to markets and resources, capital flows, and the transfer of technology. U.S. initiatives in these three areas can lead to more productive, mutually beneficial relations. The basic approach we recommend would restructure market relations in the mutual interest of all nations of the hemisphere; it would support and reinforce a renewed respect for national sovereignty in the political sphere as well.

A. ACCESS TO MARKETS

1. *Tariff Preferences*

The Commission urges the United States to fulfill its pledge to grant generalized preferences for imports of manufactures from the developing nations. Favorable access to the largest market in the world would be of special importance to many Latin American countries. The product per capita in the region now exceeds $600 a year, a gain of some 40 per cent since the beginning of the 1960s. The composition of the region's economic output has changed: agriculture now accounts for less than 15 per cent of total production, while manufacturing comprises almost 25 per cent. More importantly, the manufacturing sector has been growing at an increasingly rapid rate, 9.2 per cent, for example, in 1972. The most industrialized nations of the region—Argentina, Brazil, Colombia, Mexico—have an obvious interest in securing greater access to the markets of the developed world for their manufactured goods. These nations have moved beyond import substitution and now look outward to the rest of the world. How the United States responds to their desire for market access will have an important effect on their economic policies and their commitment to economic and political cooperation. Our responsiveness also will have a significant impact on the policies of other countries—Peru, Chile, and Venezuela—whose industrial capacities are growing.

The Commission believes it is in the interest of the United States to encourage freer trade in manufactures and commodities. More liberal trade arrangements are likely to result in increased U.S. sales abroad, as well as lower-priced imports. The latter, by helping to bring about a more efficient domestic allocation of resources, will be an important weapon in the battle against inflation. Temporary dislocations and hardships, although inevitably painful and requiring generous transitional assistance for certain segments of the economy, should not deter the United States from policies which are needed to bring about more efficient national and global economic structures.

While a universal, non-discriminatory, most favored nation framework for global trade relations is essential, the Commission favors generalized tariff preferences for developing countries as a means to support their development. The Trade Reform Act of 1973, currently being considered by Congress, provides such preferences, but they would be of very limited benefit to Latin America. The proposed legislation excludes from the list of eligible products many of the manufactures in which Latin America might possess comparative advantage. The limitation on products admitted with preference to $25 million or 50 per cent of U.S. imports whichever is less, restricts potential economies of scale and the likelihood that new investment will be stimulated. In fact, the two restrictions—on type of products admitted and dollar volume—would deny preferences to about 80 per cent of dutiable exports from Latin America and to some 90 per cent of total exports. Among Latin American countries, only Mexico stands to gain much from the trade bill as it is currently written.

The Commission feels that the preference scheme in the proposed trade bill should be extended to provide greater benefit to Latin America without serious adverse domestic repercussions. The size, and growth, of the United States market can define realistic limitations that are both more generous and more economically sound. The upcoming multilateral tariff negotiations in the GATT will also offer opportunities to cooperate with Latin America on additional steps to liberalize trade relations.

Recommendations:

20. The United States should enact a generalized scheme of tariff preferences for developing countries. However, both the list of products to be admitted and the limitations on dollar volume should be drawn with a view to providing increased benefits to Latin America.

21. The United States should cooperate with Latin American nations in the forthcoming multilateral tariff negotiations to achieve tariff reductions on products which would be of mutual benefit.

2. *Export Subsidies and Countervailing Duties*

A second and related element in hemisphere trade relations is the matter of export subsidies and countervailing duties. The temporary use of export subsidies by developing countries whose overvalued exchange rates are disadvantageous for their exports can help ease the transition from the high tariff structures found in most of those countries to less protectionist systems. Because exchange rates are expected to move closer to equilibrium over time, the use of export subsidies should be a temporary phenomenon with their phaseout linked to adoption of more realistic exchange rates. Current GATT rules relating to the use of such subsidies should be reviewed and revised to better regulate existing practices.

Threats to quickly impose countervailing duties in response to subsidized exports have been a source of tension between the United States and several Latin American countries. The proposed trade bill provides for a waiver of a countervailing duty under certain conditions, thus permitting a more flexible response to export subsidies. The special circumstances of developing nations could be taken into account in determining whether and to what degree countervailing duties would be imposed. While the waiver provision is desirable, it is not a sufficient or long-term solution to the subsidy-countervailing duty problem. The United States should take the lead in negotiating new international rules that more realistically define the magnitude and conditions under which temporary subsidies by developing countries are permissible. If such rules are not developed, the issue will give rise to increasing frictions between the industrialized and the developing nations generally, and with Latin America especially, as the developing nations seek to extend their exports of manufactures. Negotiation of fair and enforceable regulations on export subsidies that are related to the level of economic development, the structure of protection, and size of exports is in the interest of all nations. Once negotiated, it would be the obligation of all nations—developing and developed—to observe those rules.

Recommendation:

22. The waiver provision on countervailing duties should be included in the Trade Reform Act. The Commission further recommends that the United States, in concert with other nations, begin to review and negotiate new and more appropriate international rules to govern the temporary use of export subsidies by developing nations.

3. *Domestic Adjustment Assistance*

More liberal import policies will impose some temporary hardships on certain domestic sectors, affecting individual firms and workers. These short-run dislocations must be eased if foreign policy aims are to be reconciled with domestic obligations. Present adjustment assistance provisions are hedged with conditions that render them inadequate. They need to be strengthened by increasing and lengthening the benefits, and by providing more effective training for displaced workers so they can fill desirable new jobs. Adjustment assistance should be selective and limited in duration so as not to become a permanent subsidy. Its objective should be to improve the allocation of resources by aiding the transfer of workers and firms from uneconomic activities to economic enterprises.

Recommendation:

23. The U.S. government should determine which segments of the domestic economy will be disrupted by more liberal trade policies, including tariff preferences, and should develop a selective, but generous program of adjustment assistance. This assistance should be integrated with national and local economic policy plans as well as with other measures directed toward more efficient domestic allocation of resources.

4. *Commodity Arrangements*

The previous discussion focused primarily upon trade in manufactures; trade in foodstuffs and raw materials poses equally vexing problems, but also provides constructive opportunities. Of late, many Latin American countries have benefited from the rapid rises in commodity prices. Although the short-term prognosis for some commodities is one of global scarcity and consequent high prices, the long-term outlook is less certain. Prices may stay high, or increased supply may exceed demand, depressing prices again as in the 1950s.

In no other area is the mutuality of interest between the Americas so clearly demonstrated: Latin American countries want insurance against oversupply of raw materials and consequent low prices; North Americans want protection against shortages and rapidly inflating prices. Both have an interest in maintaining adequate commodity flows at reasonable prices. The obstacles to harmonious trade in commodities, however, are obvious: definitions of what is "adequate" and what is "reasonable" may differ, and a trading nation seldom wants to stabilize prices and quantities when the terms of trade are running in its favor. The commodity problem provides a major opportunity for hemispheric initiatives toward world cooperation.

The United States and Latin America together can, in the first instance, assure that information concerning projected demands and supplies is shared among individual countries so that internal policies are not developed in isolation. Coordinated either through the OAS or the Inter-American Development Bank, such efforts can help to perfect and anticipate the operations of the market. Because this information is in itself insufficient to guarantee against the risk of excessive production or to prevent large, but temporary, price fluctuations, additional mechanisms are required.

The commodity agreement approach sometimes favored in the past cannot by itself provide a solution. No one technique is likely to be sufficient to deal with the complexities of commodity markets. A variety of approaches may be more promising. One possibility the United States and Latin American nations might consider is compensatory finance arrangements: for example, differences between actual and stipulated prices for a range of commodities could be partially offset by monetary receipts from, or payment into, a hemispheric facility managed by the IDB. If prices declined below an agreed level, which itself would change in response to shifting demand and supply, producing countries would have a claim to transitional financial assistance. If prices exceeded a maximum, owing to inadequate supplies, consuming countries would have the full inflationary impact diluted by repayments from this facility. This arrangement could be used in conjunction with the more modest finance now available from the International Monetary Fund, and could be extended to global dimensions.

As an alternative or complementary approach, long-term supply contracts could provide another mechanism to help assure adequate supplies and reasonably stable prices. The United States might explore means to underwrite or otherwise encourage long-term contracts for the purchase of selected commodities. Such efforts at price and quantity stabilization would serve U.S. interests by offering Latin American countries an incentive to provide adequate and accessible supplies. They would improve the Latin American countries' prospects for continuous, favorable export receipts, while reducing the fear of sudden balance of payments difficulties brought on by declining commodity prices.

However the actual arrangements are carried through, they must remain compatible with the realities of global economic interdependence. It is not in the interest of the United States to encourage the world to shatter into exclusionary bilateral agreements reminiscent of the 1930s. Rather, the United States should work to expand commodity production to satisfy world demand, and to remove monopoly elements from commodity, manufactures, and technology markets.

Recommendations:

24. The United States should encourage the establishment of a regional system for the exchange of information on commodity supply and demand projections.

25. The United States government should examine means to limit and offset the effects of wide fluctuations in supply, demand and prices of selected commodities. Alternatives which should be considered include compensatory finance arrangements, long-term supply contracts and commodity agreements. Such arrangements could be initiated on a regional basis, but should be consistent with Western Hemisphere interests in expanding total global production and maintaining orderly and equitable global trading arrangements.

B. CAPITAL FLOWS

1. *Public Capital*

Extensive bilateral concessional assistance from the United States to Latin America is largely a thing of the past. Yet some groups of the population, and some countries within Latin America and the Caribbean continue to require concessionary aid. Annual per capita income in several countries is still below $300. What assistance is available, in both bilateral and multilateral forms, should be targeted to yield the largest benefits. The United States, in cooperation with the countries involved, should focus its assistance on projects designed to better the living conditions of Latin America's poorest citizens. That means attention to specific problems—low productivity agriculture and inadequate food supply, infant mortality, education and population growth—and to specific regions and countries—Bolivia, Paraguay, parts of Central America, and much of the Caribbean.

The Commission believes the United States should cooperate with Latin American nations and multilateral development institutions in programs to narrow the disparity of incomes and to help the poorest in the region. Such undertakings could perhaps serve as a model for joint efforts by developed and developing nations to ameliorate desperate poverty in the world. Poverty hn its most severe forms is self-regenerating. It makes large families an economic necessity and keeps children from attending school because their incomes are necessary to mere family survival. It limits techniques in the agricultural sector to the most traditional. It means malnutrition and disease, and an inability to realize one's economic potential.

Eradication of poverty does not lend itself to simple panaceas directed only at certain symptoms. Family planning, however necessary, will prove inadequate in the absence of expanded economic opportunities and improved incomes. Modern inputs in the agricultural sector in the absence of better distribution of income will not be sufficient. Low-income housing without more jobs will be but a temporary expedient. Increased access to education without the economic capacity to finance attendance offers little benefit to the poor.

While the problem is difficult, much can be accomplished if there is continuing commitment and attack on many fronts. The United States should play a leading role in efforts to eliminate poverty, not only because it may promote political stability in the long-run, but because the United States, along with the more prosperous Latin Americans cannot help but be affected—morally and practically—by the wasteful and inhumane consequences of islands of poverty in this otherwise dynamic and rapidly developing region.

Limited, but effectively utilized funds provided through the Agency for International Development and the Inter-American Foundation can have significant impact on the processes of economic and social development. They can be augmented from other sources. Multilateral lending agencies themselves have begun to concentrate their funds on the poorer nations and regions. Wealthier Latin American countries can contribute. Venezuela has already made large contributions to the World Bank and the Inter-American Development Bank conditional on the funds being used to finance projects in the poorer countries. While few other nations are so advantaged, many can afford to do without the IDB's "soft" loan resources (the Fund for Special Operations) and thus make at least some additional sums available for their poorer neighbors. These varied resources can permit significant accomplishments, especially if objectives are limited and defined clearly. It is important that the United States exercise its leadership by fulfilling its own commitments to the IDB and World Bank. At the present time, the United States is in arrears on its commitments to the IDB's Fund for Special Operations by $500 million, and on its commitments to the World Bank's International Development Association by $320 million. United States calls for cooperative hemispheric efforts will ring hollow if the United States does not live up to its own pledges.

Recommendations:

26. The United States should target its bilateral assistance to the poorer countries in Latin America and the Caribbean, and in cooperation with the countries concerned, to projects within countries which will better the lot of the poorest segments of the population. The United States should endorse attempts by multilateral lending agencies to apply similar criteria in their programs.

27. The United States should fulfill its own commitments to the Inter-American Development Bank and to the World Bank, and should encourage the wealthier nations of Latin America to make more of their resources available for development assistance in the region.

2. Foreign Private Investment

Foreign private direct investment, by U.S. or other international investors, has made and can continue to make important contributions to Latin American development. Yet foreign investment, especially in its direct equity form, is often an emotional issue to the people of both Americas. It is an issue loaded with suspicions and misunderstandings. North American investors are concerned about instances of capricious treatment from Latin American governments, in disregard of written agreements, while many Latin Americans are concerned that powerful multinational companies, unwilling to subordinate their global business interests to national economic aspirations, will exploit them. But times are changing and so are the terms of foreign investment.

Latin American countries have become more self-confident and technically more competent in their dealings with the multinational corporations. Competition among investors from the United States, Europe and Japan enables the Latin American countries to strike better bargains. More and more natural resource exploration and exploitation is conducted under national policy direction and with joint participation between the host country and the foreign firm. Licensing arrangements and joint ventures are more common, providing a framework for local investors to participate in eventual profits. Investors from many different countries have combined, for example, in the Atlantic Community Development Group for Latin America (ADELA) to take minority positions in joint ventures with local private and public capital to start new industries. Investment that simultaneously brings benefits to the host country in the form of more jobs, better production techniques, increased opportunities for exports, and ultimate domestic ownership, as well as yielding returns to the foreign investors, is becoming more prevalent. Correspondingly, the potential for direct and irreconcilable conflicts of interest is diminished as foreign firms see the advantages of the large and growing Latin

American market and recognize the desirability of responding constructively to host country concerns.

Inevitably there is a tension in the foreign investment process between the investor's need to remit earnings home and the host government's need to retain the largest possible gains internally. What makes the conflict ultimately resolvable to the mutual advantage of all concerned is the increased output of goods and services made possible by the investment and the continuing need for capital and technology by the host Latin American countries.

Host country demands for renegotiation of initial terms and conditions which may have initially attracted particular foreign investments have become commonplace occurrences in Latin America. Such modifications can take various forms, including increased taxation of foreign profits, or requests for equity participation. While many renegotiations have been concluded successfully, others—most often in the area of natural resources—have precipitated sharp disputes between U.S. companies and Latin American governments. They have resulted at times in U.S. government involvement to influence a settlement.

The Commission believes that relationships between United States investors and Latin American countries are best conducted on a direct basis, with minimal U.S. government involvement. The policy of the U.S. government should be to encourage the probability of mutually advantageous, private solutions. Arbitrary and unilateral disrespect of contractual obligations by any government must not be condoned, but at the same time, the U.S. should avoid actions which escalate private disputes to the level of governmental confrontations. That is one reason for the Commission's previously stated recommendation against the threat or use of automatic sanctions in expropriation disputes.

The United States should remain receptive to Latin American attempts to develop codes of conduct applicable to foreign investors. As multinational firms, whose economic size and power may exceed that of host countries, play more of a role in Latin America, there is understandable concern on the part of host countries that they be able to deal effectively with such enterprises. There is an equal interest on the part of the U.S. government that these vast corporations conduct themselves in accord with the U.S. national interest.

Serious discussion to define the rights and responsibilities of foreign investors and governments is needed. It is not enough to assert that "international law" protects foreign investors, nor can we realistically urge U.S. or other foreign companies to accept without any diplomatic recourse, the application of host country laws and practices to their companies when those practices contradict prevailing international norms. The availability of impartial and generally accepted mechanisms for effective fact-finding and arbitration, however, could eliminate the need for diplomatic involvement in investment disputes. The establishment of such mechanisms, whether under global or regional auspices, would go a long way toward minimizing the damage investment disputes often do to inter-American relations. A structure of mutual expectations could be established which would guide the dealings between U.S. companies and Latin American governments, without the unnecessary and sometimes counterproductive involvement of the U.S. government.

Recommendation:

28. The United States should collaborate with the Latin American nations in the development of codes of conduct defining rights and responsibilities of foreign investors and governments. Together, the United States and Latin America should work to develop impartial fact-finding mechanisms and utilize impartial dispute settlement procedures to help in the resolution of investment disputes.

3. OPIC Guarantees

The Overseas Private Investment Corporation (OPIC) guarantee programs in Latin America could be modified appropriately to further reduce governmental involvement in private investment matters. Large investors can assess and assume risks on their own. For them the insurance provided by OPIC is largely unnecessary, and where used, it may be questioned whether the investment should have been undertaken initially. Moreover, claims under a guarantee can bring the U.S. government more directly into dispute with the host country.

OPIC guarantees might usefully be applied, however, where mutual policy objectives are agreed upon and there is little likelihood of contention. Such guarantees could encourage medium and small firms with needed skills and capital but little foreign experience to take the risk of investing abroad. They could also assist projects approved by host governments that are intended to have a favorable impact upon the poorer segments of the population. By attracting and helping to direct additional resources to the most needful regions and sectors, such guarantees can supplement the policy initiatives previously recommended.

Recommendation:

29. The Overseas Private Investment Corporation guarantee programs in Latin America should be modified to emphasize primarily medium- and smaller-size firms and projects intended to have a favorable impact upon the poor.

4. *Capital Markets*

The present uncertainties in the world economy offer another opportunity for constructive U.S. government initiatives. In the last few years many of the Latin American countries have had unparalleled access to the capital markets of the developed countries, and in particular, the Euro-dollar market. Such an inflow has permitted rapid growth in imports of capital goods and intermediate inputs without balance of payments strains. However, new deficits in the developed countries brought on by the much higher cost of petroleum have made access to their capital markets more difficult. The development prospects of many Latin American countries, particularly oil importers, will be dealt a severe blow if they are unable to attract continuing inflows of money capital. For some it would mean curtailing present rates of growth and a turn again toward inward-looking development; for others it would pose serious problems of timely debt repayment and possible default.

While the amount of public funds to meet these requirements is obviously inadequate and unlikely to materialize, the United States government can help to assure that international facilities used for the transfer of oil revenue dollars give due consideration to the needs of the developing countries. It can likewise explore the possibility of attracting private U.S. capital to participate jointly in certain bilateral and multilateral public projects, thereby expanding the total capital inflow available. The United States should also be prepared to consult with other creditor nations to try to assure that Latin American development efforts are not impeded by heavy debt burdens acquired when the global economic outlook appeared more favorable.

Recommendation:

30. The United States should collaborate with the countries of Latin America to assure that facilities used for the international transfer of oil revenue dollars give appropriate weight to the requirements of the developing countries.

C. TRANSFER OF SCIENCE AND TECHNOLOGY

Developing countries have become aware of the critical importance of scientific knowledge, and its effective application, to economic growth. Capital accumulation, foreign exchange availability, and elimination of other conventional constraints are insufficient in themselves to assure high, and self-sustaining rates of economic progress. These measures can foster per capita income increases only in conjunction with the productivity increases made possible by more efficient technology.

It is no accident, then, that the transfer of technology appears near the top of every Latin American list of current issues in hemispheric relationships. Latin Americans are keenly aware of the extent to which they import much of their technology—in form of machines and managerial techniques—from the United States and other industrial nations. They are concerned about this dependence, and what it implies for continuing foreign participation in their economies, particularly if equity investment becomes the only medium for such transfer.

The issue is complex, for unlike commodity trade in which transfer can be effected by a simple exchange of goods, science and technology are not always embodied in a simple physical form. Such activities reach down into the cultural matrix of societies. And short-term policies that seem to work may be inimical to longer-term solutions.

The United States, as the world's foremost producer of industrial technology, can enhance Latin America's development prospects by encouraging the flow of technology southward. Our concern for a stable world and hemispheric political order also suggests that we facilitate development of scientific and technological bases within the Latin American countries. For only with an ultimately sophisticated technological infrastructure can the process of scientific application be internalized.

The United States can take measures to assist in both dimensions of the transfer process. Development of scientific and technological capacity is time consuming and costly. The U.S. should lend its official efforts to bolster Latin American capabilities, avoiding wasteful duplication of energies and resources within the region. For a long time now such a role, as distinct from manufacturing and marketing techniques on a commercial basis, has been left almost exclusively to private foundations and individual scholars.

Technology transfer takes many forms. The institutional and organizational ability to use it is as important as access to the technology itself. The Commission believes a United States-based public foundation acting in concert with Latin American counterparts to facilitate their access to scientific and technological activities in the United States could make a useful contribution to this process. It could help to match Latin American needs with scientific and technological capabilities in the U.S.—in universities, government laboratories, research institutes, and private firms. The corresponding Latin American groups, some perhaps involving more than single countries where national units are small, would be locally funded and would coordinate their own research and development priorities.

Initiative in such an arrangement would rest with the Latin Americans and be shaped by their priorities. Such a facility could usefully supplement existing international agencies and build upon the long and successful hemispheric intellectual interchange under private auspices.

Recommendation:

31. The United States should assist the development of scientific and technological capabilities within the Latin American countries. To support

this process, we recommend establishment of a publicly-funded foundation to cooperate with counterpart Latin American institutions.

The Commission would like to point to one specific area where expanded cooperative research programs are greatly needed. The recent Law of the Sea Conference has made very apparent mankind's insufficient knowledge about the location and magnitude of marine resources. More intensive programs of marine research are needed and would facilitate agreement on a new international code regulating exploitation of marine resources. In particular, the Latin American nations have much to gain. We therefore encourage mutual research with Latin America to improve and share our knowledge of the seas.

Recommendation:

32. The Commission recommends that the United States undertake cooperative research in marine science. Consideration should be given to the establishment of international or regional Marine Research Centers in Latin America and the Caribbean in which scientists from member countries could jointly undertake marine research projects and studies, thereby strengthening local research and scientific capabilities.

This assistance speaks primarily to the long run. For the present, capital is, and will remain for some time, relatively scarce in many Latin American countries. Basic research is extremely costly and produces tangible returns only after long periods of time. Resources invested in training high-level manpower subtract from those available for assuring mass literacy and educational access. What is of more immediate significance is freer availability of the technology of the more advanced nations that can be utilized without duplication of the steps involved in its initial development. The Japanese experience may serve as a useful model, with its simultaneous reliance upon foreign patents and licenses and emphasis upon adaptation to local conditions.

The Commission recognizes that most of the United States technology available for immediate application resides in private hands; most transfers correspondingly result from private decisions of corporations, typically in the form of equity investment. There is a legally recognized monopoly through the patent system that is bestowed upon possessors of technology; and firms legitimately seek to protect and defend against imitation and competition even in the absence of such formal authority.

In these circumstances the potential for governmental direction or regulation of the transfer process is circumscribed. And the market-place, because of the monopoly elements inevitably present, will not always yield equitable solutions. This is the crux of the matter: for Latin American countries often are persuaded that they are paying higher prices and receiving inferior quality. Such a sense of discrimination and abuse contradict the tenor of the United States approach to hemispheric relations we recommend.

Constructive measures can be undertaken. The market for technology might be improved if better information about terms and prices of technology were recorded and shared. The technical competence of Latin American countries in dealing with technology transfer is growing; most nations now routinely collect information on licensing agreements. The United States should cooperate to assure fuller dissemination of that information without violating the confidentiality of specific contracts. This information, collated from hemispheric countries and coordinated through some regional organization, could do much to eliminate foundless charges and identify true distortions. It also would foster competition among the developed countries themselves, and in that way permit the evolution of a more efficient market.

Internally within the United States, efforts can be made to encourage medium-sized and smaller firms to make their technology available for sale. They, too, lack information concerning the opportunities available to them in Latin America. By restructuring OPIC guarantees, as previously recommended, and including a clearing house function among the activities of the aforementioned public foundation, more diversified participation by American business may well be forthcoming.

Recommendation:

33. The U.S. government should cooperate with Latin American countries to collate and disseminate information relating to the terms of licensing agreements, royalty payments, etc. Similarly one function of the new public science foundation recommended previously should be to provide a clearing

house of information on technological services potentially available from middle- and small-sized firms in the United States.

These measures taken together will not make the issue disappear. The very nature of the transfer of technology precludes such optimistic identity of national interests. But these policies can help lead to elimination of the dangers of technological dependence. Expeditious implementation can make clear our appreciation of the Latin American position and our commitment to act within the realm of the possible to resolve the problems surrounding the transfer process.

VII. *Directions for the Future*

Our conclusion is clear: the time is ripe for a new U.S. approach to inter-American relations. Neither old rhetoric nor new slogans will suffice. A fundamental shift in the premises underlying U.S. policies is required.

We must base our actions in the future on the recognition that the countries of Latin America and the Caribbean are not our "sphere of influence," to be insulated from extra-hemispheric relationships. Nor are they marginal to international politics. Rather, they are increasingly active participants on the world scene, nations whose friendship and cooperation are of growing value as we confront the realities of global interdependence.

We must also recognize that the nations of the region are not homogeneous. They are diverse, with varying goals and characteristics, at different levels of development. They are not, and need not be, replicas of our country, nor do they require our tutelage. They are sovereign nations, able and willing to act independently, but whose interests in forging constructive solutions to regional problems will often coincide with ours.

Our mutual concerns in the hemisphere center not on military security, but rather on the critical issues of economic and political security in an uncertain world. The growth of our economies, the well-being of our citizens, the coherence of our societies, and the protection of our individual liberties—these are the goals we share, and which we now recognize cannot be attained in isolation from—or at the expense of—our neighbors.

By understanding today's Latin America as it is, and by making clear to Latin Americans how our conceptions have evolved, we in this country can lay the foundation for a new era in U.S.-Latin American relations.

The approach we suggest is based on the proposition that the United States cannot neglect, exploit or patronize its hemispheric neighbors. It is based, too, on the proposition that justice and decency, not disparities of power and wealth, should be the guiding forces in hemispheric relations. Both self-interest and our fundamental values require that we nurture our common interests and historic ties in the Americas, and that we cooperate in helping to build a more equitable and mutually beneficial structure of international relations.

The approach we advocate looks toward a future in which the peoples of the Americas will work together in confronting regional and world problems—maintaining peace, relieving poverty, eliminating hunger, and respecting human rights. It looks toward a future in which we will join together to harness human and material energies, to develop and conserve human and natural resources, to share the richness of our diverse cultures. Only with such an effort can all Americans, from both North and South, look forward to decent and satisfying lives.

THE RELEVANCE OF LATIN AMERICAN DOMESTIC POLITICS TO NORTH AMERICAN FOREIGN POLICY
Kalman H. Silvert

For years it has been customary to say that one cannot speak of a "Latin America"—and then proceed to do so anyway. One reason is that for some purposes "Latin America" does indeed exist. But another reason is that building categories in which to place Latin American events and situations is difficult and controversial. Categories are statements of theory. The taxonomer sets up his limits on the basis of a commonality *that he imputes to them.* He argues that his system of boxes is useful to understanding, description, prediction, diagnosis, and so on. Accordingly, categorical systems should not be lightly accepted; they set the agenda, suggest what is significant and what can be neglected, and tag what is variable and what is constant.

Latin American politics cannot be discussed with refinement without passing through the construction of categories. Perhaps we can speak with sense about Latin America's generic characteristics: language, ethos, religion, world position, or historical experience. But any similarly general political statements are absurdities. They are of the order of Latin America's "chronic political instability," the "hot blood of the Latin temperament," or the "need for personalistic,

charismatic figures in a population that admires the 'macho' spirit."
Those stereotypes could as easily be given an opposite twist. For
example, political turmoil reveals Latin America's unquenchable thirst
for better and more open governance. Or, Latin Americans are willing
to risk their lives in the pursuit of the ideal of improved governance.
Personalism and charisma are elitist excuses for governments of force,
evidence of their unwillingness to accede to the never-ending popular
quest for a meaningful and effective voice in affairs of state. Even
though we know that every stereotype contains some truth, the
problem is how much truth for which countries, and for which groups
within which countries.

There is no opportunity to fully indicate the theory lying behind my
selection of categories. Consequently, I will hew as closely as possible
to conventional wisdom in order to highlight the links in the
reasoning.

I assume that one of the basic elements playing in politics, whether
domestic or international, is power taken pure. Power can be viewed as
the ability to force others to do what you wish them to, despite their
opposition. It can also be taken to mean the simple ability to take
effective action even in the absence of an antagonist. I will take power
in both senses in this analysis.

I also assume that power—as coercive ability, knowledge, and
available instrumentalities—is always in its applications mingled with
preferences. "Pure" power and "pure" ideologies, preferences, and
tastes come together to give us politically effective desires, the political
analogue of what economists call "effective demand." Political victory
is only sometimes unequivocal for individuals, and almost never so for
states. And, more importantly, the origins of power have to do with
social organization, classes and "races," idea-systems, and profound
cultural values as they all filter through consensus, legitimacy,
institutions, and policy. These themes are the subject matter of
international politics, here defined as the power-infused relations
among formal states in pursuit of varied doctrines of the national
interest, and concerning all subjects which become consciously
attended, from war to cultural exchange. This definition covers only
those relations which fall into the overtly political sphere. It is for this

reason that I have chosen to use the term "international politics" and not the more inclusive "international relations." To assess the relevance of domestic factors:

—We want to know something about the kinds of power that can be brought to bear at any given moment by governments.
—We want to know something about the kinds of power that can be brought to bear *for certain purposes* by governments.
—We want to know the range of alternatives that can be seen by governments, interest groups, intellectuals, parties, and other interested and organized groups in a society.
—We want to know something about tendencies in the above three respects.

Societies create and structure public power in Latin America in the following ways:

—*Patrimonial states.* A small ruling group uses a large non-nationally organized group for economic purposes of a low order of complexity. Only very small numbers of persons can be recruited for tasks at the national level, for there is hardly a "nation" in other than formalistic senses. If the upper groups are cohesive, such governments can be effective for their own limited purposes. They are fragile and weak in the face of external threat, but they can be persistent if internal division is avoided and social change at lower levels is not promoted. Haiti, Nicaragua, and Honduras are classical examples of this kind of governance.
—*Partially "organic," corporate states.* The purpose of corporatism is to permit the growth of institutional differentiation and specialization in the accomplishment of tasks, but without scrambling the class order. Hierarchy is institutionalized within and among the clergy, the landowners, the industrialists, the military, the bureaucracy, the merchants, and the trade unionists. The concept of citizenship exists, but is strained. The notion of *citoyen* from the French Revolution is that all persons are equal before the state; corporatism provides a minimal equality within an occupationally derived, structured system of inequality. Several

Latin American countries show signs of organic corporatism: Mexico's political party structure is corporate in form; the thinking Chile's incumbent government is overtly corporatist, and it is pursuing policies to bring such a state into existence; Peronism and the present Brazilian government both show strong traces of this persuasion.

—*Liberal partial nation-states.* The nation-state seeks to integrate the universal *citoyen,* who can overcome the class-based accidents of birth and assume equality of condition before the state. No nation-state anywhere has succeeded fully in achieving the goal of complete equality of condition in political matters. But some, obviously, have come closer than others. Clearly, the political goal of Allende's administration in Chile was to mitigate, if not erase, class-rooted impediments to complete citizenship. Substantive equality before the laws and structures of the state was much more true than false for most members of the Argentine and Uruguayan upper and middle groups throughout this century, until very recent years. It was the loss of this class-related equality that caused great distress in Brazil after the military came to power in 1964. The attempt to build the social nation characterizes the present Venezuelan polity. The class-inhibited partial nation-state is the political form which has been most characteristic of Latin American ideals (not practice) during the past fifty years. Attacks upon it in the attempt to substitute corporatism provide the fundamental pattern of domestic political strife in the more complex societies. The emergence of the nation-state as ideal form has given rise to two fundamental areas of political clash in Latin America, as well as in the Western world generally. They are the clash between nation and class at the level of total social organization, and between sacred and secular legitimation within the formal state itself.

—*The clash between nation and class.* The idea of the secular nation-state is to provide "marketplaces" in which equality of condition can play itself out in a rationalistic interchange which, it used to be supposed, would allow ever-growing efficiency within a self-correcting and thus self-sustaining mechanism.

Citizenship, religion, and public education would be equally available to all. These were the ideals, and however imperfectly they were realized, in many nations they promoted mass mobilization of populations to new economic tasks, the emergence of popular (and populist) nation-states that could count on the willingness of masses of citizenry to die in defense of the polity, and they contributed to strengthening middle classes and changing the nature of upper classes. However, nowhere has the construction of national communities of universal membership come to completion. In every case, including the United States, national movements have created vast new social and political powers, but they have also created a class order that can effectively resist the completion of essential structural equality.

The second crisis has to do with the form of the state most suitable either for the pursuit of national ends, or for the attempt to restrict expansion of national community. In all countries, of course, there are major segments of the population totally outside the "national question": the Indians of Mexico, Guatemala, Peru and Bolivia; semi-nomadic populations in Brazil and Paraguay; and persons living on society's margins in both rural and urban areas.

As I see it, then, the three grand families of Latin American politics are those of patrimonialism, of anti-national sacralism, and of pro-national secularism. So far we have been speaking of authoritarianisms, totalitarianisms, and democracies only by implication. The reason is clear: national community is a precondition for both the secular republicanism of democracy and the sacred paternalism of totalitarianism. Political situations in non-national societies are in a class by themselves, falling into types of authoritarian regimes far removed from either the voluntarism of the perfectly integrated society or the coercive control of totalitarianism.

Social organization as inferential of power creation was the first category considered here. The second dealt with the quintessential problem of all national states. And the third, political systems, deals with the formal structures evolved for day-to-day governance. It is clear, however, that some rough correlation must exist between the national social organization and the kinds of political systems possible.

Thus, based on estimates of national integration (derived from economic statistics, urbanization, literacy, mobility patterns, cultural and racial homogeneity, extent and complexity and completeness of social services, and hunches concerning citizenry loyalty and anticipatory obedience to law), the Latin countries can be rated on an approximate scale of national community.

The most complete social nations:

> Cuba
> Chile
> Uruguay
> Argentina

Harsh class divisions, but strengthening traditions of participation and social access to national institutions:

> Costa Rica
> Venezuela

Harsh class and regional divisions, racially reinforced stratification, but with growing access to national institutions, with general exception of effective and continuous political participation:

> Mexico
> Brazil
> Peru
> Colombia
> Panama
> El Salvador

Harsh class divisions, very sharp urban-rural differences, sometimes racially reinforced stratification, and little growth in access to national institutions including the political:

> Guatemala
> Paraguay
> Ecuador
> Dominican Republic
> Bolivia
> Nicaragua
> Honduras
> Haiti

(I have omitted formerly British Caribbean republics from this list, for by tradition and circumstance they constitute a special problem.)

It should now be obvious that, given the bases of this argument, the countries which can effectively choose quasi-democratic or quasi-totalitarian forms of governance must come from the top half of the list. This exercise is not an idle one. If it had been gone through at the time of the Bay of Pigs, the planners of that operation might have been less ready to apply a technique learned from Guatemala, one of the most fragmented of Latin American countries, to Cuba, a country socially ready for nationhood. Similarly, an Assistant Secretary of Inter-American Affairs warned a conference several years ago that the United States "is on a collision course with Haiti," implying that if we did not treat "Papa Doc" well, he would opt for a *fidelista* course. Nonsense. But it was not nonsense to have viewed the urban guerrillaism of the early 1960s in Venezuela as bearing a functional relation to the choices then recently made in Cuba. The two countries share many characteristics, and their potentialities are still not radically different. In short, this array of cases suggests the limits of choices effectively open to the societies concerned. It also suggest that as one goes down the list, leadership can express ever-widely varying opinions—being unconstrained by any complexity of followership—but that their ability to actually affect change is limited. Thus, the governments of Arevalo and Arbenz in Guatemala could call for revolutionary change, but could probably not bring it about with a population that was over half Indian, over three-quarters illiterate, and about 90 per cent rural.

This categorization is useful for understanding some of the reasons for the present array of governmental situations. It also allows for the application of easy (and necessarily somewhat slovenly) labels:

In full crisis of nation vs class.

Cuba—a socialist authoritarianism, totalitarian in national political affairs, participant and democratic in many local affairs.

Chile—totalitarian military corporate state in the making at both national and local levels. Not yet fully settled down.

Uruguay—totalitarian corporate state under military tutelage.

Argentina—quasi-democratic state, unstable, undergoing attempt to establish a traditional liberal democracy with a populist cast.

Building nation, not yet upon the nation-class confrontation.

Costa Rica—traditional liberal partial democracy.

Venezuela—traditional liberal partial democracy.

Totally mixed situations, politically and structurally.

Mexico—mixed situation, with some elements of corporatism, some of liberal partial democracy, and remaining strong vestiges of patrimonialism, especially in rural and Indian area.

Brazil—mixed situation under military control, with some elements of corporatism (strong), some of liberal partial democracy (weak), and remaining strong vestiges of patrimonialism in lower groups in both city and country.

Nationalizing elites, lagging populations.

Peru—developmental military rule attempting to move from patrimonialism to some of the choices open in the Mexican and Brazilian scenes.

Colombia—civilian rule, using the forms of partial liberal democracy within the social structure and social habits of patrimonialism.

Panama—essentially patrimonial with some of the trimmings and promise of traditional liberal democracy.

El Salvador—the same.

Pre-national.

Guatemala—classbound military patrimonial rule, traditional in a slowly modernizing social setting.

Paraguay—the same.

Ecuador—the same.

Dominican Republic—the same, but with civilian oligarchical government.

Patrimonial.

Bolivia—the same politically, with little social modernization.

Nicaragua—the same.

Honduras—the same.

Haiti—the same.

It should be noted that all five of the lowest ranking countries—as well as some others—have in the past been the objects of direct military intervention by the United States. Non-national states geographically close to a major power are always inviting targets for the impatience of military intervention: they are pushovers, simply put. At the other end of the list, covert activities have an inviting chance of succeeding when countries experience the ultimate crises of national existence, and are willing to seek assistance from abroad to confront their profound crises at home. It is this kind of opportunity which the United States is accused of having taken in Brazil, Chile, and other countries.

Intervention, in broad terms, involves North American stimuli to and reactions toward Latin American situations. But there is the narrower matter of interventionism. Obviously, the U.S. "intervenes" by existing; our cultural and ideological impacts on Latin America have been strong and continuous for a century and a half. Also, the nature of our economic system and economic presence in some countries at given times has been taken as the basis of *dependencia* thinking in Latin America. Approaching the subject with such breadth, however, precludes reasoned discussion. Economic and cultural dimensions, therefore, will be dealt with only as they become the subject matter of political intercourse. Some patterns of what may vulgarly be called "interventionist" international politics include:

Coercive intervention: The direct use of armed forces, almost always in the smaller, weaker, and neighboring republics. As the Cold War recedes and security becomes redefined, this style of behavior is becoming passé. It has been superseded by the indirect use of coercion.

Indirect and implied coercive intervention: The major case is the training of Latin American armed forces in techniques of civic action and internal policing. These programs were related to doctrines of internal warfare common in the early 1960s, but have since been employed by some Latin American armed forces to create political devices unforeseen and unintended by U.S. advisers. Covert operations also belong in this category, such as operational activities undertaken by intelligence agencies.

Ideological interventions: There are many examples. To wit: the Alliance for Progress, the *abrazo* for the democratic friend and the handshake for the authoritarian enemy. The Hickenlooper Amendment. The individual actions of some U.S. ambassadors.

Economic interventions: Especially protection of individual U.S. enterprises; the establishment of policy for the Inter-American Development Bank, the World Bank, and similar agencies, including the interesting history of the Eximbank in this respect. These economic interventions are also heavily freighted with ideological considerations, of course. The blockade of Cuba, the policy of economic denial applied to Chile, and certain recent reticences in the Peruvian case are examples.

Cultural interventions: The USIA, bilingual schools, traveling exhibitions, scholarships, the academic developmental activities of USAID, etc.

Interventions cannot be avoided, but there should be conscious control over how and why and for what ends. Given the very differing Latin American situations, no single set of techniques can very well be employed. In all instances, however, the United States should seek to increase the ability of Latin American polities effectively to make ever broadening sets of choices. Areas for legitimate U.S. "intervention" would include:

—National communities—We should support nation-building endeavors; they provide the "effectiveness" in the choice-making.
—Democratic organization permits self-correction and provides for meaningful choices reinforced by public acceptability. Thus, when possible, we should support partial democracies where they are to be found and recognize the costs of their absence.
—Academic freedom and university autonomy, civil liberties in their full range, and the existence of strong artistic and intellectual

THE AMERICAS IN A CHANGING WORLD / 72

communities are critical to meaningful choice-making. We have many governmental devices to encourage the creation of such practices and communities. They should be employed, and the United States should not hesitate to be a haven for persons threatened because they have exercised such freedoms.

Taking a look at two broad areas may help to spell out the meaning of this posture in foreign policy decision-making. One concerns atrocious political behavior such as torture and mass murder, and the other the issue of socialism. But first, several steps which I think the U.S. should *not* take, even in such cases.

—We should not use diplomatic relations as a sign of approval or disapproval.
—We should totally eschew overt or covert coercive behavior.
—We should assume blockades and economic denial to be the ultimate sanctions we will employ (unless, obviously, we find ourselves in a state of legal warfare), and use them only as emergency measures, with Congressional approval.

In the realm of atrocious practices, it is immediately clear how complex the subject is. After all, the United States is widely accused of committing atrocities at home as well as in Vietnam. In Latin America, it may be that as many as 300,000 persons died, some the victims of quite spectacular techniques of murder, in Colombia's *violencia* between 1948 and 1960. A dwarf in the Dominican Republic was alleged to have specialized in biting off testicles in the Trujillo period; it is said that an iron maiden was in use in Venezuela during the Perez Jimenez era; impalement is not an unknown police practice in Guatemala; torture and some attendant death has been taking place regularly in Brazil for most of the past decade. The problem is to decide which type of horror may legitimately be an issue of inter-governmental concern.

The United States should remind signatory states to the Universal Declaration of Human Rights of their obligations; it should apply moral suasion against and, if necessary, adopt a policy of cool and sharply limited diplomatic interchange with all states which commit atrocities *as an intrinsic and institutionalized part of the governmental process*. I think a legitimate case can be made that both Brazil and Chile have done this: Brazil, in order to still opposition from the Liberal elite, from potential trade union leaders, and from intellectuals. Its economic development policy demanded the country be made attractive to capital flows from abroad by restraining unionization (not a difficult job), by ousting or weakening certain national industrialists, and by silencing the voices of left nationalism. Relatively little killing was necessary; torture and attendant fright broke not only the nascent urban guerrilla movement, but also stifled most public protest, and muted demands for internal equity in income distribution. Brazil's governors think the price low for a high rate of industrialization, on which basis they promise later to build a better society. Others disagree.

As for the Chilean incumbents, they have destroyed the country's political party system, its national trade unions, and its interest group structure. In the absence of institutions which permit free expression of opinion and consensus, they are left with the practical necessity of substituting the coercive effects of fright for routine acceptance of law. They argue that they were forced to such extreme measures in order to forestall civil war. Others disagree. In any event, in both cases the practices continue long after the end of the heat of revolution, and have become a part of day-to-day governance. But there the resemblance ends, for Chile is on its way to totalitarianism, Brazil is not. In Brazil there are still places to hide, to express dissidence, to wait for a better day, to be silent. In Chile such havens are hard to find. The difference is akin to that which distinguished Nazi Germany from Franco Spain. That distinction is not an innocuous one; for many millions of persons it has been the difference between life and death.

The suggestions flowing from this are:

—Except for routine diplomatic relations, the United States government should in no way assist by word, economic aid, or any other action any Latin American government which is totalitarian. All such governments rule through inducing fright; all such governments sooner or later fall, for by definition they exclude the practices of self-correction. No Latin American government, as I have said, is as yet in this happily exclusive club, but Chile is on its way.

—The U.S. government should publicly state its displeasure to any government using terror as an instrument of governance, and should not in any way reinforce the specific governmental agencies employing terroristic devices, or reward the purposes of the use of atrocities.

The finding of fact in these cases will not be easy. But it can be done. I am well aware of the arguments that "nobody appointed the United States to be the world's policeman." I agree with the statement. I do not agree, however, that Americans do not have a sense of mission. Most of us are infused with the democratic ethos, and we would like to see other countries pursue the promotion of personal and group freedoms. Some say we have neither the knowledge nor power to pursue such goals; others say that our own international situation should serve as moral example; still others are more activist. The real issue is what modalities and techniques we can and should employ in helping to build a comfortable world.

The other area concerns socialist regimes. The only recommendation I can logically fit with prior statements about totalitarianisms is that if the socialist state is truly total dictatorship, then we should extend no friendliness. But socialism is not automatically totalitarian. It is also no assurance of its own major promise, egalitarianism. Neither, of course, does capitalism assure democracy. Economic systems and types of governance are not in a one-to-one relationship.

In actual practice our government has treated attempted socialisms in Latin America as I have suggested we treat totalitarianisms, and it has treated harsh authoritarianisms and nascent totalitarianisms with policies more appropriate to more realistic, pragmatic, and open societies. I do not view this selective diplomacy with equanimity. It reveals a hidden basic preference which is frightening.

I do not wish to imply that the United States should disregard stripping American citizens and companies of their assets by a nationalizing or socializing foreign country. But we should banish religious fervor from our reaction; after all, every major economy in this world, and most minor ones, are either completely or heavily collectivized—not subject to the accountability of a free market, monopolized, planned, relatively non-competitive. The real issues have to do with private versus public collectivization, with which segments of the economy have been removed from the market, the nature of planning, and the degree to which national economies contain government or are contained by government. We must expect more socialization and nationalization in Latin America, unless all those countries turn into corporatisms for the protection not of private enterprise, but merely of private ownership. A proper diplomacy will seek to minimize loss to North Americans and not attempt to combat the evolution of Latin American political-economic forms.

Thus, I do not agree that the fate of American investors overseas is not a governmental concern, on the argument that the risk of expropriation was well known to them before they ventured forth. Rather, equity-seeking mechanisms of many sorts should be established, ranging from a reinforcement of present law to specialized courts of arbitration to appropriate and economically feasible insurance schemes internationally underwritten, if possible. North American policies in Latin America need a broad constituency for successful and consistent application. Businessmen are an important part of that constituency, and should not be written off or otherwise heedlessly abandoned to their own devices. Reaction to their needs, however, should be taken as a *political* problem, not as a labor of Messianism.

Apart from macro-politics, there are a number of common difficulties which affect all nations of the world in varying degrees: ecological matters, population dynamics, urban-rural relations, education and citizenship, education and employment, patterns of industrialization, and communications, among many others. If the stakes are global, they are also particular to each nation and to every person. Thus, these themes are obviously testing grounds for styles and types of international relations and organization. One way to test the utility of my earlier typologies is to learn to what extent a nation either recognizes or has any interest in any of these subjects. For example, countries at the top and bottom of the array of states tend to have little problem with undue population expansion. The least developed "benefit" from high death rates, as in Haiti; the most developed have self-governing populations, as in Argentina. The in-betweens have rapidly expanding populations, as in Brazil, Mexico, and Costa Rica. The least developed have few ecological problems, as in Honduras. The most developed have populations that worry about the environment, as in Argentina. Again, the intermediates emphasize the quantitative over the qualitative, as in Mexico, Peru, and Brazil.

But matters affecting the nature of populations, especially evidenced in education and communications, are of a different order. They are unavoidably ideological in nature. In the last century the purpose of education was to prepare an elite to build economies, polities, and societies. In this century education serves to supply manpower; labor is seen as a commodity, becoming but another factor of production. Communications, to take another example, can be used to promote sales, or to "prepare" people for occupational roles. Or, communications can be regarded as necessary for the enrichment of human experience and understanding. The transfer of international experience and knowledge in these fields is a first-order task with profound long-term political implications.

Policy, therefore, is the sum of an explicit preference system which includes guides for application and a statement of appropriate styles and instruments of application. In this view, policy is akin to the common law, and opposed to civil law pretensions to anticipate all possible human behavior. I have deduced this paper from Latin American cases, but have also suggested prescriptions that may well have much wider application. These prescriptions, however, are intimately and particularly linked to the countries of the Americas. They presume the existence of a "special relationship." I see the particularity in Western hemisphere affairs as having something to do with the following elements:

—Republicanism is a long-standing common ideal of governmental structure in the Americas.
—The ideal of egalitarian democracy has, until very recent years in some countries, comprised a key element in the ideological constructions of all reigning groups.
—Capitalism, as a market economy of private participants, has also

until recent years been a dominant ideological commitment, if decreasingly an actual practice.

—Until very recently, all states as they have grown competent have moved toward an extension of educational systems and other aspects of public welfare.

—The existence of class and racial barriers has been generally seen as undesirable, even while the privileges they confer have been enjoyed and defended.

—The crises of republicanism and of class and nation have become the common property of all the more developed societies, including the United States.

One could extend this list, simultaneously introducing elements which more clearly distinguish American from Western European experience. But I wish only to suggest that it is reasonable to assume that indeed there has been a "Western Hemisphere Idea." If structures and practices have partially belied the idea, the fact of a widespread common commitment is a subtle and profound potential instrument for collaborative and controlled change.

THE INTERNATIONAL SYSTEM AND U.S. POLICY TOWARD LATIN AMERICA
Stanley Hoffmann

The author of this paper is not an expert on Latin America or on the relations between the United States and Latin America, and therefore cannot discuss them as if he were. The purpose of this essay is to describe the main trends of the present international system, from the viewpoint of American policy, and to examine briefly how these trends relate to American interests in and policy toward Latin America.

I. *The Present International System*

1. It is difficult to analyze a system that is in constant flux. For many years, students agreed that it was bipolar, that the conflicting power interests as well as rival ideological conceptions of domestic and world order resembled the classic description of a similar contest by Thucydides, that the world was dominated by security fears and military calculations, that third parties faced an agonizing choice between joining a camp or trying to stay in a safe shelter. Experts disagreed as to whether bipolarity would, as in the past, lead to disaster, or whether nuclear weapons would tame the competition. They also disagreed about the durability of the system. But there was

little doubt about the shape of the elephant, so to speak. Consequently, while sharp debates raged over what U.S. foreign policy ought to be—between supporters of the "Acheson-Dulles line" (build "situations of strength," resist all transgressions and forms of aggression in the hope of forcing compromise) and critics who thought that more of an effort ought to be made toward accommodation through mutual disengagement and arms control—these debates were circumscribed in one important way: both sides assumed the primacy of the Cold War.

In the past six or seven years there have been so many changes that there is no more any agreement as to whether we are even dealing with an elephant! I have elsewhere tried to describe some of the alternative formulations which are being proposed and will not repeat this discussion here.[1] Whereas everybody acknowledges the changes that have made the system of the postwar years apparently obsolete, there is deep disagreement over whether they are lasting or merely temporary, and (even if they are lasting) whether or not they radically transform the essence of international politics as we have known it for centuries. Is it still a contest of state interests in which the absence of any broad consensus and the resort to force turn into something infinitely weaker than political and social contests within a reasonably well-functioning state? Or have the enormous risks of nuclear war and what Raymond Aron called "the dawn of universal consciousness", as well as the many manifestations of material interdependence, begun to create a "global society" more like the domestic societies of its members? It is clear that depending on the answer, the prescriptions for U.S. foreign policy are likely to be quite different. And it must be said that the Nixon-Kissinger foreign policy has very skillfully avoided telling us what its own diagnosis was: the constant talk of "stable structures of peace" is at so general a level as to be compatible with any view, and while the tactics and style have not exactly been congruent with what might be called the "global society" interpretation, there have been lofty speeches that pay at least lip service to it.[2]

Ambiguity may actually be the better part of wisdom. For a system is what its members decide to make of it. Whether the profoundly new features will last, and even more whether they will affect the traditional murderously competitive and divisive essence of world politics, is not predetermined. Here, the responsibility of the great powers is obviously huge, although one of these new features may well be that their grasp, today, is far smaller than their reach. What follows is an attempt to describe the main features of present international relations.

2. The traditional field of competition of the states is what Aron has called the "strategic-diplomatic" field: the chessboard on which the pawns are weapons and armies, diplomats and spies, and legal advisers; the stakes are people and territory, domination and submission; the moves are threats and wars, alliances and guarantees. This chessboard remains, of course, of vital importance, but it has been drastically transformed.

a) It continues to be dominated by the competition of the superpowers (of which there are still only two, although the split between Moscow and Peking, and Peking's nuclear progress, have obviously complicated the picture). But if one compares that rivalry today with what it was 20 years ago, one finds—without having to decide whether "detente" is a trick or a trend, a convenience or a necessity—three moderating factors. One might be called nuclear wisdom, i.e., awareness not only of the perils of nuclear confrontations, but also of escalation, and consequently a determination to avoid any direct military clashes between the U.S. and the U.S.S.R. If they occasionally bare their teeth, it is—as in the universe of Konrad Lorenz' beasts—in order not to have to fight.

The second moderating factor is the legitimacy of the nation-state, cornerstone (however porous) of the international order. This means, on the one hand, that naked aggression and overt domination have to be disguised or sheathed; on the other hand, that even weak powers, or very recent ones, find ways of resisting or of exploiting their limited assets to good advantage. Superpowers must now take into account the complexities of local situations, and the extraordinary diversity of issues in a world of ideological, ethnic, political and economic fissures. All of this has made it impossible for the superpowers to fully absorb into their contest all the troubles, disputes and issues of a highly heterogeneous world. For instance, while the great power rivalry heightens the peril in the Middle East, it did not create the Arab-Israeli conflict, any more than detente suffices to solve it. Nor was the

Indochina war merely an episode of the struggle between Moscow, Peking and Washington.

These moderating factors have two important effects on the great powers' rivalry. The first is that it tends to be increasingly regulated: one could almost codify the rules of competition, some of which are tacit, others explicit. Some are so "highfalutin" as to be meaningless (the renunciation of unilateral advantages is tantamount to giving up foreign policy), some are so vague as to be useless, and some (as in SALT I) are so limited as not to corset the competition very much, and even incite bulges wherever the corset stops. Yet the existence of rules reflect the states' desire to avoid disaster and to develop restraining mutual ties. Secondly, the stake of a partly reined-in competition tends to be influence rather than control;[5] and influence is far more elusive and evanescent. It means that the game is never over, and that any defeat (or "breakthrough") may well be a mere setback (or temporary gain). This, in turn, should contribute to defuse the contest (cf. the history of Soviet-Egyptian relations).

b) The huge changes in technology have radically transformed the military security problems of the superpowers. It is not only that they are incapable of developing an annihilating first-strike capability (unless some unpredictable revolution in anti submarine warfare occurs), it is also that it releases the superpowers from some of their dependence on outlying bases. The new submarines, the new bombers, and of course the ICBM, have enormous ranges: the home territories and the oceans suffice. This does not mean that bases (for instance in the Eastern Mediterranean or the Western Pacific) have lost their importance for regional military operations, or that U.S. and Soviet troops in the two halves of Europe have lost their multiple functions. But this, too, contributes to the dissociation of the strategic, i.e. the survival-levels, from the other levels of the great powers' competition.

c) This does not mean that the world can breathe safely. For the trends mentioned effect a displacement of danger, away from a general war between the superpowers, in two directions.

(i) One might be called localized interstate chaos. It results from the very heterogeneity mentioned above, and from the fragmentation of the international system into regional systems that remain ultimately connected with the central nuclear balance, but only ultimately. Such localized violence is of course more or less dangerous, depending on the degree of superpower implication: in Europe it is so deep that total combustibility has actually insured deterrence and peace; in the Middle East there is just enough of a balance of local turbulence and great power involvement to make the area the most dangerous powderkeg in the world. But even when the great powers are not deeply involved, or (as in Latin America) when only one of them is, localized chaos is dangerous for several reasons. One is the difficulty of control: in a sense, control is easier when the risk of superpower confrontation is greater (cf. the repeated ceasefires in the Middle East). Another is the risk of contagion: ultimately any "stable structure of peace" will depend on the ability to cope with violent conflict in several parts of the world. A third reason is the deliberate contribution to chaos by several major powers. Either by failing to curb their own nuclear arsenals, or by selling nuclear materials under conditions that do not adequately prevent proliferation (I do not suggest that they could in any case have prevented it: this is one realm in which their loss or lack of control is a rather bitter victory for pluralism and equalization in the world jungle; but there is a difference between not being able to stop something, and making it more likely). On the other hand, competitive weapons sales to eager clients—as if Migs were figs, or Mirages perfumes—by major states in search of political influence and commercial gains have escalated irresponsibly and provoked local arms races, inevitably. By contrast with nuclear weapons, conventional weapons have always ended up being used, between states that have good or bad reasons for conflict, and where the possession of military hardware provides pretexts for toughness and opportunities for mischief.

(ii) The second direction might be called non-interstate chaos. It has two familiar forms. One is large-scale internal genocide, in countries tormented by deep divisions and hatreds (cf. Biafra, or Bangla Desh, or Indonesia in 1965, or Cambodia and South Vietnam today). Here too, the possibilities of outside control are limited, especially by the taboo about "non-intervention in domestic affairs". The other form is not internal but transnational: individual or group terrorism, taking advantage of weapons available for spectacular massacres, and of opportunities for disruption which the delicate network of world production, transportation and communications affords. Thus, overall peace between the most potent does not mean general peace between states; it can coexist with extraordinarily bloody or selectively destructive violence distinct from interstate conflicts.

3. The other great transformation is the increasing saliency of new chessboards of world politics. There are important fields of competition whose subject-matter is economic, monetary or technological, and whose importance to the contestants is enormous. This saliency results both from the evolution of the world economy toward economic development and social welfare, and the increased role of the state in these areas, as well as from the displacement of the "game of nations", away from the excessively perilous minefield of strategic-diplomatic affairs, toward new fields where gains may be more rewarding and less elusive, and where the contest only rarely or obliquely entails the use or threat of force.

A key reason for this new trend is that modern nationalism means, above all, a desire for economic security and not merely military safety. This means having safe access to the raw materials, sources of energy, or agricultural and industrial products that one needs to import, having markets available for one's exports, capital for expansion, and means of financing what one must buy. A second reason for the importance of the new chessboards is the appearance of actors besides the states. Some are quite simply and traditionally national interest groups, but groups of such economic importance that they tend to exert considerable influence on the state's policy (for instance, shipping and fishing interests, or labor, or farmers, or even central bankers). Others are transnational, the so-called multinational companies, which develop their own strategies and are (either through their fiscal policies, investments, capital movements, or agreements among themselves or with customers), often able to thwart decisions of the states in which they operate. Other new actors include international agencies with regulatory functions.

A third reason lies in the ambivalent nature of economic and technological interdependence. On the one hand, the fact that economic issues are now at the core of governmental responsibilities instead of being left largely to private enterprise, means that the manipulation of interdependence has become the core of interstate politics. Each state tries to make the relation of interdependence one in which it will be less, and the others more, *dependent*. On the other hand, what might be called the neo-mercantilist politics of interdependence coexists with a highly non-mercantilist phenomenon: the *loss* of national control, not merely by some nations to the advantage of others as, for instance, between oil-importing nations and OPEC members (which *is* a "neo-mercantilist" phenomenon), but by all, due partly to the new non-state actors, partly to phenomena resulting from an international economy which states either do not know how to control, or else are afraid to control by unilateral measures that might cut them off from the world economy on which they depend.

What are the chief characteristics of the relations between actors on these chessboards?

a) The *stake* can best be defined by the late Professor Arnold Wolfers' distinction between two kinds of state goals: possession goals (such as territory, colonies, bases) and milieu goals (obtaining a favorable environment for one's activities).[4] I have noted that on the traditional chessboard, influence was replacing control as a state goal, implying a shift from possession to milieu goals. On the new chessboards, even if a state's concern is with securing certain goods (for instance, a guaranteed amount of oil, or national control over its own resources), it aims primarily to shape the milieu in such a way that the coveted possessions may be secured by common consent. In other words, influence rather than control is at the heart of the process: who will have a greater or even a determining role in shaping the framework or setting the terms of the relationships?

b) The *form* of this competition for influence is the politics of global bargaining and overlapping coalitions. It is here that the resemblance to domestic politics is greatest—but to the domestic politics of a nation with extremely weak central institutions, and with the competing or coalescing interests recognizing no higher goal than their own advantage. It is only because of the spectacular impact of OPEC that we have even become aware of the emergence of global bargaining and overlapping coalitions. But a study of the politics of international communication satellites, of world monetary reform, of the International Atomic Energy Agency, of confrontations between the U.S. and the European Common Market, or of the negotiation of international commodity agreements, would yield the same conclusions. The current conference on the law of the seas shows how complex and fierce such bargaining can be, and how varied national strategies are. Weak states that share one valuable asset tend to "gang up" in order to exploit it to the hilt, while states that want some part of or access to it bring to bear whatever assets *they* have in other realms.

c) The *theme* of the contest could be termed the dialectic of nationhood vs. management. Each state wants to retain as much control as possible, and to regain control where it has lost it. But the very scope of the problems at stake, the obvious fact that a maze of national regulations would easily destroy the world economy and therefore backfire, the need to protect resources from unbridled exploitation, the ease with which worldwide "diseases" are circulating, all of this necessitates the collective management of problems, with institutions and provisions for enforcement.

d) The *issues* around which the contest takes place can be divided into two categories.

(i) Problems of delimitation: how far are states and other actors allowed to go in the exercise of national sovereignty or economic maximization? This is at the heart of the problems of contemporary international law, which has to deal with areas formerly beyond its reach, or where previous rules no longer apply because of technological change and the growing activity and greed of states and economic interests (cf. the current problems of the sea, where everything has to be redefined). And it is also at the heart of multiple confrontations of recent years, at UNCTAD, or GATT, or at the UN, or around OPEC. Can producers who enjoy a quasi-monopolistic position pretend both to set prices and to regulate production? How can the interests of foreign investors and those of the host state be reconciled? Should the same, rather liberal rules of international trade apply to the developing as well as to the industrial nations, etc. . . . ?

(ii) Problems of international regimes. Joint management, with the transfer of various regulatory, executive and even redistributive powers to common institutions, is likely to be if not *the,* at least *a* wave of the future, and a focal point of international bargaining. The current haggling over an international regime for the high seas, with its own revenues and licensing rights, is a good example. An eventual reform of the Bretton Woods system would inevitably entail a strengthening of the IMF, as regulator of floating or "adjustable" rates and as manager of the SDR. To deal with the problems of pollution, or food shortages, the necessity for international authorities becomes even more apparent. But they will make global politics more complex, by providing new arenas for the contest of influence, new actors, and new constraints on the existing actors.

4. Let us put together the different elements we have listed. They point to a paradoxical world: a rather comforting modicum of *global* peace, but almost limitless opportunities for local disruption and functional maneuvering; joint management, consequently, as an imperative and central theme, but probable unmanageability given the number of danger points, the diversity of regional and national situations, the instability and narrow basis of interstate coalitions, the uncertainties of the world economy, and above all the fact that the new and the old chessboards are not entirely disconnected, so that in a variety of still uncharted ways, states whose economic interests are threatened may want to reintroduce the threat or the use of force.

This rather bewildering world poses special problems for the U.S.

a) In the contest for influence, the U.S. has extraordinary assets: no nation has greater means to punish and to reward, no nation has established so many forms of presence in so many parts of the world, no nation has such an impact on the setting or upsetting of the rules and frameworks of world economic relations. And yet, these vast advantages easily turn into embarrassments, both because they make the U.S. the frequent and almost unavoidable target of foreign grievances, and because they permanently threaten to reduce the flexibility, impede the mobility, and deepen the commitments of the U.S. In the new international system, a great power may easily find that its responsibilities far exceed its rewards: its "privilege" is to be concerned lest local violence or functional chaos threaten the framework of world order which it requires to protect its interests and its influence. Its physical safety and material advantages are paid for at the high price of permanent fear, not only for that framework, but of excessive entanglement.

b) Dealing with this kind of a world is alien to both of the traditional approaches of U.S. foreign policy. One has been isolationism: the avoidance of military and political obligations, leaving U.S. private interests fully active around the world, under an official protection that isn't called into operation unless those interests are threatened. It is blindingly clear that the world in which such a policy made sense has gone, and that the pleas for neo-isolationism—based on the fear of military implication and escalation—ignore both the imperative of influence (which persists unless one simply decides to opt out of any attempt at shaping the international milieu), and the new dimensions of international economic affairs.

The other approach has been a crusading one. While it may still be true, in the words of both George Ball and Henry Kissinger, that the U.S., among non-Communist nations, is the only one with "global responsibilities", it is clear that the trends discussed here have made a policy of global containment, focusing on the cold war and on the traditional chessboard, rather obsolete. Mr. Kissinger has understood it, insofar as he has changed the mode of operation of American diplomacy. Yesterday, we often seemed like a puppeteer pulling the strings of sometimes reluctant puppets. Today we have given up the puppet show, and merely try to build the roads on which others will be allowed to walk. But despite its special assets, one single nation can no longer be so decisive in shaping the milieu: world engineering may have to be democratized.

II. *On U.S.-Latin American Relations*

There are too many issues, and above all too many countries, for any overall discussion of the relevance of these generalities to Latin America to make much sense. Indeed, a blanket discussion is usually an attempt to evade the real issues or to smother them in platitudes, and the frequent tendency to deal with them either by labeling U.S.-Latin American relations ("community" or "partnership") or by celebrating the dawn of a New Spirit, is a combination of evasion and dishonesty (both of which have their diplomatic uses). I will not be specific either, for sheer lack of expertise. But I will try to point out in which ways the trends of the international system are relevant.

1. Given those trends, the threads that should guide U.S. foreign policy in the labyrinth of Latin American affairs could be described, or rather prescribed, as follows:

a) A first imperative is the avoidance of any direct collision between the U.S. and the rising nationalisms of Latin America. The depth of American official and unofficial involvements, the very tendency of Latin Americans either to turn to Washington—which breeds resentment—or to make Washington responsible for their own problems, the North American habit of taking Latin America for granted as a zone of influence and *chasse gardée,* all of this seems to make collisions inevitable. But local collision in one part of the world could be contagious elsewhere: the imperative I propose is derived partly from the vulnerability of the U.S. to nationalist "insurrections" all over the world. Secondly—still on the traditional chessboard—it is such collisions which could provide Moscow or Peking with opportunities to try and dislodge Washington's influence and establish their own. This temptation could dangerously reverse what I have called the dissociation of the central strategic balance from the regional balances, and the moderating impact of the former even on non-nuclear confrontations between the great powers. Thirdly, such collisions would severely disrupt the conditions of mutuality and interdependence which exist between the U.S. and Latin American nations on the "new" chessboards. The unevenness of interdependence makes collisions possible (cf. the complaints of many Latin Americans about the behavior and effects of U.S. companies, concerning their national economic development and their internal politics). But interdependence exists, and a great deal of mutuality as well (cf. the need Latin American nations have for outside capital, markets for their industrial exports, and credit). There is a fourth reason for avoiding collisions; it has to do with our second imperative.

b) The U.S. ought to do all that is possible to promote the entry of Latin America into the world of multiple management. The gravest danger here is the rise of diverse and often antagonistic nationalisms among states that, for reasons of domestic "social mobilization" and of their emergence on the world stage, may be tempted to behave like the European nations a century ago. Nationalism would thus be both a way of overcoming deep domestic fissures, and a way of cutting a grander figure.

Clearly, collisions between Washington and Latin American nations would only foster such a temptation. But Latin American rivalries unconnected with the "Yankees" may make a world threatened by local chaos and unmanageability an even more unruly place. Insofar as the U.S. is in fact a great power (which does not mean it is a repository of global wisdom), it cannot shake off *some* responsibility for the way in which Latin Americans will act on the world scene, even though it must not tell them what to do and what not to do. In other words, an excessive swing of the pendulum from the extreme of overbearing arrogance to that of "benign neglect" (recommended by some as a tough but necessary cure for both sides) would be a mistake. Thus, it is easy to see that each imperative is difficult to follow, and that they aren't easy to reconcile.

2. One way of showing how they can be promoted and reconciled is to describe what the U.S. national interest in Latin America is *not*.

a) It is not primarily strategic. From the viewpoint of the contest on the traditional chessboard, the U.S. national interest is to continue to deny military bases and positions of strong political influence to its chief rivals. But, on the one hand, as long as Latin America is in effect a zone from which these rivals stay away militarily, and in which Russia has no other ally than Cuba, the U.S. needs no bases of its own, especially in light of the technological changes discussed. The first imperative suggests that establishing new bases would be an error. It also suggests that it may be in the interest of Washington not to maintain such irritants as Guantanamo base or sovereignty over the Panama Canal Zone. In the latter case, guarantees of free passage can more easily be obtained if the sovereignty issue is removed from the diplomatic agenda: nothing is to be gained by delaying tactics or by making the transfer of authority appear excessively and directly conditional. On the other hand, the greatest opportunities for Soviet (or eventually Chinese) military and political penetration would be provided by acute confrontations between the U.S. and a nationalist regime in Latin America: Cuba should serve as the negative model *par excellence*. It is hard to imagine a Latin American nation offering bases to, or becoming a diplomatic satellite of, Moscow unless it felt so pushed to the wall by Washington as to prefer a distant protector to a close one. In its overt dealings with the Allende regime in Chile, the U.S. seems to have learned that lesson—which does not, however, mean that Washington was beyond reproach. To wit:

b) The U.S. national interest is not to maintain only certain kinds of regimes in power while undermining or even trying to overthrow others. The external manipulation of domestic politics is wrong from the viewpoint of both imperatives—to try to avoid clashes with Latin American nationalism by having "understanding" regimes risk provoking hyper-nationalistic reactions among the manipulated nations as well as among "friendly" countries, which will be tempted sooner or later to establish their nationalist credentials and authenticity. Moreover, the promotion of multiple management will remain fragile as long as the voices that speak for Latin America in the conferences and organizations in charge of such management are not the true spokesmen of genuinely national regimes. No action taken by such regimes can be so seriously destructive of U.S. interests as to justify U.S. interventions *unless* it opens up major channels of strategic and political control to our chief rivals. As this would result only from the failure of a U.S. policy of support for weak or corrupt regimes (as in the Cuban example), there can be no overriding argument for U.S. overt or oblique interference with domestic affairs.

To be sure, some regimes are likely to provide a more favorable milieu for U.S. public and private interests than others. Some have argued that it is legitimate for the U.S. to support regimes that provide unfettered opportunities to American investments and which adopt policies compatible with those of the U.S.; that it is normal for the U.S. to try to prevent or to embarrass regimes hostile to American economic interests and policies. They have argued that it is therefore proper for the U.S. to train Latin American police forces for counterinsurgency warfare and to provide, so to speak, technical aid against guerrillas and subversives. But this would mean linking the U.S. to the fate of certain types of regimes at a time when the uncertainties of influence require flexibility and the careful preservation of changes for influence, even with originally hostile or "difficult" regimes. Since the regimes that almost invariably receive U.S. support happen to be the most oppressive or the least authentically national, this first position is a recipe for disaster in the long run.

Others argue that the U.S. ought to promote democracy and respect for human rights and elementary freedoms throughout Latin America, and to ostracize tyrannical or corrupt regimes. Despite admirable intentions, this policy too would condemn the U.S. to recurrent entanglement. Moreover, it would sooner or later lead to a double perversion. Regimes fought by the U.S. would find easy, demagogic opportunities to give a popular or populist basis to their excesses by posing as victims of U.S. hostility. And the U.S. would just as easily lapse from altruistic and idealistic objectives into self-interested ones; it would not be the first time that the self-appointed promoter of lofty ideals would end up cloaking imperial designs and selfish economic or power interests in the language of virtue. This does not mean that the U.S. should not, along with other powers, try to prevent internal genocide in foreign nations. Nor does it mean that in deciding on aid or loans, or on investments, the U.S. government or U.S. interests should treat representative and unrepresentative, free and tyrannical policies alike—especially in an area where there is no strategic reason for closing one's eyes to the sorry spectacle of tyranny or decay. But there is a difference between a U.S. preference for regimes that truly express the ideals of self-determination and self-government, and a policy of deliberate intervention which would, *ipso facto,* violate them. For—as we have discovered in Vietnam—neither nation-building nor the imposition of democracy can be imposed from the outside, short of circumstances as radically exceptional as, say, the occupation and reform of defeated nations like West Germany or Japan.

3. What, then, *are* the essential interests of the U.S., leaving aside the economic realm (which I consider by far the more important, but which is treated elsewhere)?

a) There is one crucial issue of delimitation. It concerns U.S. strategic interests, and it also affects the capacity of nations to manage adequately their joint interests. I refer to the new definition of states rights on the sea. While some of the proposals made by the U.S. at the conference on the law of the sea are eminently debatable insofar as they would give the more powerful fishing fleets and the more industrialized nations vast advantages in exploiting the resources of the sea and the seabed, nevertheless Washington's position is essentially correct on three points: the need for a narrow (12 miles), not a huge (200 miles) scope for the territorial sea; the need for states that will be given extensive rights on a broad zone contiguous to the territorial sea to grant free passage there (and through straits) to all ships—including submarines—i.e., not to apply the restrictions traditionally applicable in the territorial sea, and not to treat that zone as one of full sovereignty; the need for an international authority to deal with the resources of the high sea beyond that zone, and which could have some say in the management of resources of the zone but not under the full jurisdiction of the coastal states.

Clearly, there is a risk of collision between the U.S. and the Latin American states, whose demands and claims have been extreme. The best way of avoiding it is surely not to yield to national greed which, however, means that the U.S. must also be willing to curb the greed of some of its own shipping and oil- or raw material-extracting interests. In exchange for a considerable reduction in the national demands of the Latin Americans (and other coastal and developing countries) the U.S. must also accept a restriction on "free enterprise" (which benefits the more advanced) on behalf of joint management.

b) Then there is the problem of avoiding "localized interstate chaos" in Latin America. The traditional rivalries and territorial contests between neighbors, the unevenness of economic development which gives a state such as Brazil the temptation of regional predominance, the fondness of military regimes for acquiring and parading advanced weaponry, all of this creates serious potential dangers. They pose a difficult problem for the U.S. We have a "milieu goal" of safeguarding peace *between* Latin American nations so as to preserve an adequate international environment for economic activities and other forms of comity. Moreover, a "stable structure of peace" will require that the major powers accept, as the counterpart of their importance, a special responsibility against localized chaos (cf. at the present writing, the role of Britain in Cyprus). Depending on the regional configuration, this responsibility will be more or less collective or shared. In the case of Latin America, the U.S. may well have trouble getting anyone to share it, even if we wanted to.

Two problems in particular are involved here. One is that of nuclear proliferation. As I said earlier, we cannot prevent it, either by ourselves or in conjunction with the U.S.S.R., short of resorting to force in order to stop the threat—which would not be a perfect recipe for world order. But we can, and should, show more imagination in the search for incentives for nations *not* to "go nuclear", and for disincentives against those who do. This is important especially in situations where the accession of one power to nuclear status would be felt by others as a direct threat or as a step toward regional hegemony, which would trigger more proliferation. While agreements on non-nuclear zones may be helpful, they may not suffice. It may be necessary for the U.S. to provide far greater assistance for the development of the peaceful uses of nuclear energy, in order to preclude the development of nuclear weapons, but under far more stringent controls than up to now. And it may also be necessary for the U.S. to make it clear to any new nuclear power whose entry into the "club" could provoke a chain reaction that we are ready to provide threatened rivals or neighbors with aid—economic and military—aimed at redressing the balance, yet without further proliferation.

The other problem is that of the peaceful settlement of disputes. There is a need here to re-enforce not only the machinery but the attention paid to potential conflicts, so that one could act before an explosion. Such an effort should take place within a multinational framework such as the OAS. (This would also make it possible gradually to take collective steps against "non-interstate chaos".) Such a framework would dilute the possibility of direct collisions between the "peacemaker" and one aggrieved party. Yet without permanent vigilance and ceaseless efforts of peacekeeping, there will be no chance for joint management.

4. Let me end with two question marks: two issues on which the national interest of the U.S. strikes me as anything but clear-cut.

a) One is that of arms sales to Latin American countries. There are many arguments for them, apart from the purely domestic one of helping the U.S. balance of payments and the survival of our huge war industry. One is that if we should discontinue these sales, the Latin American nations would turn to our competitors, who would thus gain influence and strongholds, often damaging to our own legitimate interests. The other is that only by persisting in our policy can we mold more or less satisfactory "balances of power" between suspicious neighbors. It is clear that the major weapons-exporting countries are far from ready to give up that method for economic and political influence through collective restraint. And yet an urgent need for restraint exists. Otherwise the U.S. might find itself heavily responsible for interstate (and domestic) bloodshed, and condemned to choose between the unsavory position of Pontius Pilate, and the unhappy one of Sisyphus. Maybe the answer lies in drawing a fine line between a rather repulsive "hard sell" of our weapons so as to dislodge any competition, and a policy of limited and discreet sales aimed only at preserving balances—while losing no opportunity to push for generalized arms control agreements.

b) The other problem is that of a reform of the OAS. The overwhelming presence of Washington has many drawbacks. It serves as a pretext for displays of Latin American nationalism, for manifestations of excessive and ritual dependence (or reliance) on Big Brother, or for perfectly vapid compromises. On the other hand, a U.S. withdrawal aimed at fostering Latin America's capacity for collective management (and depriving it of excuses and fake targets) might weaken the OAS' capacity for peaceful settlement, and actually accentuate "scapegoatism" by heightening the Latin American sense of neglect. Here, again, the solution may have to be subtle: maintaining the OAS, yet providing within it for separate organs that would include only the nations south of the U.S. border for several ranges of issues.

Obviously, this is no more than a sketch. But its purpose is to provoke argument, and perhaps also further thought.

NOTES

(1) "Choices," *Foreign Policy*, Fall 1973.

(2) For further elaboration, see my contribution to *Pacem In Terris III,* Vol. I, Center for the Study of Democratic Institutions, Santa Barbara, 1974.

(3) "Weighing the balance of power," *Foreign Affairs*, July 1972.

(4) See Wolfers' *Discord and Collaboration* (Baltimore, 1962).

THE CHANGING NATURE OF LATIN AMERICAN INTERNATIONAL RELATIONS: GEOPOLITICAL REALITIES*

Riordan Roett

Introduction

The international relations of Latin American nation-states are now beginning to manifest a startling degree of heterogeneity and fragmentation. It is no longer feasible or practical, for the purposes of policy, to speak of the international politics of Latin America as though they were no more than a reflection of traditional United States-Latin American relations or a mere reaction to international systemic forces.

Other papers prepared for the Commission have touched on some of the external reasons why this is true: the movement away from

---

* As used in this paper, "geopolitics" refers to geopolicy, or the dynamic aspects of those combined geographic and political factors that influence the options and strategies of a nation's foreign policy. There is no attempt to relate historical interpretations of geopolitics by Mackinder, Mahan, Haushofer, Sypkman *et al.* to contemporary Latin American international relations but merely to emphasize the emergence of geographic factors as part of subsystem politics.

bipolarity to multipolarity; the growing world demand for Latin America's natural and primary resources; the increasing willingness of the Latin nations to act collectively at the international level;[1] the emergence of a series of authoritarian/corporatist governments that have given real meaning to the "state" in the "nation-state" concept for the first time since independence; the increasing freedom and cross-linking ties created by multinational actors; and the search for European and Asian allies in specific issue-areas such as arms supplies, trade agreements, and others, in the face of United States disinterest or unwillingness to deal with these issues.

The significance of these and other changes is that many Latin governments are now able and willing to identify, extract, and employ human and physical societal resources for national purposes. Governments will no longer tolerate the interference of private interests or "private governments" in national policy-making. Previously able to countermand or neutralize feeble efforts at national policy-making, private interests must follow the government's policy for development, if they want to survive.

Latin governments, all of which are heavily influenced by the military on the continent (with the exception of Argentina, Colombia and Venezuela), have emerged in the last six to eight years as increasingly developmentalist. Emphasis is primarily on internal security and development; as power is consolidated and policy-making centralized in the national government, the authoritarian regimes are increasingly able to consider the external or international implications of national development.

Whether authoritarian-left as in Peru, authoritarian-right as in Brazil, or authoritarian-centrist as in Ecuador at the moment, Latin governments are becoming aware of the international dimensions of policy-making and increasingly able to "play the game." The old

---

1. The collaboration of the Latin countries in the June 1974 OPEC meeting in Quito is clear. ARPEL, the organization of Latin American oil companies is increasingly active as is OLADE, the new Latin American energy organization. The recently formed IBA (International Bauxite Association) promises to become increasingly aggressive in its demands. Peru and Chile are leading members of CIPEC, the copper exporters organization.

geopolitical realities—a quiescent continent of "democratic," free enterprise republics united in a paternalistic Inter-American System—are no more. The Latin American subsystem, for better or worse, has begun to come of age. The United States will have to respond in diverse ways to new demands and situations.

Some of the dynamics of the new international relations, and the implications for United States policy, follow. Implicit in the discussion are the following assumptions: (1) Brazil, Peru, Venezuela, and perhaps Mexico are the principal candidates for geopolitical leadership in Latin America; (2) the philosophical underpinnings of the governments under discussion—democratic vs. authoritarian or democratic vs. socialist vs. totalitarian—are less significant in the geopolitical sense than the governments' capacity to act independently for national purposes; (3) the British Caribbean is not included, except where it is explicitly introduced; (4) the major world actors relevant to Latin America in the foreseeable future are Japan and Western Europe, not Eastern Europe and the Soviet Union (with the clear exception of their role in contemporary Cuba); (5) Asia and Africa are subsidiary interests for Latin America although the Third World concept is useful, and will be employed increasingly by Latin states at the international level for diplomatic and propaganda purposes. (Africa will increase in relative importance for Brazilian trade and resource purposes as well.)

Specific Areas of Concern

Brazil and its subsystem. Geopolitical reality demands that the United States no longer consider Brazil as a "big kid" growing up too fast; realism also requires the United States to bury the assertion that "as Brazil goes, so goes Latin America." Brazilian foreign policy has been oriented towards a continental and world role throughout most of this century, but only with the change in government in 1964 has that operating premise become a possibility.

Brazilian foreign policy has three dynamic aspects. The first is the geopolitical outreach into the neighboring tier of states, Bolivia, Paraguay, and Uruguay. The second is its clear interest in diversifying its trade and economic contacts away from dependence on the United States towards Western Europe and, more significantly, Japan. And the third concerns Amazon development and relations with Peru and Venezuela.

Slowly but surely, Brazil is creating a security perimeter of border states. Brazil's techniques are not military conquest and occupation; more subtle and effective economic and cultural strategies are employed. In Paraguay, the signing of the Itaipu hydro-electric power project binds Paraguay to Brazil, economically, for the foreseeable future. The only natural resource advantage Paraguay possessed has been tied to Brazilian development. The old balance maintained between Argentina and Brazil by Asuncion has been tilted in Brasilia's favor, even though Paraguay signed a supplementary hydro-electric agreement with Argentina farther down the river. The Brazilian cultural influence has been preponderant in Asuncion for years; a senior member of the Brazilian foreign service is always posted to Paraguay. The Paraguayan-Brazilian border has become an area of free transit and the Brazilians have begun to import workers, build schools, and suggest informal "colonization" in the area around the site of the power project.

With the assumption of power by General Banzer in Bolivia, following the overthrow of the populist-left Torres government, and the heavy hint that Brazil supported its removal, Brazilian influence in La Paz has increased dramatically. Trade agreements, the signing of a contract for natural gas concessions, and general economic assistance has given the Brazilian government a strong foothold in Bolivia for the first time in decades; Bolivia, again, had formerly been a traditional area of Argentine influence.[2]

---

2. In May 1974 the Banzer and Geisel governments agreed that Brazil will assist Bolivia to create a "pole of development" in the Santa Cruz area, in exchange for the sale of natural gas. Brazil has agreed to prepare feasibility studies for the construction of a Santa Cruz-Cochabamba rail link. At present, the only route to cross the continent from Brazil to Chile is via Argentina. The line would have strategic as well as economic importance.

The recent agreement between Paraguay and Bolivia to further economic and cultural exchange underlies the growing symmetry among the bordering nations and again underscores the predominant, although not exclusive, influence of Brazil. Uruguay, the third of the countries included in this security perimeter, has long been an area of land purchase and settlement by Brazilians moving down from Rio Grande do Sul. Increasing ties between the Brazilian military with their counterparts in Montevideo, and direct economic interests, have further strengthened Brazil's informal but significant presence in Uruguay.

Growing Brazilian influence in these three neighboring countries does not suggest imminent takeover; there is no need for such destabilizing conduct. Economic penetration, diplomatic maneuvering, trade and concession agreements, arms supplies, land purchase and informal colonization all provide flexible mechanisms for accomplishing eventual pre-eminence. Brazil's motivations are primarily economic, with some geopolitical or military security emphasis as well. The security of Brazil's borders, as well as the natural influence it holds over three potentially non-viable nation-states, justifies present policy. The fragility of these states and the bleak economic future of each is apparent.

The second aspect of Brazilian foreign policy is the increasing diversity of economic ties away from the United States, towards Western Europe and Japan.[3] Both the Common Market and Japan provide increasing attraction as trading partners, and the Brazilian "economic miracle" has produced a variety of goods that are of considerable appeal in Europe. Brazil ranked second last year, after the United States, in terms of Japanese overseas investment. Their growing ties are based in part on the large Japanese immigration to Brazil—Brazil's Japanese community is the largest outside of Japan. It also rests on the willingness of the Japanese to provide risk capital and to invest in safe, but security-related projects (such as port and dock construction, ships, and related materials). Increasingly friendly and

---

3. The announcement of diplomatic relations with Peking has a strong economic rationale and trade may justify a complete re-evaluation of Brazil's relations with Cuba, particularly after the Argentine car deal.

profitable contact has been established between them. Some would go so far as to speak about the probability of a "partnership," giving Brazil the Pacific outlet it desires for trade and diplomatic purposes, and preparing the Brazilian navy to assume a "two ocean" stance by the end of the decade through the rapid modernization of its facilities with Japanese assistance.

There is no intention to suggest the creation of another "co-prosperity sphere." Nor can one speculate that Japanese-Brazilian relations will necessarily "hurt" the role of the United States in Brazil. But it is a fact to be remembered in the context of Japanese sensitivity to being "overlooked" time and again in U.S. policy-making. Brazil's belief that it should be consulted by the U.S. in the future may well provide a sufficiently coherent nexus between the two nations for economic as well as political purposes.

The development of the Amazon basin provides a third, distinctive aspect to the "new look" in Brazilian foreign policy with geopolitical implications. While the primary motivation for the massive development program in the Amazon appears to be internal—opening the last frontier, securing borders, drawing off excess population from the Northeast, and so on—Peru and Venezuela perceive Brazil's Amazon policy to have its external aspects as well. This will be explored in discussing the Andean Pact.

Argentina and Chile. Argentina and Chile are the states which have lost the most in the dramatic opening of an era of geopolitical maneuvering in Latin America. The old rivalry between Argentina and Brazil may continue at the psychological level, but it has little significance in terms of armed conflict unless Argentina undergoes a dramatic shift to the left, which appears unlikely. Brazil has outdistanced Argentina in the last decade in economic growth, international outreach, and maneuvering among the three nations that both have considered their spheres of influence. Buenos Aires will need more than the next decade to recuperate. Recuperation will depend on the government's ability to settle internal social and political issues, particularly the terrorism of the left and right, and to deal with the continuing decline of the once prosperous and expansive Argentine economy. Argentina is presently isolated. Without economic force it cannot challenge Brazil. Given its geographic location, it is not a logical candidate for membership in the Andean Pact.[4] The traditional Chilean-Argentine rivalry does not suggest any immediate or successful effort to forge a Santiago-Buenos Aires linkage. The new reality is that Argentina is weak, demoralized, and increasingly marginal in continental political considerations.[5]

The overthrow of the Allende government in Santiago in September 1973 merely confirmed this. With the decisive imposition of a military authoritarian government, thus far without developmental pretensions, the tragedy that is Chile has been laid bare. Economically, the nation remains a one-mineral exporter: copper determines its economic future whether in the hands of multinationals or in the hands of the state. The agricultural dilemma, recognized for decades, remains without remedy. A power in the 19th century, Chile now confronts a growingly powerful Peru to the north and stronger demand for a solution to the Tacna and Arica controversies with Bolivia—both countries which Chile defeated in the War of the Pacific at the end of the last century.[6]

---

4. It should be noted that a 150 man delegation of Argentinian business and industrial leaders visited Peru in June 1974 in what was seen as an initial effort to establish contact with the Pact.

5. This does not mean that Argentina has lost all flexibility on the continent. Its efforts to establish counterbalancing economic agreements to those of Brazil, in Bolivia and Paraguay, indicate a capacity for survival that is as much reflex as new initiative. Argentinian activity in Paraguay and Bolivia today must respond to Brazilian initiative; fifteen years ago it was the reverse. The activities of the recently revived River Plate Basin Organization demonstrate this point nicely. This confirms my assertion that Brazil can now entertain the notion of improved diplomatic relations with Argentina because of Brazilian preponderance in the region.

6. It would appear that Chile is rapidly being drawn into the Brazilian orbit. There exists an ideological affinity between the authoritarian-right governments in power. Chile, a traditional rival of Argentina and Peru, complements Brazil's interest in isolating Argentina and neutralizing Peru. The meeting of General Pinochet of Chile with President Banzer of Bolivia in Brasilia in March 1974 came about through the good offices of the Geisel administration (Bolivia and Chile have not maintained diplomatic relations for twelve years). The Pinochet visit to Paraguay, another Brazilian satellite, indicates a growing affinity among Brazilian dependents on the continent.

Diplomatically isolated because of the brutality of its internal policies, desperate for external arms to prepare for the worst (or the inevitable) from Peru, economically wrecked and socially bifurcated, Chile remains a shadow of the bourgeois democracy that we knew and loved but ten years ago. The possibilities of either redemption or renewal are dim for the remainder of the decade.

The Andean Pact. The Pact is a convenient way of discussing Venezuela and Peru, its two most important members and the only nation-states on the continent, other than Brazil, with realistic ambitions of power and influence beyond their present borders. The Pact itself may well assume a more important continental role but that role will reflect the leadership of either Peru or Venezuela or both; the other countries in the Pact (Chile, Bolivia, Ecuador, and Colombia) are subsidiary actors at best.

With the ouster of Fernando Balaunde Terry in October 1968, Peru "found" itself. The authoritarian, albeit reformist, military government severely weakened the "private governments" that had challenged the capacity of the state, and has proceeded selectively to mobilize segments of the population previously ignored. Peru has successfully settled the IPC controversy with the U.S. on its own terms. Arms and military equipment are now regularly purchased from suppliers other than the U.S. The diplomatic leadership of Peru on issues such as the 200 mile territorial sea is a recognized fact; its position on international fishing along its Pacific coast is clear. Peru's expanding international role reflects both the internal political and economic changes of recent years as well as its historical role in the Pacific area, often discussed but never realized.

Perhaps just as significant, Peru stands as a logical candidate to oppose any expanded Brazilian role in the Pacific, either through the shared Amazon territory or through their common neighbor, Bolivia. Peruvian plans for settlement on the eastern side of the Andes are aimed at forestalling Brazilian infiltration. The Peruvian military regime, possessing the most coherent and identifiable "ideology" of development on the continent, looms large on the Pacific coast as the most important and forceful leader among the Spanish American Republics.

A final aspect of Peru's pivotal role is the irredentist claims for the territory seized by Chile in 1879 during the War of the Pacific. In Lima and in Santiago there is a good deal of discussion about the possibilities of conflict. The recent purchase of Soviet tanks, apart from its implications for U.S. arms policy, demonstrates to some that Peru will attempt to regain its lost territory before the 100th anniversary of the War; in such an encounter Bolivia would be an active, if meaningless, collaborator.

Venezuela is a more complicated subject for analysis. With the recent increase in oil prices, Venezuela finds itself in the most preferred position, economically, in the hemisphere. As the "showcase" democracy remaining on the continent, it offers a contrast to the at times repressive, limited participatory governments of the military regimes. The principal questions that relate to Venezuela's international role in the Americas are whether or not the country sees itself in competition with Peru for leadership in the Andean Pact; whether or not Venezuela seeks greater influence in the Caribbean; and whether or not Venezuela's fear of Brazilian expansionism through the Amazon is real or imagined.

An overriding factor in Venezuela's role in Latin America will be the decision by the new Carlos Andres government of whether or not to turn inward and reinvest oil profits in domestic social reform and economic diversification, or seek international prestige at the expense of meeting its more difficult and challenging internal needs. Can Venezuela do both? Will a limited internal investment program forestall social upheaval and guarantee national income after the depletion of petroleum reserves? The government must soon deal with these issues.

Quite clearly Venezuela foresees a Caribbean role for itself. Both Cuba/Hispaniola and the Enlgish Caribbean are seen as economically profitable and politically necessary for Venezuela's long-term security interests. The recent loan to the Caribbean Development Bank is only one manifestation of this interest.[7]

Will Venezuela challenge Peru for Andean Pact leadership?

---

7. Increasing Venezuelan activity in Central America should be noted. Talks are underway to construct a refinery that will provide 400,000 barrels for the Central American market. Other projects financed by Venezuela in Central America have been signed or are being negotiated.

Certainly former President Caldera's decision to opt for membership despite the opposition of internal business groups (primarily Fedecamaras, the main interest group "combine" in the country) was motivated by both economic and political considerations. Venezuela's concern with Brazilian activity in the Amazon (realizing that Brazil does not possess petroleum), and Caldera's frantic and unsuccessful trip through the hemisphere last year to initiate what many thought to be an anti-Brazilian alliance, indicate Venezuela may turn to the Andean Pact as a logical mechanism for forestalling Brazilian expansion or infiltration through the Venezuelan Amazon. That Peru shares similar feelings should encourage a dialogue between the two countries on at least that issue. The resolution of potential differences between Peru and Venezuela over the political and economic objectives of the Pact will determine Venezuela's role in the hemisphere; it will not necessarily reduce or impede continued Peruvian-Venezuelan collaboration or conflict on other questions.

Mexico and Central America. As indicated earlier, Mexico is one of the four nation-states in Latin America with the potential for increased power and influence, but it is not clear what course it will take. Mexico is not overly popular with the Central American republics, and Guatemala resents any Mexican encroachment because of its own pretensions to leadership, two facts which preclude a major role for Mexico in the foreseeable future. Whether it develops a stronger interest in the Caribbean, through the Gulf of Mexico, will depend to a great degree on the attitude—and success—of Venezuela, as well as its changing relations with Cuba.

Mexico's efforts to be recognized as a major spokesman for the hemisphere have met with relatively minor success.[8] President Echeverria's recent peregrinations, both worldwide and in Latin

---

8. One result of Echeverria's recent trip through Latin America may be the exploration of closer collaboration with Brazil. As others have indicated, both countries follow similar economic development programs and both share a close and long-standing relationship with the U.S. Science and technology offer areas for potential collaboration. A Brazilian "opening" would give Mexico its desired access to the continent.

America, have confirmed what was suspected: that the President prefers to be out of Mexico, to preclude dealing with the inconsistencies in the PRI coalition. Moreover, Mexico's reputation is far stronger abroad, especially in the Third World, than at home. Mexico's geographical proximity to the United States, and its *de facto* economic integration with North America, present real obstacles to a hemispheric-wide role. A possible, and intriguing, combination would be that of Venezuela and Mexico, with explicit interests in the Caribbean, superficially similar political philosophies underpinning their governments, and relatively well advanced economic infrastructures.[9] Such a coalition, while not an immediate possibility, should not be discounted, particularly now that Venezuela has moved closer to Mexico's traditional position with regard to Cuba.

There is relatively little to be said for or about the Central American Republics. Economic integration appears stalled at a low-intermediate level of development.[10] Political cooperation has made little, if any, headway, as the 1969 "Soccer War" demonstrated. The wide variety of political regimes, ranging from pluralist Costa Rica to paternal Nicaragua, bode ill for immediate change. Guatemala's internal contradictions preclude a larger regional role. Composed of mostly non-viable nation-states, eventually some sort of confederation or integration appears inevitable for the region.

The Caribbean and Panama. A distinctive area in the hemisphere, the

---

9. Mexico and the Caribbean Community (CARICOM) established a joint commission to strengthen economic, cultural, and technical relations after Mexican President Echeverria's visit to Jamaica in August 1974.

A British Caribbean summit meeting in July 1974, the first since the establishment of CARICOM in 1973, again foreclosed any action on political unity but did decide to establish formal relations between CARICOM and the Andean Group and the Central American Common Market.

10. Witness the continuing failure of the UPEB, the organization representing the seven most important banana exporting countries of Central and South America. In May 1974 the planned summit meeting of Central American presidents was postponed indefinitely because of their inability to agree on any possible restructuring of the common market. The El Salvador-Honduras hostility continues to poison all efforts in Central America to initiate renewed progress for the market.

Caribbean does not lend itself to the same treatment as the other cases examined and only a few, brief comments will be made. The Caribbean must be divided into the British Caribbean and the "traditional" or Cuba-Haiti-Dominican Republic Caribbean. The British Caribbean poses a particular set of problems in that they are not united by either culture or language to the Spanish and Portuguese parts of the hemisphere. Recently come to independence, the region is made up of a series of micro-states, few of which are economically viable, and a good deal of political and social instability. This "encouraging" thumb-nail sketch is completed with the knowledge that the former European colonial powers have withdrawn or are attempting to do so with a few glances backward. The early efforts at federation and integration, i.e. the 1960s, resulted in failure. The few bright spots, such as Jamaica with large bauxite reserves, promise little over the long run. The British Caribbean, then, may well be susceptible to a Venezuelan or other presence if the initial barriers of language and culture can be overcome. The possibility of a Canadian presence in the area has been mentioned by some, but there is little evidence that Canada has more than passing economic interest in the island republics. The probability of internal strife in the islands is high; the possibility of inter-island strife somewhat less, given low levels of military preparation, manpower, and leadership.[11]

The "other" Caribbean of Cuba, Haiti, and the Dominican Republic pose a different set of questions and problems from those raised in this

---

11. The importance of economics and natural resources is again dramatically illustrated in the Caribbean with the bauxite example. Jamaica, Surinam, Guyana, the Dominican Republic, and Haiti produce 42% of the world's supply of bauxite, and supply the U.S. with 90% of its needs. The nationalization of Alcan by Guyana in 1971 and the recent backdated 7½% production levy imposed by Jamaica on one Canadian and five U.S. companies indicates a rapid change in Caribbean bargaining power. Will the newly created International Bauxite Association be able to enforce its price demands? Will the construction of locally owned aluminum smelters bring added friction of a cessation of Caribbean protests against foreign exploitation? Will bauxite profits be reinvested, where, and for what purposes? Will bauxite begin a movement towards collaboration between the Dominican Republic and Haiti and the British Caribbean?

paper and should be considered in a separate analysis.[12] All three island republics are more directly related to issues of U.S. security and less to the possibilities of geopolitical movement in Latin America. Panama falls into the same category; it is a "one issue" country; once the Canal question is resolved it is difficult to foresee anything more than continuing insignificance, in political terms, for Panama.

The United States and International Relations in Latin America. What is the role of the U.S. in the context of this new era of international relations in Latin America? It seems clear that the old formulas will not work again. A more imaginative, but not necessarily more involved response (which may or may not be a "policy"), is required. Neither crusading paternalism nor benign neglect is appropriate. The U.S. must first recognize the new configurations of power that are emerging, and deal with them in their various manifestations—political, economic, and social. As the principal Latin American nation-states take charge of their own destinies for the first time, they must be shown the same deference that all newly emerging "powers" receive. Latin America is no longer one undifferentiated mass of countries; an international and regional "pecking order" has emerged. Brazil, Venezuela, Peru, and Mexico should be treated with more seriousness and more purposiveness by the U.S. than before.

This does not mean that the other nations of the hemisphere are unimportant. It means that the geopolitical realities of the 1970s require a different response from the 1930s when a Good Neighbor Policy sufficed; from the 1950s when Cold War concerns required and imposed a uniform security mold on the hemisphere; or from the 1960s when well-meaning social reformism and economic growth were the responses in all the republics to good vs. bad, democracy vs. communism, free enterprise vs. socialism. It is not that these policies

---

12. It is clear that in the Cuban case, the U.S. runs the risk of being left behind by its neighbors in the hemisphere if it doesn't revise its inflexible hostility. Informal channels indicate this is being done. In order to diffuse a possible "time-bomb," the U.S. needs to at least keep pace with the majority of (and most significant) nations in recognizing the regime in power since 1959. There is no evidence that recognition will have a negative impact on trends now emerging for collaboration or conflict in the hemisphere.

were necessarily inappropriate, though many would argue that they were at least insufficient, but they should not be employed as guides for current policy.

The reality of the situation is that the U.S. will have a decreasing role to play in the power politics of Latin America in the decades ahead. There will no longer be the justification for or the acceptance of the Inter-American security need for U.S. hegemony. Trade and economic questions will create issues that divide rather than unite the hemisphere. Competition among Latin American nations will involve the U.S. to a lesser degree as new overtures to Western Europe, Japan, and other nations provide more diverse international options. Increasingly, the small countries will defer to the larger. While a country like Argentina, and possibly Colombia or Chile, may eventually move into a position of greater importance, there is no likelihood that Paraguay, Bolivia, honduras, or Panama will ever lay claim to the power and influence of Brazil or Venezuela.

These facts lead us to examine the implications of conflict among the major actors in the Latin American subsystem, and among their allies or dependents. The U.S. will no longer possess the "veto" it previously appeared to have when the control over arms supplies largely determined the level of response to perceived threat for each Latin American nation. With growing independence in arms purchases, and the national capacity to produce small armaments and other material for war, the leverage the U.S. possesses will be employable, ironically, with the un-influential and not with the nations of power. What the latter cannot get from the U.S. they will purchase elsewhere.

More important, decision-makers within a strong, centralized authoritarian state, will determine their national interests with decreasing concern for the attitude of the U.S. Not that the major actors in Latin America will be unconcerned about the U.S. response, or be hostile, merely that the U.S. will become one of several factors to be considered.

The role of the U.S. will become one of persuasion and diplomacy, in many instances. Threats may be employed with nations where economic and military aid programs continue at a level at which the threat is credible. The U.S. presence, diminished, may become more that of a "balancer" among competing groups or factions within the hemisphere. U.S. might and assistance could be decisive in one side's victory over the other. To "play sides" would be disastrous, but to use good offices and work quietly through our allies would be an acceptable form of statesmanship.

There is no assumption here that the U.S. will not have a future role in Latin America. The assumption is that the U.S. will be influential, not hegemonic; less able to utilize the security threat as justification for overt and/or covert interference; less able to satisfy the new and important economic needs and demands of many of the Latin American nations; and less able to impose hemispheric responses on what will have become basically bilateral concerns.

It would be unfortunate if the U.S. were to view this prospect with such dismay that it attempted to withdraw from the region. Withdrawal is not the question; the ties between the Northern and Southern continents are too ingrained to allow such a complete reversal in policy. Nor would it be in our best interests to do so. The U.S. must use what influence it retains to persuade and at times cajole; to remain interested but not to interfere.

U.S. involvement should not be at the level of pontifical promulgation or mere threat. It should attempt to work with those new and powerful actors who understand both the responsibilities and the limits of power. Opposing territorial change merely because it is change would be unwise; counselling against the outbreak of war between Chile and Peru would be both appropriate and necessary.

What institutional mechanisms are needed for a new role for the U.S.? One salutary effect of the new geopolitical realities in Latin America may be a restoration of the authority of the embassies the U.S. maintains in each Latin American nation. If it is clear that there is no "one" policy, broadly conceived and unworkable at the national level, closer contact and negotiation may result in a greater flow of accurate information and appraisal for utilization in Washington.

The question of the OAS arises, of course. I do not foresee any greater or any more diminished role for that organization in the political and military-security areas.[13] Secretary Kissinger's recent

---

13. Mexico's Echeverria stated in Buenos Aires, on his recent Latin American tour, that the OAS has practically disappeared. He proposed to President Isabelita De Peron

dialogue with the Latin American foreign ministers, deliberately outside the OAS framework, indicates that when the U.S. needs to consult with its neighbors on a multilateral basis, the audience is there. It would be unwise to move all issues to a multilateral level though; hopefully, there will be a return to bilateral negotiations and contacts. Not all questions require international dialogue. By making issues multilateral, even the transnational and science and technology questions now under discussion, multilateral "posing" is required, that is, a policy position by "them" to counter "ours." The less of that there is in the future and the more serious the exchange between the U.S. and Venezuela, Brazil, Peru, and Mexico, the better for the future of U.S.-Latin American relations.

I would anticipate that the U.S. would maintain modest economic assistance programs with some of the smaller states in the hemisphere. Humanitarian aid certainly will be maintained and increased where appropriate. In those nations with which the U.S. is able to retain a modest arms program, a relatively higher degree of influence will be wielded. By shifting as much of U.S. economic assistance as possible to international institutions, specifically the Inter-American Development Bank and other OAS educational and health agencies, the more the U.S. will assure Latin American nations that its interest continues while its intentions have changed.

There is no attempt made to ignore the fact that from time to time a legitimate security threat will occur in the hemisphere; appropriate procedures exist and can be employed to meet such a contingency, if so recognized by a majority of the nations. Nor is there the assumption that the U.S. will soon be confronted by strident, swaggering military regimes attempting to redraw the frontiers of Latin America at any cost. Conflict is possible, not inevitable. National power increments are facts which the U.S. must accept. National interests among the Latin nations will more and more be determined by leaders less susceptible to intimidation and threat and far more concerned about the development of their countries than any of their predecessors.

Not all military governments are "good," but then not all civilian

---

that an exclusively Latin organization replace the OAS. Echeverria did not indicate why he thought a new entity would be more successful than the old.

governments are good either. National purpose at this time in Latin America requires more forceful leadership and more effective policies. There is, however, no need for the U.S. or other nations in the hemisphere to be paranoid about this.

The sale of Soviet tanks to Peru, the building of warships by Brazil, the movement of Venezuela into the Caribbean—all are part of a changing geopolitical situation. It is not that the U.S. should "favor" Peru or Brazil over Chile or Ecuador, but the realities of power, resources and leadership require the U.S. to recognize and deal with those states acknowledged to be most influential by other Latin nations. While the U.S. may not "like" one regime compared to another, it will be far wiser to emphasize pragmatism in future U.S.-Latin relations. Certainly such a policy cannot fail anymore dismally than previous efforts, and may indeed reap benefits unimagined even by the most optimistic observers of politics in the hemisphere.

U.S. POLICY TOWARD CUBA: A DISCUSSION OF OPTIONS
Jorge I. Dominguez

Games and Stakes

Several international "games" are played concerning different aspects of the relations between the United States and Cuba. The games are played individually but the moves and strategies are interconnected. The players define the stakes.

The first game is played primarily by the United States and the Soviet Union. At stake is the Soviet military presence in the Western hemisphere. Will the Soviet navy make active and intensive use of Cuban ports and facilities for its ships, especially to increase the time on station of its nuclear submarines? Will the Cuban military posture be shaped by the Soviet Union to pose a meaningful threat to U.S. security, or will Cuba be equipped primarily with weapons limited to defend itself against an external attack? Will Soviet personnel offer only advice or will they also be engaged in operations? What will be the level, scope and intensity of the Soviet non-military presence in Cuba?

The second game is played primarily by the United States and the

Latin American governments. At stake is the structure and the policies of the institutionalized inter-American system. How are decisions made and changed concerning pariah states? How much compliance will there be when sanctions are imposed without unanimity? Should collective sanctions still apply to Cuba? Should Cuba somehow be reincorporated into the inter-American system? Some Latin American politicians may be buying radical support by pursuing an ardently "pro-Cuban" foreign policy. These leaders often have a greater stake in the continuation than in the solution of the Cuban problem. Will the inter-American system eventually be altered to exclude the United States in order to form an all-Latin American organization? Will the presently emerging two-tier system become institutionalized and thereby have a less drastic though comparable effect?

The third game is played by the United States and other governments as well as by multinational enterprises. To what degree and for how long will U.S.-based multinational enterprises comply with the American trade embargo against Cuba? How willing will other governments be to request official U.S. exemptions for subsidiaries of these enterprises operating in their countries? Will they decide not to honor the extraterritorial features of U.S. legislation?

The fourth game is played by Communist governments and movements; here Cuba is a direct player. What are the dignified and efficient ways of conducting the struggle for liberation, especially in Latin America? Is armed struggle the only way, or one way, or no way? What policies should Communist governments pursue toward Communist movements, toward non-Communist radical movements, toward non-Communist conservative governments, and toward each other?

The fifth game is played directly by the United States and Cuba. How do they communicate and deal with each other to affect the moves, strategies and outcomes of the other games? How do they settle specific disputes between them—in the Gulf, the Florida Straits, Guantanamo, and regarding international movement of persons and transportation? How can they resolve issues concerning the international sugar market, and Cuba's share in the world and the U.S. sugar market; or compensation for the nationalization of U.S. property in

Cuba and the settlement of outstanding economic disputes; or the status of the Guantanamo base treaty.

Background

Cuba has undergone a major transformation in its foreign relations since 1968. It is today more active and more successful in its foreign policy than at any time since the early days of the revolutionary government. Its specific—and narrower—foreign policy goals are being achieved. But it is also less dependent than at any time since the beginning of the revolution. Cuban dependence on, and responsiveness to, the Soviet Union has increased in the past six years.

These two consequences stem from the Soviet Union's reassertion of hegemonial authority over Cuba since 1968, leading Cuba to limit its foreign policy goals and concentrate its resources on their achievement. Cuba's transformed foreign policy has become markedly less militant in fact, though not yet in rhetoric. It may have entered its international Thermidor.

Originally, Cuba wanted to support revolution in several countries, in opposition to the policies of the Soviet Union.

In the mid-1960s Cuba sought independence from, and sometimes defiance of, the Soviet Union, China and the United States. Systematic efforts to promote and support armed struggle in Latin America were the means to these goals. But the guerrilla policy failed, leaving Cuban foreign policy with one instrument less. Moreover, by 1968 the Soviet Union had had enough. It had been accused of being no better a trading partner than the imperialists. It had been accused of collaborating with Cuba's enemies and of forgetting revolutionary solidarity. It had been accused of plotting the overthrow of the Cuban leadership in 1967–1968. The Soviet Union then struck back. It froze the level of petroleum deliveries to Cuba while increasing petroleum production and selling more to any other Latin American country; and it delayed the signing of the annual trade protocols. Cuba caved in. The public turning point was Fidel Castro's endorsement of the Soviet invasion of Czechoslovakia. The Soviet leadership warmly welcomed the return of the prodigal son.

The Soviet share of Cuban trade in recent times has ranged between 50% and 52%. Cuba's cumulative trade deficit with the Soviet Union amounted to 1,508 million rubles by the end of 1970; its total debt is larger, though it is difficult to establish by how much. The level of the debt has risen since the Cuban policy reversal in 1968. The debt has also been rising at a faster rate since 1968 than before (except for 1970). The Soviet Union has paid a premium for Cuban sugar, as high as three times the world price in the late 1960s. The Cubans may have paid a premium, too, for Soviet goods, some of which Fidel Castro described as "old junk."

In December of 1972, Cuba and the Soviet Union signed five trade agreements. The two nations have also established institutional means for widespread economic collaboration. The Cuban-Soviet Commissions for Economic, Scientific and Technical Collaboration, established in December of 1970, link Cuban and Soviet Ministries, agencies and local enterprises. Joint production agreements exist in such areas as the production of agricultural machinery and equipment, the management of the Cuban satellite communications station (with broadcasting and receiving capabilities) and fishing. In the summer of 1972, Cuba joined the Council for Mutual Economic Aid (COMECON).

Cuban economic dependence involves the whole Socialist bloc. It has relations with China; and even when the Soviet Union was coercing Cuba in 1968, Rumania signed a petroleum agreement with Cuba—the very item which the Soviet Union was using as a club. The North Koreans, the North Vietnamese, the Vietcong and the Rumanians sent high ranking delegations to express solidarity with Cuba.

The level and rate of military dependence on the Soviet Union has also increased. The Soviet navy has visited Cuba regularly since 1969. Cuban ports are used to give submarine crews free time on shore, do minor repairs, and re-stock general supplies. In the early 1970s Cuba's military posture shifted. The size of the standing armed forces shrunk and the military budget's share of national income declined, but the actual sums spent for the military increased. These expenditures were used for modernization, and to insure a capability for full and swift reserve mobilization. The Soviet Union has supplied weaponry free of charge and Soviet technicians have served as advisors.

Congressional testimonies of the U.S. Defense Department and the intelligence agencies suggest that Cuba does not pose a military threat to the U.S. or Latin America. Cuba has a "bee sting" capability, that is, it can inflict considerable pain on any would-be attacker, but it cannot launch an attack on its own.

The failure of guerrilla movements and the emergence of friendly Latin American governments also caused Cuba's foreign policy to change. Cuba now has diplomatic relations with Peru, Argentina, Guyana, Trinidad-Tobago, Barbados and Jamaica. Mexico and Cuba had never broken relations. And while not formally recognized, relations with Venezuela and Panama have improved. Colombia, Costa Rica and other Central American states may re-establish relations soon. A Latin American majority to remove the collection sanctions imposed on Cuba in 1964 exists, but U.S. and other abstentions resulted in fewer than the required two-thirds vote at the OAS Conference in Quito in November 1974. The Cuban government has been denounced by its erstwhile guerrilla allies for abandoning the armed struggle, but it still provides some support to Latin American revolutionaries. Cuba's rhetorical commitment to revolution has, moreover, not wavered. In sum, there is a quantitative and qualitative change in the character of Cuba's activity in the area of exporting the revolution—far less than before, still well above zero.

Since 1970, however, Cuba has concentrated mainly on its own internal economic development. Its foreign policy shift coincides with this emphasis. First, it has obtained many economic benefits from the Soviet Union by effectively harvesting the fruits of international dependence in a hegemonial system. Secondly, Cuba has contributed to the erosion of U.S. influence in the Americas by courting Latin American governments rather than trying to overthrow them. The result has been that the wall of isolation, built by the United States around Cuba, has cracked.

U.S. Policy Options

OPTION 1

The first option for the U.S. is to seek to change its relations with Cuba. American policy has sought to reduce Cuban military relations with the Soviet Union, and reduce its export of revolution to Latin America. U.S. policy has also been not to change until these conditions are met *a priori*. The main weapon has been the embargo on economic relations. But the structure of the inter-American system and the extent of American extraterritoriality over U.S.-based multinational enterprises have become linked as possible costs of pursuing these policy objectives.

The crucial argument that makes this "status quo" option viable is that U.S. policy is in fact sufficient to maintain necessary minimum relations. U.S.-Cuban cooperation on well-defined and practical issues has existed for several years. The Swiss embassy in Havana is an adequate conduit, and on occasion the Mexican government has served as go-between. Current policy has been sufficient to agree on an exile airlift in 1965, and on the return of hijackers and hijacked property. Cuban and U.S. weather bureaus collaborate on hurricane tracking. Procedures exist for travel to Cuba by U.S. citizens, and for visits by American sports teams to Cuba, and by Cuban teams to Puerto Rico. Scientific publications are exchanged. And procedures are developing for the showing of Cuban films, and for the distribution of Cuban books in the United States. The possible expansion of Soviet naval facilities in Cuba may be a matter to take up with the Soviet Union directly.

Cuba is not China; relations do not have the same obvious political benefits. There is little to be gained from formal relations that cannot be gotten under existing arrangements. And this American policy toward Cuba is relatively costless. Despite objections from some Latin American governments, attempting to change the U.S. posture does not seem to be at the top of the policy agenda of most of them.

The cost of a policy of sufficiency arises from whether U.S.-based multinational enterprises will press for unlimited authority for their subsidiaries in other countries to trade with Cuba. Will other governments insist that they be permitted to do so, or that they by-pass the U.S. government altogether? On April 18, 1974, the U.S. Department of State authorized General Motors, Ford and Chrysler subsidiaries in Argentina to trade with Cuba, pursuant to the demands of the Argentine government. The Canadian subsidiary of U.S.-based Studebaker Worthington has signed a contract to sell 30 locomotives to Cuba for $14 million, with a Canadian government guarantee that the contract will be honored. If the U.S. forces American subsidiaries abroad to apply the embargo against Cuba, it will be against considerable opposition from foreign governments and U.S.-based multinational enterprises. The issue involves not so much the value of the Cuban trade—though this is not insignificant—as the application of U.S. legislation in other countries: whether multinational enterprises are something other than the extension of U.S. enterprises attached to American foreign policy.

OPTION 2

The second option is sufficiency with forward movement. No basic change should be made, but the U.S. may *react* to specific challenges. It will take few initiatives and no cognizance of real changes in Cuban policies, but when confronted, the U.S. may yield. This perhaps characterizes more closely the current policy. The decision with regard to subsidiaries in Argentina was explained by Secretary Kissinger as follows:

> to permit American companies that are chartered in foreign countries to comply with the laws of the countries in which they are located—to deal with an anomaly of our legislation which makes American companies that are incorporated in foreign countries subject to United States law rather than to the law of the country in which they are domiciled in case there is a conflict . . . Therefore, the behavior of American companies in those countries will depend on the policies the countries pursue vis-a-vis Cuba.

However, other statements by U.S. officials strongly indicated this was a one-time exception. Yet, the U.S. has gone along with an

Argentine initiative to invite Cuba to the next meeting of foreign ministers of the hemisphere to be held in Buenos Aires in March 1975. The arguments for sufficiency apply also to this option. The chief difference between the first and second alternatives lies in the willingness to try to enforce sanctions against Cuba.

Arguments Against Policy Change

The case for options 1 or 2 is bolstered by the costs of changing current policy. There are domestic costs: the large and vocal Cuban exile community is not monolithic, and not unanimously opposed to improving relations. On the contrary, in the last two years some Cuban groups and publications in the United States have supported a new openness toward their country of birth. Nevertheless, most Cuban exiles do oppose any significant change, and would use their political leverage to prevent it.

There are also international costs. Brazil, Chile, Bolivia, Uruguay and Paraguay, half of the South American countries, have hostile relations with Cuba, independent of U.S. pressure. Many Central American and Caribbean countries are also anti-Cuban. Others, though they may vote for Cuba's reincorporation into the inter-American system for internal political reasons, still want reassurances of U.S. protection in case of Cuban subversion. A new policy may provide Cuba with outlets from which to intervene in the internal affairs of other countries. It would entail the reconstruction of the inter-American system wherein the U.S. could well find itself more isolated.

There are ideological costs. Although American policy is not now aimed at the overthrow of the Cuban government, a major policy change may actually guarantee its survival.

But a policy of supporting either internal insurgency or an exile effort to overthrow the government, can no longer be considered a viable option. There still is discontent in Cuba, turnouts in local elections are lower than in pre-revolutionary Cuba, there is non-compliance with government-promoted, new patterns of behavior. But virtually all of this is now increasingly "within the system." Cubans seem to want to improve their living conditions, not to overthrow the government. The government has responded by abandoning some of its oppressive policies. Nevertheless, if the overthrow of the Cuban government is not a viable option, neither is strengthening it. It is, then, both a factual and a value decision whether further change should occur.

One may also oppose change in U.S.-Cuban relations on the basis that the integrity of the Cuban socialist revolution is predicted upon isolation from, and hostility to, the U.S. It was in the crucible of the internal struggle against the American presence that the socialist character of the revolution emerged in the early 1960s. The most radical policies of the revolutionary government were developed in the heat of combat against the U.S. This argument holds that scarcity has led to virtue; luxury would lead to decay. From a leftist viewpoint, therefore, if one is not disposed to risk such an outcome, one should oppose any policy change.

Argumentation

OPTION 3

There is an alternative way for the United States to pursue its two objectives of reducing Cuban-Soviet military relations and reducing Cuba's export of revolution. Containing the Soviet military presence in Cuba should be pursued primarily as a part of U.S.-Soviet relations rather than U.S.-Cuban relations. The policy objective for Cuba should be solely to prevent its export of revolution. U.S. treaties with Latin American countries seem to require that this remain an important U.S. aim.

The chief policy instrument would be to induce a Cuban Thermidor—a further turn toward more conservative internal policies as the zeal for revolution declines. A Thermidorian policy would induce Castroism in one country. The U.S. could stimulate Cuban concern with economic growth; it would welcome the shift away from moral incentives toward material incentives for labor; it would support every effort toward relaxation of the Cuban social system. Instead of preventing trade with Cuba, this policy would stimulate it, for the U.S. as well as for American subsidiaries.

Under this third option the structure and policies of the inter-American system would have to be reformulated. Those countries which have loyally supported the U.S. on the Cuban question must be reassured that they have not been abandoned. The issue of compensation for confiscated U.S. property will arise. Some Cuban exiles will seek to attach Cuban property in American courts; terrorist groups may attack Cuban government crews and property at U.S. ports. The status of Guantanamo may be on the table, alongside the sugar quota. The alternative formulation sets aside ideological objections to the Cuban government. It risks contributing to the economic success of the regime because it acknowledges the consolidation of its rule. Thus, it would be an interim step looking forward to—and risking costs in—a whole set of new negotiations.

Current U.S. policy is open to criticism, mainly in that it has been irrelevant to Cuba's behavior for several years. Cuban policies toward the Soviet Union and Latin America (the two areas of American concern) have varied, independently of U.S. policy. The effect of the embargo, great in the early 1960s must be attributed to Soviet pressure to Latin American changes, and to internal Cuban changes. U.S. policies seem not to have had much influence.

During the past 15 years there has also been an inverse relationship between Cuba's closeness to the Soviet Union and Cuba's support for guerrillas, since the Soviet Union has opposed their support. Therefore, U.S. efforts to reduce Soviet influence may increase Cuban recklessness; the reduction of Cuban militance may only be achieved as a result of increasing Sovietization. International order in the hemisphere may actually benefit from the dead hand of Communist orthodox. U.S. policy instruments are counterproductive. One effect of the embargo was to increase Cuban export of revolution in order to fight the U.S.; continued isolation makes it more likely and necessary for Cuba to depend on the Soviet Union. And the U.S. has shown a declining ability to affect policies of other countries on this issue. Compliance is decreasing.

Moreover, though existing channels are sufficient for many purposes, it is obviously more effective to have direct relations. The general argument for diplomatic relations with all types of government applies. Though the U.S. did not cause and cannot alone sustain Cuba's abandonment of militancy, a new policy would not require or promote Cuban opposition. Zero-subversion is not a likely prospect, but it may continue to decline. In addition, direct relations with the U.S. would give Cuba more leverage with the Soviet Union, and may prevent additional Sovietization. This last argument must be understood narrowly. The U.S. would probably not aid Cuba in a serious dispute with the Soviet Union; Cuba is not likely to trust the U.S. government very much, nor would it be likely to exchange certain Soviet assistance for U.S. promises. And, given the need for a degree of Sovietization to restrain Cuban militancy, the leverage argument should not be pushed too far. The reconstruction and the redefinition of the inter-American system is no easy task, but present policies should not continue out of fear of the effort to build a new relationship.

There is, in fact, a threat to the structure of the inter-American system under the second (current) option. If every request by U.S. subsidiaries must be handled on a case-by-case basis, the result will be a series of challenges to U.S. policy. If the Argentine decision set a precedent, then the present policy will eventually become useless by attrition. The welcoming of Cuba to inter-American meetings presents another problem. This system has been evolving informally into a two-tier structure. The Latin American nations caucus in advance of their meetings with the U.S. The prospects are for Cuba, but not for the U.S., to participate in the Latin American caucus and for Cuba to press for a continental organization to exclude the U.S. If Cuba purchases American products from overseas subsidiaries without dealing with the U.S. directly, and if Cuba participates in inter-American meetings without bearing any collective responsibilities, its current policy goals of breaking through U.S. political and economic isolation will have been achieved. Cuba does not want to rejoin the OAS unless it is drastically changed; under option 2 it could break through political isolation without having to rejoin formally.

Cuba wants access to American goods without having to change too many internal or international policies. Trading with U.S. subsidiaries would accomplish this. There would not be the embarrassment of an active U.S. embassy in Havana. The United States would remain enough of an enemy to invoke for internal policies. There would be no need to come to grips with relations with those overseas Cubans who are no longer counterrevolutionary. There would be no threat of cultural penetration, or uncontrolled economic luxury, that would weaken the moral fabric of socialism. Because the trade would be through subsidiaries who have been explicitly freed from U.S. government oversight, the U.S. would get no political leverage from increasing trade with Cuba. The settlement for nationalized property or the regulation of Cuban fishing in the Gulf and Florida Straits would remain non-topics. One possible long-run effect of option 2 is that Cuba may receive maximum benefits at minimum cost.

The internal effects in Cuba of extensive American contact would probably lead in different directions. It may insure the survival of the incumbents for a longer period of time. But, as the socialist critic feared, it may also change the character of incumbent rule. Cuba has not been cut off from the United States so long that its attractiveness has vanished altogether.

There are also human rights arguments to support a policy change. The economic embargo has become counterproductive, and it is also indiscriminate. It hurts pro-Castroites and anti-Castroites in Cuba alike, but the injury to the Cuban people is unintended. There have been provisions in U.S. legislation to mitigate it but the dislocation of the Cuban economy has meant the curtailment of foreign exchange reserves to buy food and medicines. The embargo originally may have been a sound policy but it has become inappropriate. A new policy could help undo the injurious effects of American policies on Cuban internal life. Although the embargo formally remains in effect, it is always possible to find ways around it.

Even by the most conservative estimates, there are some fifteen to twenty thousand political prisoners in Cuba. A continuation of present policies will not have a positive or ameliorative impact on their fate. Unilateral and collective efforts, in a context of international hostility, have not been able to improve the treatment of political prisoners. Should international tensions recede, a political amnesty in Cuba may be possible. A more flexible policy may also facilitate international travel and migration to and from Cuba. It may make possible the reunion of some Cuban families, on Cuban soil, who have been divided by previous migration. There is no expectation that current policies will make this flow possible.

A Critique of Option 3

Advocates for policy change have assessed U.S. policy erroneously. It is not irrelevant: on the contrary, the policy has worked. The embargo has not been exclusively responsible for the dislocation of the Cuban economy—internal mismanagement and lack of consistency probably account for most of the troubles. But the embargo has contributed to dislocation, and has consequently raised the cost to the Soviet Union and Cuba of their policies. The Cuban leadership finally felt the pain, and aided by domestic protest, was forced to turn away from foreign adventure to concentrate on internal economic growth.

The success of American policy is not yet complete. The U.S. should continue to rely on policies which have proven successful, and continue to raise the cost to the Soviet Union of its Cuban policies. Just because some aspects of Cuban policy have changed is no excuse to reward the Cuban government with a massive influx of U.S. goods. The argument that isolation provides a disincentive for Cuba to be reasonable and less militant has been belied by the facts. Cuba did turn away from militancy. The argument that current policy plays into Cuban hands is misleading. If extraterritoriality is limited or eliminated altogether, trade by U.S. subsidiaries in other countries would admittedly reduce the impact of the embargo, but Cuba's continuing inability to trade with the U.S. itself remains a formidable instrument of foreign policy pressure. It is unlikely that Latin American countries will be persuaded by Cuba, even if it attends the Latin American caucus and the U.S. does not. The proposition that an internal relaxation of the regime is the best guarantee against foreign policy recklessness remains unproven.

Anti-Castro Cubans overwhelmingly disagree with the human rights arguments which purport to help them. They suggest that a change in policy will guarantee the survival of the regime that has repeatedly violated elementary human rights, and that anti-Castroites in Cuba are willing to pay the cost. There is no guarantee that a policy change will open the prison gates. Exile from Cuba under current conditions is difficult but possible. And only traitors, who are few among Cubans in the U.S., would be willing to live once again under a tyrannical government in Cuba when they have the alternative of living in freedom in the U.S.

A Scenario

OPTION 3

The first option envisions little change in current American policy. The second option envisions reactive change, if challenges occur. Only the third option envisions fundamental change, with a variety of sub-options. The purpose of a scenario is to suggest some of these. Existing international agreements, and U.S. legislation and Executive regulations bearing on Cuba, can be classified into six clusters.

The third option must begin with an end to the U.S. embargo. While this has not come to pass, one can nonetheless speculate on the consequences of such a policy. The United States would move to discontinue the measures adopted against Cuba in recognition of the fact that Cuba has ceased to constitute a danger to the peace and security of the hemisphere. If approved, the U.S. trade embargo would be repealed, the Department of the Treasury would repeal Cuban asset control regulations, the Department of Agriculture would repeal restrictions on the shipping of commodities to Cuba. There would be no immediate reason to repeal Department of Commerce regulations requiring prior approval for U.S. exports to Cuba, but the Department's policy to generally deny such requests would be changed. The President would determine that it is in the U.S. national interest not to deny foreign assistance to countries which furnish assistance to Cuba and to enter into sales agreements with countries that trade with Cuba.

These actions, taken at the outset of option 3, seek to end the embargo, to permit trade between Cuba and the U.S., and to suspend any legislative provisions which penalize third countries for trading with Cuba. Multinational enterprises, at home and abroad, will be free from U.S. legal extraterritoriality. The U.S. government, however, need take no further steps. The first sub-option, therefore, is limited to undoing negative policies.

The second sub-option would encourage change in response to

Cuban foreign policy initiatives. In all court cases in which a claim to confiscated property is asserted, the President will determine that application of the act of state doctrine is in the U.S. national interest. Such determinations will depend on Cuban willingness to reopen the compensation game. The Cuban government has recognized the legitimacy of the principle of compensation. In 1967, it signed agreements with Switzerland and France, which have been implemented, to pay for the confiscated property of Swiss and French citizens. Payment was also made for unpaid debts and for the unauthorized use of brand names. The mechanism for compensation has been linked to the existence or development of extensive trade relations. In the Swiss case, where new trade was promoted, compensation was paid from the proceeds of the trade exchange. At the depressed sugar prices of 1967, Cuba expected that approximately one-third of the proceeds each year would be used for compensation. The same mechanism is available for a possible settlement of claims between Cuba and the United States, and is presumably under consideration in the continuing discussions between Canada and Cuba.

Because compensation would be linked to more extensive trade, other measures are likely to become necessary as well, depending on Cuban responses. The U.S. Department of Commerce's regulation which prohibits the export or re-export of petroleum and petroleum products to Cuba may be repealed. Cuba is classified as a Communist country under the Trade Agreements Extension Act of 1951, which denies such countries the benefit of generalized trade preferences. Cuba would be removed from the list upon a finding by the President that "Cuba is no longer dominated or controlled by the foreign government or foreign organization controlling the world Communist movement."

Sub-option 2, therefore, would facilitate trade between the two countries more than sub-option 1, but there would still be no active effort to promote trade. Sub-option 2 does little more than remove present trade barriers. Sub-option 3, on the other hand, actively stimulates trade. The President would find it in the U.S. national interest to re-establish the Cuban sugar quota, provided diplomatic relations are resumed as required by the Sugar Act. The restoration of diplomatic relations is one of the foremost goals within the general intent of option 3. It is unlikely that the restoration of formal ties, following the experience of U.S. relations with China, would occur in the early stages of option 3, but it may come. The restoration of the sugar quota is probably necessary if the U.S. expects to receive any compensation for nationalized property as Cuban compensation legislation is directly tied to sugar sales to the United States: no sugar exports, no compensation. It also states that compensation would be paid after sales to the U.S. surpassed three and one half million Spanish tons at 5.75 cents a pound. In 1960, both conditions were unrealistic. However, with the recent rise of the international price of sugar, the second provision is not difficult to attain, and the first should be subject to negotiation.

The restoration of the Cuban sugar quota entails yet a new cost for the United States. The suspended quota is presently supported by other countries friendly to the United States. Cuba's gain would be their loss. The Sugar Act provides that the restoration of the quota to the level specified in the legislation will take no less than three full calendar years; therefore, a period of transition may soften the blow—but it will be a blow.

Other economic measures may be taken in a hypothetical sub-option 4. Some may require Congressional action. The President may seek repeal of the prohibition against furnishing assistance to Cuba, repeal of restrictions on sales agreements, and repeal of the provision to try to avoid U.N. Development Program aid from going to Cuba. And the President may seek an exemption from the prohibition against Export-Import Bank credits to Cuba.

There are, however, some acts which the U.S. would not be expected to take, and a number of others whose modification the U.S. would continue to oppose. It would oppose repeal of the resolution excluding Cuba from participation in the Inter-American Defense Board. It would oppose repeal of the resolution lifting restrictions on military aid to Latin America to enable countries to strengthen coastal patrol activities. U.S. Department of Commerce regulations prohibiting trade with Cuba in arms, ammunition, other implements of war, and fissionable materials, would be retained.

One should also place the Guantanamo naval base treaties in this cluster of policies likely to remain unchanged. There is a 1903 Treaty, a 1934 Treaty, and supplementary agreements. None of them have a terminal date. The U.S. continues to pay rent, and Cuba continues to refuse to cash the checks. This cluster of non-acts pertains to military defense. In the expectation that Cuba will remain a Communist country closely allied with the Soviet Union, it seems unwise to change these policies, and unlikely that two-thirds of the Senate would ratify a treaty to turn the Guantanamo naval base over to the current Cuban government.

The sixth and last cluster of acts does not easily fit this pattern of de-escalation. These are the international agreements and resolutions which equate the Organization of American States with an anti-Communist defense pact. These include resolutions declaring that "the principles of Communism are incompatible with the principles of the inter-American system," and they exclude Cuba from participation in the inter-American system.

One of the stakes here is precisely U.S.-Latin American relations, and the structure of the inter-American system. It would be useful to induce Cuba to abide by many inter-American agreements, of which non-intervention in the internal affairs of other countries is but the most obvious. Moreover, membership in inter-American institutions, and benefits therefrom (including Cuba's possible joining the Inter-American Development Bank), would serve as further inducements to shape Cuban government behavior in the desired direction.

It may become necessary, therefore, for these and other reasons, to re-examine the current close link between the military-defense-security aspects of the inter-American systems and its other aspects: it may be useful to consider differentiating them more clearly. Cuba could rejoin one part of the differentiated system, but not the other. This constitutional redefinition could begin at any point in sub-options 1 through 4. It is most clearly related to sub-option 3, which envisions the restoration of diplomatic relations.

The sixth cluster of acts raises the issue of the style of U.S. government conduct during the implementation of any part of this scenario. A solo performance by Secretary Kissinger would probably injure relations between the United States and Latin America. Should the U.S. revoke its trade embargo, for example, prior to the repeal of the 1964 resolutions on sanctions against Cuba, the effect would be a U.S. contribution to further undermining the authority of the

Organization of American States. Whatever the merits of a solo performance in the case of re-establishing contacts with China, it would be counterproductive in the present case. It would discard at the outset one of the gains the U.S. should seek under option 3: the strengthening and restructuring of the inter-American system.

Throughout all sub-options, the U.S. government will seek benefits from its developing relations with Cuba. One has been mentioned already, the issue of compensation for nationalized property. The U.S. would also seek vigorous implementation of the hijacking agreements. It may want to renegotiate agreements on the movement of persons in and out of Cuba. It will want to improve cooperation on hurricane tracking and other aspects of weather watching and international public health regulations. It will want to promote extensive cultural, scientific, educational and travel exchanges. The value of trade itself can be considered a benefit. It will want to negotiate a maritime agreement to regulate fishing activities in the Florida Straits and the Gulf of Mexico, pending a global settlement. It will seek to influence a continuing Cuban move away from the export of revolution, and perhaps toward a reduction of Soviet military involvement. It will try to secure Cuban adherence to the nuclear non-proliferation treaty, and to the treaty for the prohibition of nuclear weapons in Latin America.

The Cuban Responses

The critique of option 2 highlighted a Cuban preference for that option, because it would give Cuba access to U.S. goods through the subsidiaries of U.S.-based multinational enterprises without dealing directly with the U.S. It would also give Cuba access to the lower informal tier of the inter-American system without having to rejoin the Organization of American States. Cuban public statements emphasize an unwillingness to rejoin the OAS unless major changes are made (including the exclusion of the U.S.), and a great reluctance to deal with President Nixon (well before impeachment difficulties began). Thus, Cuba could diversify its trade, erode the embargo and break out of political isolation without having to risk American influence in Cuba and the loss of socialist virtue. U.S. government officials have made much of the fact that Cuba has not signaled a willingness to change.

These arguments may be misleading. President Nixon is out of office, and Cuba has yet to refuse any firm offer to re-establish diplomatic, consular or economic relations with any country on any grounds. The exception is Israel. Though Cuba refused to break diplomatic relations with Israel after the 1967 war, parting company then in yet another matter with the Soviet Union, it broke relations after the 1973 war. But there has been no other such instance; it has, for example, had extensive and profitable political, cultural and economic relations with Spain. Its negative public statements should be viewed against the record of factual change which is impressive. In sum, there is no *a priori* reason to believe that Cuba would not be responsive to new overtures under reformulated policy options.

This essay owes much to my *Taming the Cuban Shrew, Foreign Policy* No. 10 (Spring, 1973). The differences will be plain to the readers of both.

Relevant Congressional testimony cited includes: "Soviet Activities in Cuba," *Hearings before the Subcommittee on Inter-American Affairs of the Committee on Foreign Affairs, House of Representatives*, Ninety-second Congress, second session, 1972: "Soviet Naval Activities in Cuba," *ibid.*, Ninety-first Congress, second session, 1970: and "Cuba and the Caribbean," *ibid.*, Ninety-first Congress, second session, 1970.

References to pertinent international agreements, legislation and executive regulations may be found in Committee on Foreign Affairs, House of Representatives, *Inter-American Relations: A Collection of Documents, Legislation, Descriptions of Inter-American Organizations, and other Material Pertaining to Inter-American Affairs*, Ninety-third Congress, first session, 1973.

Among recent, nonpartisan and serious evaluations of U.S.-Cuban relations, the following stand out: John Plank, "We Should Start Talking with Castro," *New York Times Magazine*, March 30, 1969; Richard R. Fagen, "United States-Cuban Relations," in Yale H. Ferguson, ed., *Contemporary Inter-American Relations* (Englewood-Cliffs, N.J.: Prentice-Hall, Inc., 1972); Robert D. Crassweller, "Cuba and the United States," *Headline Series, The Foreign Policy Association*, No. 207

(October, 1971); Edward Gonzalez, "The United States and Castro: Breaking the Deadlock," *Foreign Affairs* (July, 1972; Irving L. Horowitz, "United States-Cuba Relations: Beyond the Quarantine," *Transaction* (April, 1969); and Carmelo Mesa Lago, "The Sovietization of the Cuban Revolution: Its Consequences for the Western Hemisphere," *World Affairs*, Vol. 136, No. 1 (Summer, 1973).

Two good essays on Cuba's international economic relations are Eric N. Baklanoff, "International Economic Relations," in Carmelo Mesa Lago, ed., *Revolutionary Change in Cuba* (Pittsburgh: University of Pittsburgh Press, 1971); and Leon Goure and Julian Weinkle, "Soviet-Cuban Relations: The Growing Integration," in Jaime Suchlicki, ed., *Cuba, Castro and Revolution* (Coral Gables, Fla.: University of Miami Press, 1972).

CHOICES FOR PARTNERSHIP
OR BLOODSHED IN PANAMA
Robert G. Cox

On November 2, 1903, at 5:30 in the afternoon, the cruiser U.S.S. *Nashville* arrived at Colon in the Republic of Colombia, its mission to block deployment of Colombian troops. The next day citizens in the Panamanian province revolted and declared their independence. The revolution was bloodless, except for the death of one Chinese bystander. Fifteen days later, the U.S. government and the Republic of Panama entered into a treaty, drafted by a Frenchman and consisting entirely of language convenient to the United States. Still in effect today, the treaty granted the right to build and operate forever an interocean canal, and to establish, for that purpose, an American enclave in a strip of land and water nearly half the size of Rhode Island, bisecting the Republic on an axis between its two major population centers. The U.S. consummated that right as fast as logistics and technology would permit.

The position of the United States in world politics for nearly two centuries has rested on hegemony in the Western Hemisphere. The country acquired interests during those 17 days in 1903 which included a responsibility for the emergence of a nation, for the administration of a major territorial possession, and for the management of an international public utility of both commercial and military value.

Focusing on current efforts to negotiate and ratify a new treaty, this paper submits some findings of fact and observations concerning the nature of those interests and the fulfillment of that responsibility.

Description of the Subject Matter

Although U.S.-Panamanian affairs are subject to the full range of complexities found in other binational relationships, the principal subject matter has always been, and will continue to be, the Canal and the Zone. It is too early to predict the contents of the revised draft treaty but the Canal and the Zone will predominate.

Panama, by the 1903 treaty, granted the U.S. perpetual jurisdiction as if it were sovereign over the Canal Zone "to the entire exclusion of the exercise by the Republic of Panama of any such sovereign rights, power or authority."

The Zone extends 5 miles on each side of the center line of the Canal, and has an area of 553 square miles of which 362 are land. It is larger than the American Virgin Islands, Guam, and American Samoa combined. Population was 44,198 at the 1970 census. About 11,000 U.S. Armed Forces personnel have been stationed in the Zone during recent years.

The Canal Zone Government and the Panama Canal Company are the two principal operating agencies, headed by one officer who serves both as Governor of the Canal Zone and President of the Company. The Governor is appointed by the President of the United States and reports to the Secretary of the Army. As President of the Company he reports to the Board of Directors, appointed by the Secretary of the Army. The Canal Zone Government maintains the civil executive authority. The legislative power resides in the U.S. Congress and the judicial power is exercised by a District Court of the U.S. Federal Court System. The Company operates the Canal, the Panama Railroad, and a ship which sails between New Orleans and the Zone.

Another U.S.-Panama treaty was signed January 25, 1955, increasing the annuity and granting Panama some real estate and buildings no longer needed by the Canal Zone administration. U.S.-citizen and non-citizen employees were guaranteed equality of pay and opportunity. The U.S. also agreed to build a bridge over the Pacific entrance to the Canal. The bridge was opened October 12, 1962 on the Inter-American Highway.

Panamanians have shown little immediate determination—of the kind so prevalent in Egypt 20 years ago with the Suez Canal—to assume the burdens and risks of administering the Canal.[1] Nationalization or purchase of the Canal, assuming either were feasible, might require Panama to contribute some effort to its management and defense, and would imply sharing in the losses as well as profits. In 1973, some officials of the Panamanian government considered the possibility of acquiring the Canal by purchase out of net earnings from increased tolls and services.[2] This, however, seems not to have received serious attention.

Economic Considerations

Americans have been inclined occasionally to overstate the commercial significance of the Panama Canal, but its value is nonetheless real. Adequate data exists to place it in proper perspective. The recent volume of transits, in number and cargo weight, is as follows.[3]

Fiscal Year	Total Oceangoing Transits	Cargo (in million long tons)
1968	14,807	106
1969	14,602	109
1970	14,829	119
1971	14,617	121
1972	14,238	111
1973	14,238	128

The Canal's ultimate capacity is 26,800 transits annually, with certain physical improvements.

Four categories of bulk commodities in fiscal 1973 accounted for most of the transiting cargo.

	percentage
Petroleum and its products	18.2
Grains	15.8
Coal and Coke	11.1
Ores and metals	9.9
	55.0

Since transiting cargo tends to be made up of commodities which are volatile on the world market, traffic forecasting is difficult.

Each year 18 percent of the world's total merchant fleet (4,500 out of 25,000 ships over 1,000 tons) transit the Canal. The size of an average ship transiting the Canal has been increasing over the past ten years.

	P.C. net tons
1964	5,910
1969	7,658
1973	9,100

The countries most dependent on the Panama Canal send the following percentages of the oceanborne commerce through the Canal, by weight:

	percent
Nicaragua	76.8
El Salvador	66.4
Ecuador	51.4
Peru	41.3
Chile	34.3
Colombia	32.5
Guatemala	30.9
Panama	29.4
Costa Rica	27.2
United States	16.8
Mexico	16.6
New Zealand	15.7

About 30 percent of Panama's gross national product and 40 percent of its foreign exchange earnings are directly or indirectly attributable to the Canal and related installations.

Canal Company tolls, by remaining constant in dollar terms since 1914, have decreased in real terms, and at a precipitous rate, as a result of international monetary readjustments in the 1970s. The result is a growing subsidy to Canal users.

Revenues of the Panama Canal Company were $200 million in fiscal 1973. Approximately 43 percent of regular receipts came from operations other than Canal tolls. The Company finances its own operations without budgetary support from the U.S. government despite a policy of low toll rates and minimal profits from other operations.

Proportions of the Canal Zone's product derived from various sources in 1970 was as follows:

	percentage
Canal Company	44.7
Zone Government	10.2
Military bases and other official agencies	39.9
Private enterprise	5.2
	100.0

Of total U. S. foreign trade, by value, the following percentages transited the Canal in the two most recent years for which data is available:

	Percentages		
	exports	imports	total
1971	12.1	5.6	8.8
1972	13.0	5.3	9.0

Since foreign trade accounts for less than 10 percent of U.S. gross national product, the Canal affects less than one percent of GNP. By volume, less than 5 percent of the total world trade transits the Panama Canal. By value, the proportion would be little more than one percent; an increasing percentage of more expensive cargo is being transported by air (for example, about 10 percent of U.S. foreign trade), and most Canal cargo is in bulk commodities.

COMMENTARY

The adjective most frequently applied to the Canal by Americans is "vital." In terms of U.S. trade, however, the numbers would justify more modest descriptions. Convenient. Useful. The Canal is economically vital to Panama, perhaps also to Nicaragua and a few other Latin American countries, but not to the United States.

One way to analyze the Canal's commercial value is to consider what would happen if it were not there. The figures already provided for U.S. and world trade transiting the Canal—9 percent and 1 percent, respectively—should not be regarded as representing the portion that would be lost if the Canal were inoperative. The decision to send a given shipment through the Canal is frequently a close one, and almost always there are alternative routes or modes of transportation. John Elac* has described the impact of closure of the Canal on total U.S. and world commerce as "inconsequential."

An indicator often cited as proving the Canal's essential worth is: "70 percent of its traffic either originates or terminates in U.S. ports." In the first place, the percentage is a little inflated. It should be 65 percent, but it should then be compared to a totality of 200 percent, not 100 percent, because it refers to both arrivals at and departures from U.S. ports. The indicator, even when placed in that perspective, is spurious because it implies but does not provide an impressive statistical base. Presumably no one believes that if only ten motorboats transited the Canal in 1975, four coming from and three bound for U.S. ports, this would reflect some kind of vital U.S. interest.

When we look at U.S. investment in the Canal, it is tempting to include defense costs, as Senator Strom Thurmond does when he says we have committed a total of $5,695,745,000.[4] But since the Canal is considered a defense asset, we would presumably be spending more than its costs on additional defense if we did not have it. The cost of defending it should be at least off-set by its asset value. Moreover, $5.7 billion is a small fraction of one percent of U.S. military expenditures

---

* Dr. John C. Elac is an international economist and a specialist in U.S.-Latin American relations. He was a member of the Board of Directors of the Panama Canal Company and a member of its Committee on Budget and Finance (1967–69).

during the 60 years of the Canal's operation. Indeed, the entire cost of the Canal might have been lost in the round-off of the defense budget in the fiscal years 1914 to 1973.

As for the $700 million in actual unrecovered investment, the U.S. government would have had that back by now had it not elected to subsidize the shipping operations of user nations through reductions in real toll charges while demand for transit service was increasing.

Military Considerations

By the turn of century, the United States had staked out its continental domain, subdued the indigenous peoples, resolved its main internal conflicts, established unquestioned predominence in the Hemisphere, and was ready to become a global power. On April 21, 1898, the nation went to war with Spain, and in three months destroyed the Spanish fleet at Manila, drove the Spaniards from Cuba, conquered the Philippines, took Puerto Rico and Guam. The battleship U.S.S. *Oregon* made a dramatic 16,000 mile voyage around Cape Horn to participate in the Battle of Santiago de Cuba. During the Spanish-American War, the U.S. annexed Hawaii after collaborating in a revolt there. The U.S. then responded to the 1899 Boxer Rebellion in China by sending two infantry regiments, one troop of cavalry, one battery of light artillery, and two battalions of Marines, commanded by a major general, to join in military operations with the British, French, Japanese, and Russians. A transisthmian canal, long regarded as a potential asset to burgeoning U.S. foreign trade, suddenly became a strategic imperative. The Canal has never been interrupted or seriously threatened by hostile action.

FACTS

The Canal remains a prime consideration in the planning for and accomplishment of the safe and timely movement of naval units between the Atlantic and Pacific Oceans. A saving in distance of approximately 8,000 miles is realized by Canal transit (versus rounding

Cape Horn), in the deployment of ships from one coast to the other. A time saving of up to 30 days can accrue for slower ships and at least 15 days for fast ships cruising at about 20 knots.

During fiscal 1968, a representative year of the Vietnam conflict, 33 percent of the dry cargo shipped from the continental U.S. by the military sea transport service to South Vietnam, Thailand, and the Philippines, and Guam, transited the Canal. For petroleum, oil, and lubricants the proportion was 29 percent. An unofficial estimate of the proportion of dry cargo used to support U.S. military involvement in Vietnam which transited the Canal is as high as 40 percent.

However, in 1970 there were about 1,300 ships afloat, under construction, or on order which could not enter the Panama Canal locks. There were approximately 1,750 more ships that could not pass through the Canal fully laden because of draft limitations due to seasonal low-water level.

The National Defense Study Group of the Atlantic-Pacific Interoceanic Canal Study Commission specifically noted the "vulnerability of the present canal," and stated: the fact that it could be closed by the use of relatively unsophisticated weapons is particularly significant in view of forecasts which anticipate that insurgency and subversion will probably persist in Latin America to the end of the century; interruption for extended periods to Canal service could be achieved with relative ease.[5]

If Gatun Lake were emptied by simple breach of its dam, for example, the Canal could be out of operation for as long as two years, awaiting sufficient rainfall to refill the lake.

The National Defense Study Group further found that even a sea level canal, though less vulnerable, would face threats of sabotage, clandestine mining, or the attack of shipping by low-performance aircraft or readily transportable weapons. The more traditional forms of attack—blockade, naval, or aerial bombardment, or ultimately attack by missile-delivered nuclear weapons—are unlikely, in the Group's view, because the attacker would be confronted by the total military strength of the United States.[6]

The Study Group concluded that closure of the Canal for periods of approximately 30 days, provided they could be anticipated in advance, would not have serious defense implications, but the denial of the Canal to both defense and commercial shipping for two years could have a serious adverse effect on the national defense.[7]

The original purpose of U.S. troops in Panama was to protect the Canal from a foreign aggressor. That is still ostensibly their primary mission. However, the Canal Zone is also a command or coordination center for most U.S. Armed Forces programs and activities in Latin America, including foreign military assistance and training, intelligence, and operational preparedness. The legality of these operations has been questioned. However, the Zone, as long as it remains relatively secure from renewal of the nationalistic attacks of the 1960s, provides a location of unrivaled excellence for an administrative headquarters, communications center, and training ground.

COMMENTARY

Two military issues concerning the Panama Canal overshadow all others: utility and defensibility.

The Canal's military value during the first half of this century is well established, principally by its contributions to the two World Wars. Regarding the Korean War and the conflict in Southeast Asia, its utility is less certainly established. A former senior officer of the U.S. Budget Bureau Military Division estimates that alternative modes of shipment would have had no adverse effect on the Vietnam War effort and that additional costs would have been negligible.[8] A ranking State Department expert in Panamanian affairs now terms the Canal "a military asset of declining value." [9] Nevertheless, a residual utility will remain for some time, largely because of the constraints of U.S. West Coast port facilities, particularly in munitions-handling.

As for the second issue, the Cameron report of the Center for Inter-American Relations puts it succinctly: "The Panama Canal is no longer defensible." [10] This holds for either a strategic attack or destruction by a "determined and resourceful enemy." The Canal can, of course, be held against some levels of civil disturbance. These informed but independent views do not diverge essentially from the later official judgment of the National Defense Study Group.[11]

As the strategic value and defensibility of the Canal have eroded, the

Zone has taken on a new military significance. The U.S. bases there form the operational center of American military activity in Latin America. Ambassador Jack Vaughn* thus described the situation last October:

> The U.S. military command in Panama is made of two parts: a major general from the Corps of Engineers who governs the Panama Canal Company from Balboa Heights, and a four-star general from the Army (CINCSOUTH) who directs Canal Zone military operations from an underground complex at Quarry Heights. Their overriding common objective is to maintain the status quo, and over the years they have been largely immune to the precepts and changes of U.S. foreign policy.
>
> While the Administration's policy has led to a reduction in all the U.S. military missions assigned to other Latin nations, the Pentagon has maintained its top-heavy command intact in the Zone. (The super-abundance of Colonels in the Southern Command has led enlisted men to refer to it as "Southern Comfort.") While the U.S. military in all other Latin nations is under the direct supervision of the U.S. Ambassador, in Panama independent policy control is exercised by the Pentagon. Just when President Nixon was assuring our good neighbors that the U.S. would wear a white hat in the Hemisphere, the Pentagon expanded training of Green Berets in the Zone.[12]

In May 1974, there was some indication in the Pentagon that civilian officials might succeed in abolishing CINCSOUTH as a unified command and reduce the rank of the senior U.S. troop commander in the Zone to major general.[13]

Political Considerations

The history of U.S.-Panama relations has been characterized by (1) Panamanian surprise and mortification over the implementation of the 1903 treaty; (2) increasing Panamanian agitation for revision; (3) an

---

* Jack Hood Vaughn was U.S. Ambassador to Panama (1964–1965); Assistant Secretary of State for Inter-American Affairs (1965–1966); Director of the Peace Corps (1966–1969); Ambassador to Colombia (1969–1970).

initial dilatory paternalism on the part of the U.S.; and (4) a more recent willingness by the U.S. Executive Branch to relieve Panama's grievances while influential members of the House and Senate demand retention of "perpetual sovereignty" in the Zone. For the past ten years, off and on, the two countries have been trying to negotiate a way out of the 1903 treaty.

FACTS

The Canal Zone is an American colony. In the international political context, the word "colony" has two generally accepted definitions: (1) the compact settlement of a group of nationals from one country within the territory of another while the settlers remain loyal to the mother country; and (2) a nonself-governing territory, or a dependency without full self-government, considered by the various governing powers to be a territory under the jurisdiction of the mother country, prevented by social, economic, and political restraints from being fully in charge of its own decisions. The Canal Zone conforms to both of these definitions.

In Panama City, March 21, 1973, the United States vetoed a U.N. Security Council resolution calling on both countries to negotiate a new treaty to "guarantee full respect for Panama's effective sovereignty over all its territory." The U.S. explained its veto, the third in its history, by saying it wanted to negotiate with Panama "without outside pressure." All other Security Council members voted for the resolution except the U.K. which abstained.[14]

The multinational forum then shifted to the Organization of American States where hemispheric foreign ministers have, during the past year, expressed unprecedented concern over the Canal Zone issue.

On February 7, 1974, in Panama City, Secretary of State Kissinger and Panamanian Foreign Minister Juan Tack initialed a statement of eight Principles of Agreement providing that:

> Panama will grant the United States the rights and facilities and lands necessary to continue operating and defending the Canal;
>
> The United States will agree to return to Panama jurisdiction over its territory; to recompense Panama fairly for the use of its territory; and to

arrange for the participation by Panama, over time, in the Canal's operation and defense;

The new treaty shall not be in perpetuity, but rather for a fixed period, and that the parties will provide for any expansion of Canal capacity in Panama that may eventually be needed.[15]

Senator Strom Thurmond on March 29, 1974, introduced Senate Resolution 301 on behalf of himself and 31 other Senators noting, in part, that:

United States diplomatic representatives are presently engaged in negotiations with representatives of the de facto Revolutionary Government of Panama, under a declared purpose to surrender to Panama, now or on some future date, United States sovereign rights and treaty obligations, as defined below, to maintain, operate, protect, and otherwise govern the United States-owned Canal and its protective frame of the Canal Zone;

Title to and ownership of the Canal Zone, under the right "in perpetuity" to exercise sovereign control thereof, were invested absolutely in the United States and recognized to have been so vested in certain solemnly ratified treaties by the United States with Great Britain, Panama, and Colombia . . .

United States House of Representatives, on February 2, 1960, adopted H. Con. Res. 459, Eighty-sixth Congress, reaffirming the sovereignty of the United States over the zone territory by the overwhelming vote of three hundred and eighty-two to twelve, thus demonstrating the firm determination of our people that the United States maintain its indispensable sovereignty and jurisdiction over the Canal and the Zone . . .

and resolving that:

The Government of the United States should maintain and protect its sovereign rights and jurisdiction over the Canal and Zone, and should in no way cede, dilute, forfeit, negotiate, or transfer any of these sovereign rights, power, authority, jurisdiction, territory, or property that are indispensably necessary for the protection and security of the United States and the entire Western Hemisphere . . .[16]

Writing in the *New York Times* on May 7, 1974, Senator Thurmond stated that a total of 35 Senators had, with "no great effort" and mostly in a single afternoon, been convinced to co-sponsor the resolution. He added:

> In my judgment, the Secretary committed an egregious blunder in committing the United States to a course of action on a new Panama treaty without a reasonable assurance that the requisite two-thirds majority of the Senate supported the abrogation of sovereignty.
>
> In consultations with members of Congress before signing the statement, Mr. Kissinger and his chief negotiator, Ambassador Ellsworth Bunker, were advised that surrender of United States sovereignty in the Canal Zone was not a negotiable item; they apparently chose to ignore this advice.
>
> There is no way in which the Joint Statement of Principles can be reconciled with the Senate resolution.[17]

Senator Thurmond and certain members of the House of Representatives contend that the relevant language in the constitution requires that a majority of the House as well as two-thirds of the Senate approve any agreement which cedes land to Panama. The State Department contends it is one of many constitutional grants of power to Congress which is affirmative but not exclusionary, and cites precedents which "in the specific context of Panama, . . . look two ways." [18]

The State Department has understood throughout the recent negotiations that no treaty with Panama affecting U.S. jurisdiction will be ratified without the approval or acquiescence of the Joint Chiefs of Staff. The JCS lines to Capitol Hill are time-honored and uncontested. The Chiefs have accepted the eight negotiating Principles of February 7, 1974. It remains to be seen whether they will approve the treaty, if and when it is concluded. Certainly as long as no treaty has been drafted and Senator Thurmond has a blocking third of the Senate aligned against the Principles, the JCS would have no need to take a negative stand, in any case.

In early 1958, a few Panamanian students quietly entered the Zone on the Pacific side and planted small Panamanian flags in predesignated spots. They called the foray "Operation Sovereignty." The flags were quickly removed by Zone employees. It was the harbinger of other, more serious, demonstrations to follow.

On Independence Day, November 3, 1959, crowds of Panamanians, led by students, tried repeatedly to surge into the Canal Zone and raise their flag. Demonstrators assaulted the U.S. Embassy and Information Service offices in Panama, tore down the Embassy flag, and attacked the American Consulate in Colon. U.S. Army units took up defensive positions on the Zone border. Later that month even larger crowds demonstrated and had to be subdued by American troops.

On April 18, 1961, 500 demonstrators tried to storm the Canal Zone protesting the Bay of Pigs and the role of Zone bases in the invasion of Cuba. In January 1964, rival groups of Panamanian and Canal Zone students faced each other at Balboa High School in the Zone over the issue of flying the American flag without the Panamanian flag at the school. The ensuing riots lasted for four days. Sniper fire into the Zone reached 500 rounds an hour at various times. Toll: Four American soldiers and 20 Panamanian civilians killed; over 400 Panamanians and Americans wounded or injured; extensive property damage. From 1964 to 1968 there were riots annually.

On October 11, 1968, the Guardia Nacional seized control of the country after a year of political turmoil. Over the next few months, Colonel (now Brigadier General) Omar Torrijos emerged as the dominant figure in the "revolutionary government."

Treaty negotiations with the U.S. were long underway when Torrijos came to power and were continuing on the third anniversary of the military coup, October 11, 1971. Addressing an anniversary rally of 200,000 Panamanians assembled two blocks from the Zone, Torrijos asked:

> What nation on earth would bear the humiliation of seeing a foreign flag planted in its very heart? What nation would allow a foreign governor on its territory? . . . Our enemies want us to march on the Zone today. When all hope is lost of removing this colonial enclave, Omar Torrijos will come to this same square to tell you: "Let us advance." Omar Torrijos will accompany you, and the 6,000 rifles of the Guardia Nacional will be there to defend the integrity and dignity of the people. But today we are not going to the Zone.

The New York Times concluded that: General Torrijos cannot turn back without losing face. Violence does not seem imminent, but only a satisfactory agreement will prevent future trouble" . . . [19] And the negotiations continued.

COMMENTARY

The Archbishop of Panama, Marcos McGrath, describes the Canal Zone in these terms:

> . . . the heartland, the most valuable economic area . . . In Panama today, the growth of her two major cities, Panama on the Pacific and Colon on the Atlantic end of the Canal, is hemmed in by the Canal Zone. Teaming tenements face across the street a fence and open fields or virgin jungles—space unused, space reserved, space denied. Panama City has grown from 200,000 to over 500,000 in the past 15 years. It has had to grow unnaturally along the coast five miles and then cut inland, because of the Canal Zone, creating a clumsy triangle, bottling traffic, and testing the patience of every city planner and in fact of every citizen. Panamanians, to go from one part of their country, in this day and age, still must traverse an area that, though legally it is not, looks like a foreign land: with its own police, courts, post-office, stores, and this across the very waist and heart of the nation.[20]

Senator Alan Cranston has observed that of the 15,000 workers in the Canal Zone, 4,000 are Americans, and of those, 1,289 work on the Canal while the other 2,700 are employed in schools, movie theaters, bowling alleys, commissaries, golf courses, and a zoo.[21]

The Panamanians, for their part, now have the toughest and most charismatic leader in their history. They proved from 1958 to 1967 that they can be tenacious in the drive to establish national jurisdiction over the Zone. They have also shown that, under Torrijos, they are willing to be patient as long as he remains believable. But history does not permit any national leader total control of his people's destiny, or even his own. The General has four alternatives: he can produce a supportable treaty. He can delay. He can leave office. Or he can attack the Zone. Time is running out on the first two.

Futures and Interests

The Panama Canal has five alternative futures:

A. *Closure* by hostile action, or by an effective decision that its costs exceed its benefits, or both. There is little evidence that points to such an eventuality, though it is as imaginable today as a seven-year closure of the Suez Canal was 20 years ago.

B. *Internationalization* under the auspices of the United Nations, the Organization of American States, or some other multilateral body. This is a theoretical alternative that continues to be discussed, though it would be far beyond the experience, capacity, and interest of the UN or the OAS. Only a military stalemate between the United States and Panama—inconceivable before the U.S.-Vietnam stalemate, and still most unlikely—could lead to internationalization in the foreseeable future.

C. *Ownership and operation by Panama.* The greatest disservice which the present Canal regime does to Panama is not in withholding benefits, but in withholding the burdens and problems of operating the Canal. Some argue that Panama has been cheated out of its fair share of the benefits. Others contend that Panama was handsomely compensated in 1904 for a strip of mosquito-infested, disease-ridden swamp and jungle, and that the Canal and the Zone constitute an economic windfall which Panamanians could have received only from the Americans. Both arguments have merit. But, by assuming all the burdens of running and protecting the Canal, the United States has denied Panama the experience and the challenge it needs to reach its full maturity as a nation. Panamanians consider their geographic position, which the Canal exploits, to be their principal national resource. Yet, with its management pre-empted by Americans, they are not prepared to assume control of this resource. A new treaty might permit their gradual assumption of operational authority, but Panamanians are neither determined nor able to take full charge in the foreseeable future.

D. *Continued ownership and operation by the U.S. alone.* If the U.S. government decides to hold the Canal and the Zone, it can probably do so for a period of years and perhaps until the Canal's commercial and military asset-value declines to a negligible level. The cost could be high and should be estimated in advance.

E. *Partnership between the United States and Panama.* This alternative is only feasible if the U.S. is genuinely willing to relinquish its exclusive jurisdiction over the Canal Zone. In the words of Ambassador Vaughn, "Intransigence . . . can only inflame the Panamanians, for they now feel grossly abused" by the existence of the American colony.[22] If the political, economic, and cultural insulation of the Zone were to disappear, Panama would be drawn inevitably into an evolving operational partnership with the United States in the Canal's support, management, maintenance, defense, and possibly in its further development.

The United States has only three essential objectives relating to the Panama Canal, according to the Atlantic-Pacific Interoceanic Canal Study Commission:

1. That it always be available to the world's vessels on an equal basis and at reasonable tolls;
2. That it serve its users efficiently; and
3. That the United States have unimpaired rights to defend the Canal from any threat and to keep it open in any circumstances, peace or war.[23]

An American treaty negotiator, authorized to speak for the Executive Branch, subsequently omitted the Study Commission's second objective on efficiency and added:

That the United States have the right to expand Canal capacity, either by adding an additional lane of locks to the existing Canal or by building a sea level canal.[24]

Panama's interests and intentions are clear:

• negotiate the Zone out of existence;
• failing that, try to make it too expensive for the U.S. to stay in Panama, recognizing that dollar costs alone may not be very impressive to Americans;
• either way, assume an active role in operating and protecting the Canal.

Problems of Awareness and Attitude

The real content of the Panama-Canal Zone issue may be as much psychological as it is military or commercial. No problem of current international affairs is more encumbered by national pride, convenient misconception, legal abstraction, and ignorance.

Americans have not been perceptive or even consistent about Panama. Theodore Roosevelt could boast one day, "I took Panama," and another day proclaim:

> We have not the slightest intention of establishing an independent colony in the middle of the State of Panama . . . it is our full intention that the rights which we exercise shall be exercised with all proper care for the honor and interest of the people of Panama.

For three generations American democracy has been absent in the Canal Zone, where public officials are not elected, but imposed. Civilian control of the military is inverted: the Governor is a major general, but distinctly junior to the local troop commander. The Zone economy is state socialism, with 95 percent of the productive capacity concentrated in the hands of the government.

The world may well wonder whether the United States knows what it is doing in Panama.

Options and Costs

Given the alternatives governing the future of the Panama Canal and the basic American objectives, there are only two operative choices for U.S. policy: we can pursue our goals in active cooperation with, or in opposition to, the Panamanians. Panama will not participate directly in that decision, but will presumably impose costs for either course.

MAINTAINING THE STATUS QUO

One option is to hold the Canal Zone while we have the capability to fortify and defend it against the Panamanians.

Senator Alan Cranston stated in October 1971 that the U.S. Armed Forces had—out of 40,000 officers, men, and dependents in the Zone—only two battalions of Army combat troops and no high performance combat units from the Air Force and Navy.[25] But reinforcements are available, and CINCSOUTH presumably learned from its experiences in January of 1964; for example:

—that the Guardia National cannot always be relied upon to restrain attacks upon the Zone;
—that small arms fire from the Zone into the Republic is not an adequate response even to a few snipers;
—that the command had better have its own search-and-destroy capability in any serious future confrontation;
—that some of the civilians in the Zone (including 8,000 women and 15,000 children) could become casualties or hostages almost instantly, in the absence of adequate contingency planning, security, fortification, tactical preparedness, and evacuation procedures.

Foreseeable costs of this choice could include the following:
1. Military expenditures and manpower commitments of significant, but not burdensome, levels would have to be made.
2. The United States would have to make the Zone less accessible to unauthorized entry from the Republic and less vulnerable to amphibious landing, an expensive and exacting task, but not prohibitively so.
3. Despite these defensive measures, some exposure to sabotage, guerrilla attack, or assault by regular military units from the Republic would persist. Such moves, even when easily repulsed, have already involved serious costs even though they have not yet included an act of sabotage or interruption of Canal operations.
4. An overt decision to maintain the status quo in the Zone would undermine the U.S. leadership position in the hemisphere. If it were followed by another bloody episode in or around the Zone, U.S. political leverage would be further diminished and could result in violent responses directed at our enterprises, diplomatic

establishments, and citizens throughout the region. The Latin Americans have never before been as united and outspoken in support of Panama's grievances against the United States. An issue that was essentially bilateral in the 1950s has become a matter of legitimate hemispheric concern. Even the United States has acknowledged this by accepting OAS investigation, mediation, and oversight.

5. The world community would condemn U.S. efforts to hold the Zone indefinitely. While most of the countries which use the Canal are interested mainly in efficient operation and reasonable tolls, no civilized nation can be oblivious to a breach of international peace, or the threat of it. This was, in part, the motivation for the Security Council's effort to intervene in 1973.

Most colonial powers that have tried to retain their possessions in the developing world have come to regret it. At a minimum, we should avoid striking a posture that is at once domineering and weak. We should decide in advance, as we regrettably failed to do in Southeast Asia, how many more human lives this real estate is worth to us, and for what period of time. Once the escalation begins it is too late for that kind of analysis.

PARTNERSHIP

Alternatively, the United States could sign and ratify a treaty along the lines of the February 7 Principles. This approach would not rule out Canal defense bases, but it would assume that the U.S. will acknowledge effective Panamanian jurisdiction over the land on which the bases would be located.

Loss of American property would be a direct cost. But the major disadvantage of the partnership option lies in the irretrievable loss of absolute U.S. authority over the enterprise. More specifically:

1. Once we relinquished our position in the Zone, the increasing Panamanian involvement might serve to dilute the operational effectiveness of the Canal.

2. If efficiency declined, world shipping, including our own, would suffer.
3. The United States, having assumed an obligation to the maritime nations and to world commerce, could be criticized for allowing the Canal to deteriorate.
4. Ultimately, the waterway might be closed because of some failure of the Panamanian partners, or the joint management, to perform. While the Canal is no longer a strategic asset against any conceivable enemy, it is still possible that its loss to the United States could in some future national emergency be significant, or even crucial.

In a world of accelerating and violent change accompanied by increasing uncertainty, the United States should not yield military and commercial advantages without careful analysis and commensurate incentive. However, if Americans have a national interest in protecting a distant enterprise that can be marginally useful in their defense and affects less than one percent of their GNP, the Panamanians might have even greater motivation to protect the Canal. It is on their territory, provides almost a third of their GNP, and constitutes their primary national resource.

ACCOMMODATION WITHOUT A TREATY

Even if the Administration persists in its determination to achieve an accommodation with Panama, its objectives are, for the moment, thwarted by a decisive bloc in the Senate and a potent group in the House, as well. Also, judging by past performance, the JCS is probably capable of producing additional legislative obstacles to any new treaty, if necessary. The Administration knows it could not have obtained ratification of a treaty before the November 1974 elections, which means February or March of 1975 would be the earliest. Much will depend on President Ford and the composition of the new Senate.

Should it become impossible to negotiate a treaty, the Administration—assuming it moves fast and decisively—could head off an immediate confrontation and buy additional time through direct executive action. If the same creative energy that built the Canal Zone were applied to dismantling it, that would probably be sufficient. For example, the Administration could:

1. Drastically reduce the numbers of civilian and military personnel stationed in the Zone.
2. Bring all dependents home, except those of civilian personnel whose permanent employment is critical to the operation of the Canal itself. (This would automatically reduce the visibility of the U.S. government enterprises which Panamanians find most disturbing: golf courses, theaters, commissaries, post exchanges, bowling alleys, swimming pools. It would also stimulate the use of privately owned Panamanian commercial and recreational establishments, bringing Americans and Panamanians into more natural contact with each other.)
3. Appoint a civilian Governor of the Canal Zone who speaks Spanish and who is acceptable to Panama, and give him authority over CINCSOUTH, except during a military emergency.
4. Make Spanish a second official language of the Zone for one year, and the only official language thereafter.
5. Require that (a) all U.S. military and civilian personnel study Spanish under Panamanian instructors, and (b) all personnel whose assignment to the Zone is for two years or more attain a working knowledge of the language within one year.

Ambassador Robert Anderson who headed the U.S. negotiating team from 1964 to 1973 acknowledged to his State Department colleagues that he had a recurring "nightmare" of collapsed talks, shattered expectations, exploding emotions, and the Zone under siege. The proposed course of action might avoid that kind of deterioration, provided the Administration maintained credible efforts to conclude a treaty at the earliest date.

Insofar as Panama is concerned, the Commission on United States-Latin American Relations came into being at a fortuitous moment. With the observations outlined here, and the additional evidence which will doubtless be presented by interested parties, the Commission should be able to weigh the alternatives, and reach a sound position on this urgent issue of foreign policy.

Senator Thurmond holds that "there is no way that any treaty can adequately protect and defend our interests in operating the Canal when it has as its basis the abrogation of sovereignty."

Ambassador Vaughn considers Panama "a Latin American Vietnam." He finds that through the collaboration of Congressional and military supporters of the Canal Zone, "Presidents' orders have been reversed, diplomatic maneuvers and decisions brushed aside, and the United Nations told to go to hell." And he concludes, "The tinder awaits the spark."

Neither of these admonitions can be disregarded. Likewise, we ignore at our peril the public commitments of national leaders abroad: indeed, it has been the commonest error of American foreign policy during the past four decades.

NOTES

1. Cf. Lyman M. Tondel, Jr. (ed.), The Panama Canal (New York: The Association of the Bar of the City of New York, 1965), pp. 42, 43.

2. Robert G. Cox, "Questions Concerning the Panama Canal: A Preliminary Opinion" (New York: Transnational Consulting Group, 1973), p. 24.

3. Panama Canal Company, Canal Zone Government, Annual Reports, 1968–1973 (Balboa Heights).

4. Senate Resolution 301, 93rd Congress, 2nd Session, March 29, 1974, p. 3.

5. Report of the Atlantic-Pacific Interoceanic Canal Study Commission (Washington, 1970), II-11.

6. Ibid., II-11.

7. Ibid., II-20, 21.

8. Interview, May 14, 1974.

9. Interview, May 10, 1974.

10. Cameron, op. cit., p. 4.

11. Canal Study Group, op. cit., pp. II-11, 12.

12. Jack Hood Vaughn, "A Latin-American Vietnam," The Washington Monthly (Oct. 1973), pp. 30, 31.

13. Interview with Senior Department of Defense Policy Officer, May 10, 1974.

14. For summary of the State Department position see News Release, op. cit., p. 6.

15. Ibid., pp. 2, 3.

16. Senate Resolution, op. cit.

17. *The New York Times*, May 7, 1974.

18. Subcommittee on Panama Canal, Hearings, Serial No. 92-30 (Washington, 1972), pp. 13–16.

19. *The New York Times*, Oct. 12, 1971.

20. "The Canal Question: A Christian View," address before Carnegie Endowment for International Peace, April 16, 1974.

21. *The New York Times*, Oct. 19, 1971.

22. Cf. Vaughn, op. cit., p. 32.

23. Canal Study Commission, op. cit., pp. 8, 9.

24. Hearings, Serial No. 92-30, op. cit., p. 5.

25. *The New York Times*, Oct. 19, 1971.

FUTURE U.S. SECURITY ASSISTANCE IN THE LATIN AMERICAN CONTEXT*
David Ronfeldt

Latin America has experienced great change and growth since the 1960s, when first thoughts typically called to mind wealthy oligarchs, backward economies, political corruption, personalistic military dictators, peasant poverty, incompetent elites, and weak but noisy nations in America's backyard. Academic visions of the potential for explosive revolutionary upheaval rivaled alternative perspectives that Latin American societies were too traditional and conservative to change fast or much at all. Moreover, as reflected in dependency themes, the only foreign policy issues that mattered much concerned the United States; and except for common market movements and a few minor disputes, relations between Latin American countries were relatively insignificant.

The context for U.S.-Latin American relations is very different now,

* This statement draws heavily on published Rand research, especially Luigi Einaudi and others, "Arms Transfers to Latin America: Toward a Policy of Mutual Respect," The Rand Corporation, Santa Monica, June 1973, R-1173-DOS, and Einaudi, ed., *Beyond Cuba: Latin America Takes Charge of Its Future*, Crane, Russak (New York, 1974) esp. Chaps. 3, 8 and 13.

and the old visions are outmoded. Domestically, durable institutional revolutions have occurred in the leading Latin American countries, as a new generation of well-trained, progress-minded elites have begun to work with rather than against the traditional institutions, such as the state bureaucracies, the military, and the Church. Regionally, relations among Latin American states are expanding rapidly, and neighbors are treated as serious foreign policy concerns. Internationally, the shift from a bipolar to a multipolar environment, combined with the lessening of U.S. hegemony, have afforded new opportunities to Latin American governments; and they have begun to regard all great powers with ambivalence.

New Security Conditions in a New Latin America

Threat assessments by Latin American nations reflect these changes. As the state has strengthened, internal security has declined as the major preoccupation of domestic military forces. As U.S. hegemony has declined and local foreign relations expanded, external defense against neighbors has returned as the primary traditional mission of standing armed forces. As local economies have modernized and a multipolar world economy appeared, Latin American leaders have begun to worry about their institutional defense against economic aggression by foreign powers and multinational corporations, a worry that has arisen from the perceived linkages between national development and national security. This new complexity of threat perceptions has altered the context for U.S. security assistance. Indeed, Latin American governments may occasionally regard certain U.S. interests as a potential threat.

INTERNAL SECURITY AGAINST REVOLUTIONARY VIOLENCE

Latin American governments are frequently portrayed as being under internal attack from revolutionary and radical elements. Rural and urban insurgencies have recently received great attention. During the 1960s, Castroite revolution was popularly forecast for all of Latin America, and foreign-supported guerrilla insurgencies did beset a number of regimes. By 1970, however, guerrilla bands had been defeated or contained throughout the hemisphere. Rural insurgency, though capable of provoking continuing trouble in countries with long traditions of internal violence, no longer offered a viable or appealing revolutionary strategy. Moreover, it became quite clear that conditions for their success did not exist on a national scale and could not be created even by determined bands in the countrysides of Bolivia, Colombia, Guatemala, Peru, and Venezuela.

Rural guerrillas achieved some gains mainly in physically isolated regions where impoverished populations were becoming independent from the old *latifundista* and *casiquista* ways of life, but not yet a part of national economic markets and government bureaucracies. One of the political consequences of this lack of integration was the transformation of several such areas into bases for insurgent revolutionaries. Peasant revolts have typically occurred in post-feudal regions that are just beginning to undergo a centralization and bureaucratization of political power and authority, as well as some transformation of the traditional economy. However, as the Latin American experience is again demonstrating, such regional peasant rebellions of insurgencies are neither long-lasting nor capable in themselves of producing national revolutions.

Despite (or perhaps because of) the many failures of rural insurgents, persistent revolutionaries resorted, after Che Guevara's death in 1967, to new strategies and tactics of urban guerrilla warfare. This was an attempt to create the conditions for revolution if not the revolution itself. As a result of terrorist attacks, kidnappings, robberies and bombings, urban insurgents have attained credibility as internal security problems in Argentina and Uruguay. Thus, what rural insurgency failed to accomplish during the 1960s, it has been feared—or hoped—that urban insurgency may achieve during the 1970s.

In practice, however, urban insurgency is proving to be less of a problem in Latin America as a whole than was rural insurgency. Incidents of urban terrorism sometimes appear to be quite numerous, but in fact, a seemingly anomic rise in terrorist incidents may indicate the decline and fragmentation of a revolutionary organization, rather than growing strength. Urban insurgents do not appear to be gaining a strategic advantage for themselves, whether measured by organized populist support, elite fragmentation, or institutional collapse.

Militarily, terrorists will probably continue to fail to seize power in urban settings, for several key reasons. Overall, the Latin American urban sectors are generally not revolution-oriented. Government institutional capabilities for control and responsiveness are generally stronger in urban than in rural areas. Moreover, urban insurgency alone has never succeeded militarily without rural support, which has not developed.

Not only do domestic political-strategic considerations not favor seizure of power by urban insurgents, but the external environment is no longer as supportive of violent revolution in Latin America as in the recent past. The Soviet Union, although occasionally resorting to subversion, generally gives greater weight to peaceful struggle, and both the Chinese and the Cubans have diminished their former active support for armed struggle. Simultaneously, the lowered U.S. profile in Latin America may also be defusing much of the symbolic target useful to insurgents, even as U.S. military assistance programs may have already contributed to increased local counterinsurgency capacities. Yet foreign participation in insurgencies, even at the high level of the 1960s, has rarely, if ever, been decisive in determining the outcome.

To say that revolutionary violence and insurgency will probably not constitute a serious internal security threat in Latin America during the 1970s is not necessarily to say that non-revolutionary violence will abate. Domestic political conflict will probably continue unceasingly—and in some countries it might even increase. The kinds of violent disturbances which can be expected are familiar—rural social banditry, student demonstrations, military coups, and so on. These are the most durable forms of political violence in Latin America. Indeed, it is doubtful that development and modernization can proceed without such occasional outbreaks. Where they exist, these activities may be regarded as internal security threats, but they do not necessarily threaten Latin America's prospects for development, or, for that matter, Latin America's relations with the United States.

Government and military institutions have gained such strength in recent decades that domestic political violence, revolutionary or otherwise, will probably not pose a serious internal security threat during the 1970s. Yet revolutionary violence has had, and may continue to have, significant political impact on the directions of national development.

A curious association appears to exist. In those countries where the established political institutions have remained relatively strong, the process of dealing with mainly rural insurgencies seems to have led to the strengthening of liberal or reformist elites—as in Venezuela, Peru, and Colombia. In contrast, urban terrorism seems associated with the strengthening of anti-liberal or conservative elites—as in Argentina, Brazil, and Uruguay. In the case of Mexico, the apparent rise and then restraint of reformist proposals within the Echeverria administration seems to correlate with the shift from mainly rural insurgency to more urban terrorism.

The reasons for this association are unclear, but may depend on whether the threatened elites are "in" or "out." Rural insurgency aims mainly at traditional landed elites who are generally on the way "out" as powerful figures, thus providing an issue whereby liberal and reformist elites from middle and urban sectors can improve their position. Urban terrorism, in contrast, poses a direct threat to business, financial, and government elites who are very much "in" and thus may effectively use their positions to press for authoritarian, conservative, and even repressive solutions.

Thus, a basic effect of unsuccessful revolutionary struggles may well be the unintended mobilization of new political leaders and groupings —of rightist, leftist, and moderate persuasions—who prefer institutional politics. Indeed, the containment of revolutionary violence seems to lead to additional pressures for political and economic change through the established institutions, as new nationalistic elites and ideas gain ground within the state bureaucracies, the military, the Church and other sectors.

INSTITUTIONAL DEFENSE AGAINST FOREIGN ECONOMIC AGGRESSION
AND DEPENDENCY

Latin America is experiencing growth and transformation in diverse forms. A nationalistic new generation of independent, well-trained civilian and military leaders are taking command. State institutions are gaining strength, and security doctrines have come to embrace national development as a central concern. Meanwhile, Latin American perceptions of what constitutes a security threat to economic development and national independence have also changed in unexpected ways.

Security concepts that focused on leftwing extremists and revolutionary insurgents as the aggressors in the 1960s, now include economic and social backwardness as central causes of political unrest and institutional fragility. Under this broader conception, security problems and even threats may originate from the unchecked activities of foreign interests (and allied local elites) that are thought to dominate the national economic structure, foster dependency on foreign powers and markets, and commit economic aggression. Their impact may not only interfere with independent national direction of the economy, but also seem to weaken a country in relation to its neighbors. Thus, military leaders may regard certain U.S. corporations, as well as U.S.-based multinational corporations, as external sources of possible internal security problems.

National security doctrines are closely linked to economic development policies by reform-minded officers striving to establish national independence. Doctrinal thinkers in Argentina and Peru in particular have warned against the potential dangers of foreign economic aggression, and argue that military dependence on foreign military technology may be the worst form of dependency.

These ideas are far from being purely academic exercises. Their practical implications are seen in Ecuadorian and Peruvian seizures of foreign fishing boats, Peru's nationalization of the international Petroleum Company, Chile's expropriation of ITT and release of secret documents translated by "specialists of the Armed Forces General Staff," and Panamanian claims against the Canal and Canal Zone. Echoes even appear in Mexico. At the 1974 hemispheric meeting of army commanders, Peruvian and Argentine officers proposed that the meeting consider Latin American defense against great power economic aggression, a topic they considered far more serious than leftist subversion or hemispheric defense against communism.

Such developments stand in marked contrast to previous decades when the United States represented the major "friend" against hemispheric "enemies." From the 1940s through the 1960s most Latin American governments shared enemies with the United States: Nazi Germany, Communist Russia, and later Cuba under Castro. These hemispheric bonds, though they varied greatly from country to country, helped unify Latin American security policies toward the United States, as well as toward each other. Presently, however, few Latin American leaders see distinct friends or enemies among the major powers. All are regarded with increasing ambivalence as presenting obstacles as well as opportunities for future progress. The unifying strand in regional foreign policies has become anti-imperialism and anti-dependency, rather than anti-fascism, anti-communism, or even anti-Americanism—and this has reinforced security concerns in regard to great power economic aggression.

Thus, the United States may find itself rather than Leftist revolutionaries, identified as the origin of activities that disturb internal development. Moreover, Latin American movement toward seeking diversification of arms supplies, and the establishment of local defense industries, similarly indicate the quest for technological independence from foreign powers, and the concern for external defense against neighbors.

A RETURN TO EXTERNAL DEFENSE AGAINST LOCAL CONFLICTS

While U.S. analysts in the 1960s regarded internal security as the proper role for Latin American militaries and as the way to reduce their influence in politics, Latin American officers instead found internal security to be a highly political task that sometimes interfered with the classic pursuit of standing armed forces, external defense. This was particularly the case in South American countries. The changing regional and international context of the 1970s, however, is returning external defense against neighbors to the priority it held before the Cuban revolution.

Local military conflict in South America: it is often difficult for an outsider to take such a prospect seriously. Throughout this century Latin America ranks as one of the most harmonious regions of the world. Only one protracted conflict has occurred: the Chaco War between Bolivia and Paraguay during 1932–35. While a few other limited conflicts have marred the peace, the three decades stretching from the Peru-Ecuador fighting in 1941 and the Honduras-El Salvador clash of 1969 provided occasional smoke but little flash.

We often attribute this phenomenon to the generally shared language, cultural and historical background of the Latin American countries. Yet, underneath, the differences among the countries are so great as to make one wonder whether the term "Latin America" conveys much that is real. Indeed, it has often seemed that the main thing most Latin American countries had in common was the United States.

Shared localisms, then, did not provide the foundation for regional peace. The regional predominance of the United States did, however, and a second major factor may be the relatively low level of interactions between Latin American states, combined with limited capacities to affect each other's activities.

Since the 1940s, these conditions have greatly constrained the potential for political, economic, or military conflicts within the region—while also constraining the prospects for higher levels of cooperation and integration. Both conditions are now rapidly changing, thereby raising local requirements for potential external defense.

The major change in the international context is the shift from political-military bipolarity to economic multipolarity. For Latin Americans it is accompanied by the resurgence of European alternatives for trade and other relations, the amelioration of possible Soviet-sponsored threats, and the lessening of U.S. hegemony, partly through the demise of its aid and assistance programs but also through the adoption of a low-profile policy. These changes have brought new opportunities, and indeed the diversification of relations with a variety of foreign powers has more to offer and entails fewer risks than at any time since World War II.

Thus Latin American governments may adopt considerable flexibility in their dealings with outside powers, and constantly-shifting coalitions on specific issues become quite likely. They can be particularly flexible in their dealings with the United States. Conservative governments can more easily afford an assertive policy of independence while radical and highly reformist governments (perhaps even Cuba) can more readily afford to cooperate with the United States.

Such opportunities for international diversification may, however, lead to local conflicts of interest becoming as prominent as the historic harmonies of interest. The lessening of the U.S. presence in particular may have disturbing rather than integrative effects, for in the past, strong U.S. power and influence often served to temper local rivalries and potential conflicts.

Meanwhile, regional interactions among the Latin American countries are increasing at a remarkable rate. New road transportation systems, press dissemination, marketing and investment patterns, population movements, and military contracts, for example, are bringing local governments and people into much closer contact, for competition as well as collaboration.

Accordingly, governments are turning toward their neighbors. Particularly in South America, local neighbors are receiving the foreign policy attention formerly accorded only to foreign powers. Controversy about Brazil's emergence as a subregional power; the rival ambitions of Argentina; jostling for influence in Bolivia and the other buffer states, as well as boundary tension among Chile, Bolivia and Peru have all served to raise doubts about future prospects for harmony and cooperation.

It comes as no surprise, therefore, that militaries, especially in South America, are turning once again to traditional missions of external defense. Neighbors are regarded as potential rivals for regional leadership, natural resources, economic markets, investments, and the control of borders. Indeed, there appears to be a resurgence of "frontier-minded" military nationalism, fed especially by interests in ocean resources and the claim to a 200-mile limit. Arms procurements, training, troop deployment, and doctrinal thinking all reflect a renewed emphasis on external defense—though classic arms races are unlikely, and compared to other regions Latin America still remains lightly armed.

In line with these trends, local "geopolitical" analyses are increasingly prominent elements in national security doctrines and foreign policy processes, as they were in Europe and the United States during the late 19th and early 20th centuries. This trend is particularly pronounced in Argentina, Brazil, and Peru; and relates clearly to their concerns about regional leadership and strength. In Argentina and Brazil, for example, there are conflicting interests in the hydro-electric development of the Plate River systems, and diverging interests in economic relations with Bolivia and Paraguay and Uruguay, which have historically served as "buffer" countries between them.

These new perspectives encourage the development and security of large frontier areas that are isolated, sparsely populated, and that may contain abundant natural resources, such as petroleum. Military officers in Argentina argue, for example, that the development of Patagonia is a vital precondition for eventual integration with Chile, while development of the northern provinces is needed for national security against Brazil. Other cases include: Colombia's Guajira peninsula claimed by Venezuela, the potentially oil-rich Amazon and Andean territories that border several countries, Bolivia's Santa Cruz region, and Chile's northern province once captured from Bolivia. The concern for frontier areas reflects the importance of relations with bordering nations.

Military conflicts in South America are not, however, inevitable. Positive countervailing developments—skillful diplomacy to avoid isolation, and regional organization on selected issues—mean that differences need not become fighting matters. Moreover, rather than prepare for war, most Latin American militaries aim only to keep modest but respectable forces in being, with the capacity to prepare for war if it ever becomes necessary. Nevertheless, the preceding points do serve to show why especially the South American countries take external defense missions seriously—and thereby indicate new complexities for the United States if it wishes to avoid entanglement between old friends and allies.

To recapitulate, then, the United States faces a Latin American security context that is radically different from the 1950s and 1960s. No direct military security threats to United States interests emanate from these countries, nor are any likely to develop in the future. Internal security problems perceived by local governments can be managed by their own increasingly strong armed forces and police agencies. Therefore, no significant internal, external or extra-hemispheric threats exist to justify U.S. security assistance programs as in the past. Instead, local prospects for border conflicts militate against large U.S. programs that might upset the local balances.

SECURITY ASSISTANCE AND LOCAL POLITICS

Major issues for the United States, then, concern political relations rather than military threats. Is there a political justification for security assistance? Or is it antithetical to politics as we traditionally believe in it? Indeed, it often appears that the Military Assistance Program (MAP) and the Foreign Military Sales (FMS) program have led to the unproductive diversion of scarce economic resources, fostered military intervention in politics, and facilitated the establishment of repressive authoritarian regimes. Recent events in most of the Southern Cone countries—Argentina, Bolivia, Brazil, Chile and Uruguay—raise doubt that the United States has interests in the continuation of security programs to them.

But "democratic" governments have been about as likely as "military" governments to allocate resources to military development. Increases as well as decreases in military spending have happened before as well as after coups—or the change back to civilian government. Moreover, the size of past MAP programs also appears to be statistically unrelated to military interventionism and arms demands. Propositions about the wastefulness of resource diversion from development to defense are also proving unreliable and misleading. In general, higher defense expenditures seem to correlate positively to higher economic growth rates—just the reverse of the original worry. Major defense expenditures for costly advanced weaponry, as opposed to programs that emphasize civilian skills, may burden growth potential somewhat; but one must also take into account the fact that arms purchases by Latin American countries have been fairly low by world standards. Finally, the more costly and sophisticated weapons provided through U.S. military programs, or purchased elsewhere, are of no real utility for repressing local populations. It is even doubtful that MAP programs of the 1960s contributed much to the final defeat or containment of rural guerrillas. MAP served mainly to improve the professionalism of the officer corps, especially management and technical skills.

Foreign military programs alone, therefore, cannot be used to account for, to support, or to reverse trends in local development. But they can encourage military roles in politics. As the 1960s began, U.S. officials evidently expected that counterinsurgency assistance, along with other programs, would help lay foundations for liberal democracy and economic development, while gradually separating the military from politics. Instead, the reverse happened: counterinsurgency brought a new generation of officers reluctantly into politics, resulting in the demise of liberal democracy in several countries. MAP may have inadvertently contributed to dictatorship.

Yet if this argument is accepted, then so must another: namely that U.S. efforts to export liberal democracy during the 1960s may also have inadvertently contributed to the current trend toward authoritarian executive rule. Liberal democratic experiments under civilian leadership in countries like Argentina, Brazil, Chile and Peru ultimately failed, in part because American-style democracy did not fit with local traditions. Corporatist style regimes, coming in democratic as well as dictatorial versions, appear to provide a more acceptable and stable basis for rule through civil-military coalitions.

Attributing such great influence to U.S. policies, however, seems to misjudge local factors that eventually overwhelm foreign intentions. Paternalistic and discriminatory features of U.S policies were prominent during the 1960s. In retrospect, however, the most serious difficulties for U.S. security policies, particularly in relation to arms transfers and political-military goodwill, appear to have derived from the largely erroneous assumption that Latin America is (even ought to be) so dependent upon the United States that its policies can guide Latin American behavior. This fundamental assumption overlooked four major factors that limited U.S. power and influence.

First, in many areas domestic conditions have taken primacy over relations with the United States. The defeat or containment of guerrilla insurgencies during the 1960s was determined essentially by domestic conditions and owed little to MAP activities.

Second, with the growth of European and other international

economies, many Latin American countries have enjoyed alternatives to dealing with the United States, as demonstrated by the failure of U.S. arms control intentions during the 1960s and the recent surge of arms transfers from Europe.

Third, partly as an outgrowth of experiences with counterinsurgency and social change, the interests and objectives of the new generations of military as well as other elites have coincided much less with those of their U.S. counterparts than was the case in previous decades. In the late 1960s, for example, U.S. restrictions on arms sales were viewed by Latin American officers as an act of antipathy and distrust directed especially at them.

Fourth, Latin America's institutional strength has grown rapidly in the last decade, providing governments with better bases for adopting independent initiatives while resisting traditional modes of influence from the United States. This is illustrated in part by the relative ineffectiveness of U.S. moves to influence local government policies and successions by withholding arms sales, military assistance, economic and/or diplomatic recognition.

The central importance of military leaders and institutions in Latin American politics, and their potential for making positive contributions to national development, suggests that it is important for the United States government to maintain constructive relations with them, as well as with elites and institutions in civilian sectors. Relations with military rulers need not, and for historical and ideological reasons often cannot, be close. A basic antagonism against military participation in politics, however, is unwarranted. In the past, disapproving measures have reflected prejudicial misconceptions of military and civilian roles in Latin America and, moreover, have generally proven ineffective or counterproductive.

Bases for a Future U.S. Security Assistance Relationship

The preceding points serve to recommend the formulation of a moderate, "correct" security relationship based mainly on political requirements for goodwill and interdependence in a multipolar era—and militate against the furtherance of large or concessionary aid programs based on partially-shared threat perceptions. Changing conditions require a new respect and responsiveness to Latin American interests, and reveal the inadequacy of paternalistic and restrictive principles. Indeed, restrictive attitudes toward arms transfer fostered, perhaps more than any other single element, the deterioration of U.S.-Latin American military relationships during the past decade.

Both the United States and Latin America have reason to welcome a moderate, even restrained, military relationship. To begin with, there is common agreement that the priorities for military defense in the Latin American region are low. While the United States is concerned with conflict environments elsewhere and seeks to divert greater resources to its own domestic use, Latin American governments seem to share the desire to avoid excessive dependence on, or identification with, the United States in sensitive national security matters.

OBJECTIVES

Three objectives in particular stand out as potentially useful, mutually agreeable bases for future U.S. security assistance in Latin America. The first is political: military relations are essential to maintaining constructive government-to-government relations, whether the regime in power is headed by military or civilian officials. Military relations are regarded as part of constructive political relations with the United States. They indicate that both sides take each other seriously. For the United States, the main benefit of a new security relationship may lie in counterbalancing difficulties likely to emerge in other, especially in economic, areas. The political interests of Latin American governments and militaries can be served by avoiding the unbalancing and balkanization that might occur if the United States withdrew or entirely favored one country against another, and by maintaining the United States as a potential mediator if regional differences lead to local military engagements.

The second objective is professional: security relations can provide a useful response to professional demands for the transfer of U.S. technology and learning. Latin American officers still regard the U.S. military as the finest in the world. It remains their favorite source for advice, training and equipment; and many officers have benefited from their professional contacts with the U.S. armed forces through its assistance programs. Indeed, institutional dignity through modernity may be the leading objective of many Latin American militaries.

The third objective is military: U.S. programs can help sustain the elementary contacts and understandings that would facilitate emergency cooperation and even joint operations should the necessity arise. For example, while detente diminishes the possibilities for a U.S.-Soviet war, some continued cooperation in the fields of ASW surveillance and intelligence may still have relevance in the years ahead.

INSTRUMENTS

The various forces affecting military relationships suggest that an adequate point of departure for policy would be the establishment of generally correct relations on a technical military basis between the United States and Latin American countries. The fading grant MAP approach could be beneficially replaced with a series of instruments designed to sustain correct professional relations in accord with the preceding objectives.

Arms transfers, inevitable in some form and from various countries, will play an important role in the evolution of the relationship. Though modest in their involvement of U.S. interests, they are far from modest in their potential for creating friction with the United States. While it has little to gain (and perhaps something to lose) from aggressive arms sales policies toward Latin America, the United States can only create continuing troubles by following restrictive policies that seem to discriminate specifically against Latin America. Given present modest levels of demand, a principle of unrestricted but unsubsidized military sales might be an acceptable basis for a post-grant policy on arms transfer to Latin America.

Military representation is essential to diplomacy, the coordination of military relations, and intelligence. The present advisory mission system, a legacy of the MAP era, might be changed to provide a small interservice group acting as liaison on professional problems of management, organization and training, which are increasingly handled by officers from the local military. Such a group would not engage directly in sales promotion, though it could facilitate sales contacts and discussions. The military liaison group might be integrated into the embassy country team as a Defense Section, rather than standing somewhat apart and operating mainly in terms of higher military commands.

Military training accompanies the transfer of technology and learning. Whether training should generally be provided on a grant, exchange or purchase basis is beyond the scope of this statement, although some training costs should probably be included in major equipment sales. Training programs now under MAP might be retained within the context of a revised technical, educational and cultural exchange program toward Latin America, directed under the State Department, that would be based on professional criteria and include military institutions.

A FURTHER COMMENT ON ARMS SALES

The principle of unrestricted but unsubsidized military sales would require several steps to implement, including:

- The elimination of grant materiel assistance to those few countries still receiving it;
- The termination of those legislative restrictions (against arming military dictators, seizing fishing vessels, providing sophisticated weapons, setting sale ceilings, etc.) that are aimed exclusively at Latin America; and
- The provision of sufficient government credit through the FMS system to ensure the international competitiveness of U.S. equipment.

These steps should be taken more or less simultaneously. Complete elimination of grant materiel assistance without also eliminating political restrictions would merely reinforce perceptions of U.S. unresponsiveness, and further alienate those Latin American leaders desirous of maintaining cordial, constructive relations with the United States. Credit terms should probably be commercial and should certainly not be concessional, though such terms are difficult to define precisely in the international arms markets. Taken together, these steps would serve to diminish both the restrictive and promotional elements of past arms transfer policies, and would enable the U.S. government to meet Latin American demands on an internationally competitive basis. While such changes could not lead to any sudden or massive burst of U.S. sales to Latin America, they would certainly prevent arms transfers from remaining a source of political and military friction.

U.S.-LATIN AMERICAN ECONOMIC RELATIONS TO 1980: THE INTERNATIONAL FRAMEWORK AND SOME POSSIBLE NEW APPROACHES
C. Fred Bergsten

The Collapse of the Old Order

The international economic framework of the first postwar generation has clearly dissolved.

The international monetary system is no longer based on fixed exchange rates and the dollar, as ordained by Bretton Woods. The international trading system is no longer characterized by nondiscrimination and a focus on import barriers, as ordained by the GATT. Some developing countries no longer need "foreign aid," and some of the former recipients are themselves becoming important aid donors. Thus both the basic rules and institutional framework of past international economic relations have become largely inoperative.

The old order collapsed because of fundamental changes in its underlying premises. The large and increasing economic interpenetration of national economies, coupled with the increasing role sought by governments in pursuing national economic and social objectives, sharply increased the domestic political importance of international economics. The onset of detente has simultaneously reduced the importance of security issues and the political dependence of other countries on the United States, and hence has lifted the security blanket which in earlier years often stifled economic disagreements. As a result of these two trends, economic issues are rising toward the top of foreign policy agendas everywhere. The relatively depoliticized economic order of the past—dubbed by Richard Cooper a "two-track" system within which economic issues were left to economic officials and a widely accepted set of international rules[1]—thus became increasingly unviable. This seems particularly true for relations between the United States and Latin America, where—aside from Cuba and the Panama Canal—most sources of potential conflict appear to be economic.

At the same time, the United States is no longer the world's dominant economy, and no longer can or should hold an economic umbrella over the rest of the world. Japan and several European countries, particularly West Germany, have become global economic powers. The shift from commodity surpluses to commodity shortages has greatly enhanced the economic and therefore political power of countries throughout the Third World; the oil producers are the most obvious examples, but the same is true for producers of commodities ranging from bauxite to bananas. So the political base of the international economic system has also undergone radical transformation.[2]

The result is a fluid, multipolar world political system with an even more fluid, multipolar world economic order. New options have opened for many countries, particularly those relegated to an inferior position in the first postwar generation. But new constraints on national action also have emerged, particularly for those most powerful in the previous hierarchy. In this new setting, what will be the economic and political bases for international economic relations?

---

1. Richard N. Cooper, "Trade Policy Is Foreign Policy," *Foreign Policy* 9 (Winter 1972–73).
2. For a more detailed analysis see C. Fred Bergsten, *The Future of the International Economic Order: An Agenda for Research* (Lexington, Mass.: D. C. Heath & Co., 1973), esp. pp. 2–8.

The New Bases of International Economic Relations

The most important economic change affecting international relations is the *ascendance of inflation* as the primary economic (and perhaps political) problem in virtually every industrial country.

At least since the Great Depression, unemployment has been the cardinal economic (and often political) problem in most countries. External economic policies have been used to help deal with domestic unemployment. This called for maintaining undervalued exchange rates or at least avoiding their overvaluation, erecting barriers to imports, and subsidizing exports. It meant buyers' markets for most goods, at most times. It led to vicious international economic conflict in the 1930s, as countries sought to export their unemployment to each other. As a result, the postwar international economic order aimed primarily to stop such practices: the IMF sought to avoid competitive exchange-rate depreciations, the GATT sought to bar import restrictions and export subsidies, and the IBRD and other aid arrangements tried to boost purchasing power throughout the world.

Now, however, for the first time in at least 45 years, inflation as well as unemployment is the cardinal economic problem faced by at least the industrial countries. As a result, the objectives of countries' foreign economic policies are being reversed. They now seek to export inflation, rather than unemployment.

This means they want to appreciate, rather than depreciate, their exchange rates—as many countries have sought to do during the last four years. It means that they will unilaterally reduce barriers to imports—as many have been doing. It means they may even place controls over exports, rather than subsidizing them—as many industrialized and developing countries have done in the recent past.[3]

---

3. A worst-case scenario could of course envisage active efforts by countries to export unemployment and inflation simultaneously through the application of export and import controls in different sectors, and even through multiple exchange rates. Such international policies could derive from a globalization of stagflation at high levels of both "stag" and "flation." Such a possibility appears highly dubious at this writing, though some observers have predicted that the explosion of oil prices will in fact trigger just such reactions in a number of countries.

In addition, much of our present inflation cannot be explained by the traditional references to excessive aggregate demand. Nor does it appear to yield much to wage-price controls. It thus appears that supply shortages and bottlenecks, at all stages of the production process, will probably be *the* most important problems for some time to come. Sellers' markets have supplanted buyers' markets for a wide range of both primary and manufactured products.

Because this shift in emphasis is so new, few if any international rules or institutions are prepared to deal with the new kinds of conflict which it may engender. There are no barriers to trade wars of export controls to parallel those of import controls. There are no agreements, even in principle, regarding access to supplies to parallel assurances for access to markets. Inflation has become a global problem but no foundation, even of a rudimentary sort, exists for an international response.

A second focus of international economic arrangements in the years ahead is likely to be *economic security*.

The postwar economic system, created primarily in the United States, was aimed at maximizing efficiency. Its instruments were the freest possible flow of trade and capital movements. Ironically, it was then only the developing countries which fretted over their *dependencia* on outsiders.

Now, however, economic security is challenging efficiency as the primary goal of economic policies throughout the industrial world. The oil crisis has brought this home most clearly.

The quest for economic security is both consistent and inconsistent with the new focus on fighting inflation. It is consistent in that quests for assured new sources of raw materials, for example, will trigger both an increase in their global availability—hence reducing prices—and provide security for those with clear access to them. But it is inconsistent in that some countries may have to accept some of the bilateral oil arrangements negotiated by Japan and several European countries.

A tension between efforts to fight inflation and to promote economic security will thus be an important factor in international economic relations in the years ahead. Indeed, countries will seek to pursue both ends simultaneously.

One major implication of both these economic changes is the *dramatic change in the North-South power relationship*. Since buyers' markets have become sellers' markets, the quest for economic security places a premium on those who have the resources to which secure access is sought. Thus many of the developing countries, including most of Latin America, have suddenly become "have" as well as "have-not" nations.

The transformation is obvious for the commodity producers: e.g., Brazil for soybeans and iron ore, Chile for copper, Peru for fishmeal, Guyana and Jamaica for bauxite, Venezuela and Ecuador for petroleum. But it may also be true for manufactured products, because only the developing countries have the surplus labor available to significantly boost their output without adding further to the spiral of inflation. Hence countries which possess both raw materials and unemployed labor—which is the case for virtually every country in Latin America—may be in a position to achieve major gains in the international economic environment likely to prevail into the relevant future.

Another key development is the *demise of the process of European unification*. The fundamental problem is that there now exists no rationale for European unity which is politically salable within Europe. The old fears of Soviet aggression and Franco-German hostility are virtually gone. Europe is not the right grouping to cope with most international economic issues, which require collaboration with, e.g., raw materials producers or the United States and Japan. Neither "independence from America," nor "saving the Germans from themselves," nor fears of Soviet political aggression ("Finlandization"), which are sometimes offered as new rationales for Europe, are likely to fill the gap.

This development increases the fluidity of the world economic and political scene in two ways. It obviates the development of a European "pole" in world affairs, so it becomes ever harder to envisage the "trilateral" (U.S.-Europe-Japan) management of world affairs envisaged by some. And it confirms that the European countries will be competing among themselves around the world, including Latin America, further expanding the options open to the latter.

These changes in the underlying premises of international economic arrangements include several more familiar trends. Detente is likely to limit any recrudescence of alliance systems dependent on coalition leaders (the U.S. and U.S.S.R.) for security or even survival, yet is unlikely to lead to superpower imposition of "law 'n order" on the rest of the world, as feared by some developing countries. The "new nationalism" is likely to continue to grow, with countries throughout the world increasingly pursuing their own goals. Transnational actors, such as the multinational firms and many others as well, are likely to remain active in international economic affairs and hence generate periodic tensions with nation-states.

The Evolving Economic Order

These fundamental developments have already triggered a number of basic changes in international economic arrangements, and suggest further directions in which the evolution will progress.

International monetary relations are now based on flexible rather than fixed exchange rates for most industrial countries. The new system has worked successfully to eliminate the balance-of-payments disequilibria (especially the U.S. deficits and Japanese surpluses) which fouled the previous system, and have kept markets open and functioning despite the pressures of huge capital flows and the dramatic rise in oil prices. Flexible rates are almost certainly with us for the indefinite future.

This development raises two particular issues for developing countries, such as those in Latin America. First, should they too float? Or should they peg onto a major currency, and if so, which one? Secondly, what role should they play in multilateral surveillance of national intervention in the exchange markets which will be increasingly necessary to assure stability and avoid international conflict?

The monetary side of the system is also evolving rapidly, but its direction and ultimate destination are less clear. The dollar will continue to be the most important single currency for some time to come. But the Deutschemark and, to lesser extents, several other currencies, are financing more international private transactions and rising in importance as international reserve assets. In addition, an increase in the official price of gold now appears inevitable. And most national authorities continue to espouse the Special Drawing Rights of the IMF as the primary reserve asset of the future. So the perennial issue of the financial base for the international economic system—which in the late 1960s had clearly headed toward reliance on SDRs—remains unresolved, and has become further complicated by the resurgence of gold and the growing strength of certain national currencies.

There has been concern that the international monetary system, including the new system of flexible exchange rates, will be severely strained and perhaps even fractured by the money flows triggered by the sharp increase in oil prices. To be sure, individual countries such as Italy and India do now face severe payments problems. The increase in oil prices adds significantly to the inflation problem and the constant threat of production cutbacks intensifies the quest for economic security.

But the oil money has been recycled successfully, at least so far, to those industrial countries which need it to finance their payments deficits. No country has sought to competitively depreciate its exchange rate, partly because of the inflationary consequences of doing so. The Euro-currency markets, which will intermediate most of the reflows, have grown by 50 percent in some recent years and appear able to do so in the future. There are even some signs that the oil producers (particularly Venezuela and Iran) are beginning to recognize their responsibility to channel at least some of their new-found wealth to the poor countries on easy terms. Any projection must be cautious, and major problems certainly exist (particularly for some non-Latin American developing countries) but the results so far and the outlook suggest that no international monetary collapse is likely.

International trade relations seek a new multilateral trade negotiation (MTN) to further liberalize (particularly non-tariff) barriers to imports and new rules to govern commercial relations among nations. Such efforts will probably continue, and—depending on how generalized tariff preferences are implemented—are of particular interest to the developing countries. The new focus on inflation has led many countries to unilaterally liberalize their barriers to imports. It provides protection against resort to new import barriers.

But it also induces countries to apply export controls and

aggressively use their leverage as sellers, especially through the formation of producer-country commodity cartels. Hence a major focus of international trade policy will be access to supplies, which could lead to a spate of new arrangements for specific commodities and new international trade rules. Such a process is already well underway in U.S. trade policy.

International investment issues are also rising in importance, especially in regard to the production of multinational enterprises (MNEs). Their output far exceeds the flow of international trade, yet only a few countries have national policies on the issue and no international rules or institutions exist at all.

It is clear, however, that most host countries—including virtually all those in Latin America—are planning to negotiate terms of entry for the MNEs which will increase benefits to the host countries: more jobs, more exports, more local ownership, more capital inflow and less repatriation of earnings, better technology and more local research and development, and so on. Such arrangements are often quite satisfactory to the MNEs and are unlikely in and of themselves to choke off much investment (except when carried to extremes, as in India and perhaps the Andean Pact) especially as the requirements are often coupled with tax and other incentives to the firms.

But this shift of benefits to host countries may often come at the expense of home countries, particularly the United States, whose *national* interests are not represented in the negotiations between host governments and MNEs. Viewed from one perspective, such negotiations thus represent a new means of transferring resources to developing countries. Viewed from another perspective, however, they can only intensify the already sizable pressures against MNEs in the United States, and threaten the maintenance of a liberal U.S. policy toward outward direct investment.

Indeed, this whole pattern of emulatory national policy to both attract and regulate MNEs, and the likely reactions by the United States and perhaps other home countries, suggest an uneasy parallel with the evolution of trade policies in the interwar period. Countries then sought to manipulate trade to their national advantage and triggered what degenerated into trade warfare when the Great Depression plunged national economies into deep despair. The same kind of trend appears to be developing with regard to national policies toward investment. As the GATT was created to avoid a repeat of interwar experience with national trade policies, international accords in the investment area.

Finally, *foreign aid* arrangements have also undergone dramatic change. The United States is no longer the chief donor, and even the absolute level of its help has declined as the old rationales wane and no new consensus has developed. New donors, both oil producers and other previous recipients (e.g., Brazil, Iran), are becoming increasingly important. Multilateral institutions are now channeling the bulk of the assistance flows. Alternative sources of help—the private capital markets, new "OPECs," the SDR link, the seabeds—have already appeared or have important potential. Several previous recipients no longer need help. Many of those who do, need different kinds. At the same time, a few countries in the "Fourth World" need assistance even more than in the past.

Each of the major components of international economic relations has changed dramatically. We turn now to the implications of the new environment for U.S. interests in Latin America, for Latin America itself, and for relations between them.

The U.S. Economic Interest in Latin America

The sweeping changes in world economic conditions imply a sharp increase in U.S. economic interests in Latin America.

Latin America can make a major contribution to the U.S. battle against inflation, and to the U.S. quest for economic security. It can supply large and increasing quantities of a wide variety of the primary products, both industrial raw materials and some foods, needed by the United States.

Oil is the most obvious. Venezuela is the leading Latin supplier, and has been cutting down its output, hence depriving the United States and raising world prices. But Ecuador, Bolivia, and several other Latin countries will play an increasingly important role in the world oil picture.

Latin American countries play even more important roles in some of the other primary products where shortages, and cartelization à la OPEC,[4] are distinctly possible. Chile and Peru are among the four dominant copper exporters. Guyana, Jamaica and Surinam are key members of the new international Bauxite Association. Venezuela and Brazil are among the leading producers of iron ore. Brazil, with help from Colombia, is holding up the coffee price. Seven Latin countries have just joined to force up U.S. banana prices. Bolivia is the second leading tin producer.

The prices at which Latin American countries make these commodities available, and the security of those supplies, are of major concern to the United States as well as to other industrialized countries. U.S. access to these supplies will importantly affect our international competitive position as well as the performance of our internal economy. Indeed, *securing assured access to Latin American raw materials at reasonable prices should be the primary objective of U.S. economic policy toward Latin America.* Achieving this objective will of course require agreement on what constitutes "reasonable prices" and a *quid pro quo* to Latin America in return for "assured access," to which we now turn.

The anti-inflationary efforts of the United States would also be promoted by increased imports of manufactured goods from Latin America. These imports could probably not be very sizable for many years, in view of the low elasticities of supply in most parts of their manufacturing sectors, but they could contribute at least marginally to checking price rises in the United States.

Increasing U.S. imports of manufactures from Latin America is of course more controversial than increasing U.S. imports of primary products, because at least some of the Latin manufactures would compete with U.S. production and pre-empt U.S. jobs or even create new employment. They would almost certainly be opposed by the AFL-CIO, because the skewed distribution of its membership (which is highly misrepresentative of the overall U.S. labor force)[5] compels it

---

4. See C. Fred Bergsten, "The Threat from the Third World," *Foreign Policy* 11 (Summer 1973) and "The Threat Is Real," *Foreign Policy* 14 (Spring 1974).

5. For example, the share of U.S. textile and shoe workers is four times greater in the AFL-CIO than in the U.S. labor force as a whole, while the share of workers in most

to avoid even gradual shifts in the composition of U.S. production.

As indicated, however, the scope of this risk is limited because even the maximum conceivable increase in Latin sales would be small relative to U.S. consumption in virtually every industry.[6] Nevertheless, an effective and generous U.S. program of trade adjustment assistance, to meet the real social costs which might result and the political opposition which will certainly be raised is a necessary concomitant of any such policy.[7] The costs of such adjustment assistance would undoubtedly be far less than the benefits to the U.S. economy of liberalizing imports of manufactured goods from Latin America.[8]

The U.S. anti-inflationary interest in Latin American commodities and manufactures should not, however, be seen solely in the context of intra-hemispheric trade. Increased global sales by Latin America reduce world prices, with indirect benefits to the United States. For example, increased Venezuelan oil sales to Europe from increased production would place downward pressure on world oil prices and make more Middle East oil available to the United States. At the other extreme, even a U.S. "special deal" which assured it access to Venezuelan oil might not reduce prices if Venezuela concomitantly cut back its sales to Europe and left world supply unchanged. Thus the United States must consider the overall production level of the goods in question,

export-oriented and service-oriented industries is far less. For the details see C. Fred Bergsten, "The Cost of Import Restrictions to American Consumers," American Importers Association, 1972.

6. All studies of the effects of tariff preferences indicate that the maximum additional flow from *all* LDCs under the original, liberal U.S. plan was $200–300 million. The amounts would of course be higher if non-tariff barriers were also eliminated and agricultural products were also covered.

7. For such a program see "Economic Adjustment to Liberal Trade: A New Approach," proposed by the Task Force on Adjustment Assistance of the U.S. Chamber of Commerce, chaired by C. Fred Bergsten, in *Trade Reform*, Hearings before the House Ways and Means Committee on the Trade Reform Act of 1973, Part 3, pp. 895–906.

8. The most detailed estimates of the costs of adjustment assistance for workers likely to be dislocated by imports from all sources ranges from $150–500 million annually. By contrast, conservative estimates of the cost to U.S. inflation of all present trade barriers exceed $10 billion.

and world market developments for *them,* in addition to purely bilateral considerations.

This leads directly to the U.S. interest in foreign investments in Latin America. The best of all worlds from the U.S. standpoint would be one in which the maximum feasible production increases, in primary products and manufactured goods, were assured to the U.S. in whatever quantities it needed, and were developed by U.S. firms. The U.S. would get both the real resources and the balance-of-payments benefits of whatever share of the production profits Latin American governments permitted to leave their countries.

It must be recognized, however, that the profits are the decidedly secondary interest. Multinational firms, far from promoting U.S. consumer interests, may at least tacitly add to the strength of producer-country cartels in some industries. At the extreme, U.S. interests would be better served by foreign (including local Latin) production of the resources than by production by U.S. firms which was limited by local governments and/or sold at least in part to countries other than the United States—which is in fact the traditional practice of most U.S. firms in Latin America.

At the same time, the United States does have a major interest in maximum access to Latin America for U.S. (and foreign-based) multinational firms, because they must still play a major role in expanding primary product and manufactured output for some time to come. This requires that U.S. policies respond to the Latin American goal of reaping a greater share of the benefits brought by the firms, such as increasing the degree of domestic processing of materials and value-added. It also, however, requires policies which recognize the legitimate demands of the firms for a stable and profitable environment in which to operate.

U.S. economic interests in Latin America also encompass the traditional goal of maintaining Latin markets for U.S. exports, to help support the exchange rate of the dollar and U.S. jobs. Latin America remains a less important market for aggregate U.S. exports than Canada, Europe, or Japan, but it is a more important market for U.S. machinery, and some other items than other industrial areas. Nevertheless, it is probably more important in absolute terms than ever before due to the increased wealth and income of many Latin countries, and therefore must remain an important objective of U.S. economic policy.

U.S. interests in Latin American monetary policy are more ambiguous. In the days of dollar-based fixed exchange rates, the U.S.—to the extent that it concerned itself at all with the effect of Latin American monetary policies on the U.S. economy—wanted the Latins to avoid depreciations in order not to raise doubts about the fixed-rate system, which would hurt U.S. trade competitiveness by promoting U.S. direct investment to produce there instead. There was also concern that the capital flows from the United States which were often necessary to avoid Latin depreciation would wind up financing imports from Europe, and hence increase the "dollar overhang" threat to the U.S. gold stock. Indeed, in the middle 1960s the United States sought special Latin investments (mainly from Venezuela and Mexico) in "long-term" U.S. securities to both window-dress the U.S. payments data and reduce the risk of such "pass-throughs."

In the present world of flexible rates, however, these concerns have largely disappeared. Latin devaluations now cheapen the cost of at least their manufactured goods, further enhancing their anti-inflationary benefits for the United States. It should be noted, however, that Latin devaluations probably have little impact on U.S. exports to the region because the devaluations occur vis-a-vis the currencies of our European and Japanese competitors as well as against the dollar.

As noted, however, many Latin American countries are pegging their exchange rates to the dollar rather than floating them freely à la most of the industrial countries. (Even Brazil and others who periodically alter their parities vis-a-vis the dollar maintain a close market link to the dollar at the prevailing parity at all times.) To do so, at some periods they accumulate dollars rather than let their exchange rates rise in value. The United States certainly prefers this, rather than converting the dollars into Deutschemarks or some other national currency which would generate downward pressure on the dollar in the exchange markets and accelerate our domestic inflation.

However, too much dollar accumulation by Latin (or any other) countries would harken back to the earlier dollar standard, whereby countries avoided upvaluing their currencies to such an extent that

U.S. deficits became unacceptably large both at home and abroad. There is some danger that Brazil, in particular, will be "the new Japan" not only in terms of economic strength but in failing to recognize the adverse effects on the world economic system of its nationalistic actions—which is a fair characterization of its continuing mini-devaluations at a time when its reserves are rising sharply and have become the ninth highest in the world.

Extreme action in this area would work only if the United States (and perhaps the other industrial countries) decided to use their external policies wholly to fight inflation, while the Latin American (and perhaps other) developing countries sought to use their external policies wholly to fight unemployment. In that instance, both sides would be happy with an overvalued dollar and undervalued Latin currencies. Such a pattern should not be ruled out, and need not have large trade effects if restricted to the DC-LDC framework, i.e., Japan or Italy did not take advantage of the renewed U.S. permissiveness and did not undervalue vis-a-vis the dollar. But this would be extremely difficult to maintain within proper limits and would raise political problems in any case—from labor in the United States, and from consumers in Latin America.

The Position of Latin America

In facing these U.S. interests, what is the position of Latin America? What are *its* goals? (One cannot, of course, speak heterogeneously of "Latin America," but I do so in this paper in full cognizance of the need to disaggregate carefully in practice.)

First and most important, Latin America's position is incomparably stronger than before for the reasons stressed throughout this paper. In some senses, they are not the "have" nations.

The shift over the past decade is perhaps best demonstrated by the case of coffee. In the early 1960s, Brazil and the other coffee producers literally begged the U.S. and other coffee consumers to create the International Coffee Agreement to keep coffee prices from plummeting. In 1973, the producers let that Agreement expire because they felt that they alone could drive the coffee price higher; cooperation from the consuming countries was no longer needed. So far at least, the producers have been proven right. A key reason is that Brazil, like Saudi Arabia in oil, is now wealthy enough (and, better than Saudi Arabia, economically diversified enough) that it can actually *import* huge amounts of coffee—the whole Salvadorean crop and even much of the Colombian crop this year—to maintain the price umbrella over the world coffee market.

This new economic power of most South American countries reduces the continent's need for traditional foreign aid. It reduces their need to plead for commodity agreements, though, as we will see, it does not necessarily reduce their interest in negotiating such agreements. Indeed, "concessional" help from the United States is no longer important for most Latin countries.

But this by no means signals an end to Latin nations seeking new economic arrangements with the United States. It does signal a change in the focus and form thereof.

A chief Latin goal remains the modernization and diversification of their economies, via industrialization, including increased processing of raw materials. Such evolution could contribute significantly to easing the unemployment which remains of cardinal importance in many Latin countries, and to strengthening their external financial positions. They are therefore much more likely to use the resurgent strength of their commodity positions to achieve these industrialization/modernization goals than they are to regard those goals as no longer necessary.

This is partly because the commodity outlook is always somewhat uncertain. It is possible, though in my view quite unlikely, that the current commodity boom will bust in the near future. But its longer run future is quite uncertain, as higher prices induce conservation of demand and the development of substitutes (e.g., tin for copper and ore-bearing clays for bauxite). Thus the commodity-producing countries in Latin America (and elsewhere) might welcome new kinds of commodity deals in which they would assure access for the consuming countries in return for guaranteed prices for their output. They would be particularly amenable if the consuming countries agreed to relate these prices to the overall terms of trade of the producing countries, both limiting fluctuations and providing steady secular improvement therein.

This kind of arrangement might be possible now particularly because discussions would be initiated by the consuming countries. This extra attraction stems from a second fundamental goal of Latin America today: independence of decision-making, and avoidance of any remnant of *dependencia*.

Another specific policy manifestation of this pervasive sentiment concerns U.S. investment in Latin America. Latin countries will simply insist on a greater share of control over the decisions of the multinational firms, and on getting a greater share of the benefits. The result may sometimes be transfers of jobs and exports to the host country.

At the same time, Latin America's needs for capital and especially technology suggest that it will certainly continue to want foreign investment. But the terms must be right: the investment must be perceived to promote their own goals of industrialization, better balance-of-payments positions, reduced unemployment, technological advance, and the like.

A third manifestation of the new Latin emphasis on "independence within interdependence" relates to any "foreign aid" programs. They will simply have to operate in less politicized forms than in the past, to obviate any semblance of the former donor-client syndrome. This would require significant alteration in the style of bilateral aid, particularly with regard to congressionally-directed limitations. In particular, debt relief provides a possible alternative to conventional aid which would be far superior to it on several counts. And it suggests an increased focus on multilateral aid, and particularly on assistance obtained through, e.g., the SDR link and the use of revenues from exploitation of the seabeds.

The new economic strength of Latin America has led to a dramatic improvement in its bargaining position vis-a-vis the United States. But it has also laid out the continued needs of the Latins for external markets, especially for their manufactured products, and for infusions of capital and technology.

In the newly pluralistic world economy, these needs can be met from a variety of industrial countries. Indeed, one of the elements of Latin America's new strength is its ability to go to different sources—and even play them off against each other—for imports once available only from the United States. Japan and several European countries have concluded that they must fashion their own "resources diplomacy" as centerpieces of their own foreign policies,[9] and hence Latin America is in some senses a new battleground for competition among the industrialized countries.

But there are certain commodities where the Latins do not produce sufficiently to meet their needs, and which are available only from a small number of other countries. Oil fits this category for Brazil, for example. So do foodstuffs and feedgrains, especially wheat, corn and other commodities of which the United States and Canada are the world's primary suppliers. Indeed, food problems—security of supply and price—may loom at least as large in Latin America as raw materials do in the United States. Both the North and South Americans will seek to diversify their sources, but there are obvious possibilities for reciprocal arrangements guaranteeing access to their respective supplies.

A final issue concerning the Latin American economic position is whether it should maintain and/or accelerate its various regional efforts: LAFTA, the Andean Pact, CACM, CARIFTA, and others. It might benefit from an all-out effort toward regional economic unity. It seems more likely, however, that more flexible answers to regional questions are called for. Different groups of similarly placed countries within the region may find it desirable to get together on particular issues, primarily to permit manufacturing industries to serve economies of adequate scale and to strengthen their bargaining positions. Some Latin countries may find it desirable to link with non-Latin countries on particular issues, e.g., Brazil with Korea on textiles and Chile with Zaire on copper. An all-LDC focus may be optimal for some issues, e.g., international monetary reform with or without Latin American caucuses inside the bigger group. Latin America-wide groups, such as

9. E.g., see "The Struggle for the World Product," *Foreign Affairs*, April 1974, by Helmut Schmidt, then Minister of Finance and now Chancellor of the Federal Republic of Germany.

CECLA, may be best on some issue. Hemisphere-wide coordination will prove best on still others, as in the Inter-American Development Bank.

The likelihood of such differentiated responses to specific issues is reinforced by the very real, if largely latent, potential for intra-Latin American conflict. Brazil is now becoming a global economic force, Venezuela is wielder of vast oil and financial wealth, and Mexico and Argentina have hardly abandoned their visions of leadership of the continent. So intra-Latin tension and overt competition can certainly not be ruled out. In addition, the long-standing territorial issues between some Latin countries may well become more heated as considerations of mineral wealth enter the picture. And the reduced profile of the United States lifts the hemispheric security blanket as well.

The lesson is that overlapping and even criss-crossing patterns of association appear most desirable, especially for a region whose newfound strength is not yet adequately reflected in the traditional international institutions.

Two implications emerge for U.S.-Latin American relations in the near future. First, there is no call for a U.S. push for Latin integration like the push of the early and mid-1960s. The breakdown of the drive toward European unity (the implicit model of that period) only adds weight to that conclusion. Second, any push for a comprehensive hemispheric "special relationship" seems to run counter to global interests and options which Latin America, as well as the United States, now enjoys. It would thus have to carry a powerful new rationale, far beyond those advanced in the past, to merit consideration.

Policy Possibilities for the Years Ahead

It is not the function of this paper to lay out detailed policy proposals, but only to suggest several possible directions for action.

First, a reciprocal deal appears highly feasible to encompass the U.S. desire for assured access to key primary products at reasonable prices and to fight its inflation. It would encompass Latin America's desire to increase sales of manufactured products, to reduce unemployment, and to speed and diversify its economic and social modernization. Latin America would guarantee U.S. access to its raw materials, probably through assuring a certain negotiated volume of output "needed by the United States." The United States would probably guarantee a floor price at the same time, so commodity deals arranged on a commodity-by-commodity basis could provide part of the package. Simultaneously, the United States would guarantee Latin America access to the U.S. market for manufactured products through a far more liberal set of tariff preferences than presently proposed, plus—more importantly—a general reduction of tariff and non-tariff barriers which reduced (or eliminated) the high effective tariffs on Latin American processed goods.

Various permutations on this theme might of course be negotiated. The volume-for-price floor commodity deals might be adequate by themselves, although the United States would then probably have to guarantee higher floor prices than if it also made "concessions" on imports of manufactures. In my view, the U.S. interest would be better served by using the opportunity to fight its inflation doubly, by reducing its barriers to the manufactured goods and using the ensuing benefits to Latin America to negotiate lower floor prices for the Latins' primary products.

A critical issue is whether any such arrangement should be couched solely in purely hemispheric terms, in view of the "spheres of influence" implications thereof. The same concept could be applied either by the United States toward all developing countries, or by the industrial countries together toward the developing countries.

There are arguments in favor of both approaches.[10] The hemispheric approach might prove easier to negotiate initially and to manage subsequently, if only because fewer countries are involved. The United States might thus steal a march on its main industrial competitors, since Latin America is clearly the most advanced and resource-rich of

---

10. If the essentially liberal world economic order of today were to break down, regional arrangements to salvage at least some of the benefits of economic interdependence would of course look much more desirable—and perhaps even necessary—even to those, such as most Latin Americans, who would deplore the *dependencia* implications thereof.

the developing regions; any efforts by Europe and Japan to form rival North-South blocs would leave them worse off, except in the highly unlikely circumstance that one of them could line up exclusive access to Middle East oil. A regional initiative in the Western Hemisphere might be the only way to jar Europe sufficiently to get it to back away from its own expanding network of special North-South ties.[11]

But there are also strong arguments for the more global approach. As noted, only increases in *global* output can really give assurance of adequate supply at reasonable prices; a Latin Qaddafi or a thoughtless move by the U.S. Congress could break off any new "special relationship" and leave the United States worse off than before. Deals in most commodities would be hard to work out without the cooperation of non-Latin countries (Malaysia on tin, Australia on bauxite, Zaire on copper). Any U.S. move to form such a regional bloc would (rightly) be regarded by Europe and Japan as an act of economic aggression, and undermine the delicate structure of interdependence as necessary for U.S. firms as a special hemispheric relationship.

From the Latin standpoint, such a deal—though its terms would clearly manifest its new economic strength—might represent a throwback to the days of abject reliance on the United States. Worse, this would occur just at a time when the "new nationalism" rejects such binding ties, thus fueling internal political opposition. Pragmatically, it would undermine Latin America's possibilities for allying with Western Europe and/or Japan against the United States on the numerous issues where it may prove to be in the Latin interest to do so. And it would reduce the opportunity for Latin America to use its new power to affect reform of the global economic order.

There is probably no single answer to whether this array of new arrangements should be pursued bilaterally, hemispherically, or globally. But the most promising approach to achieving the overall

---

11. Some Europeans (notably the French) might, however, welcome such a move as justifying their own approach and undermining the persistent U.S. efforts to interfere with their own "special relationships." For a good, recent study of the whole issue of North-South arrangements, which concludes that special deals are being pursued only by Europe although the potential exists for Japan as well, see Ernest Preeg, *Economic Blocs and U.S. Foreign Policy* (Washington: National Planning Association, 1973).

commodities-for-manufactures exchange might be within the framework of the forthcoming multilateral trade negotiation (MTN). The United States and Latin America already have a number of common interests which they should pursue jointly: e.g., a reduction in agricultural protectionism in Europe, elimination of Europe's preferential deals with the developing states associated with the Common Market, elimination of Europe's continuing import quotas against Japan (which induce the Japanese to focus their export drives excessively on the United States and, increasingly, Latin American markets).

In addition, careful U.S.-Latin coordination to pursue the high-level tradeoff suggested here could dramatically focus the MTN on the most serious international economic issues of the foreseeable future. The United States could seek to develop a joint offer by the industrial countries covering floor prices for particular commodities, liberalized tariff preferences (in terms of both commodity coverage and safeguard provisions), and across-the-board reductions of especially those tariffs and NTBs which limit the manufactured exports of developing countries. The Latin Americans could seek agreement among the commodity producers to guarantee access to their supplies for the consuming countries, for limiting recourse to export controls like the GATT limits on import controls, and to decide what floor (and ceiling?) prices and other industrial-country concessions would be acceptable.

The goal would be a wholly new, cooperative and relatively stable economic relationship between the United States and Latin America, within the framework of a cooperative and stable new relationship between North and South globally. "Regionalism within globalism" would supplement "independence within interdependence" as new themes for U.S.-Latin relations. Institutional innovations would be needed to implement new arrangements.

Trade would be the focus of this approach, since all of the other key aspects of international economic relationships in this post-aid era—investment and monetary relationships—serve largely to generate trade and affect the direction of its flow. These other issues are also important for U.S.-Latin relations in their own right. Therefore:

Second, the United States should gear its policies toward foreign direct investment in Latin America to the clear Latin desire for independence and a fair share of the benefits brought by the MNEs, in return for guarantees of a stable environment for the firms themselves. For example, OPIC might sharply modify its policies to insure investments on the basis of host-country attitudes. The Andean Code need not be fought, though its faithful implementation must be assured. The Hickenlooper and Gonzales Amendments must go. These are only among the more obvious examples; investment relations call for perhaps the most creative new thinking of any of the economic policy issues. Indeed, there may be ways in which the United States could serve its own national interests while meeting legitimate Latin American (and other LDC) interests in "decoupling" the packages of technology, capital, marketing organization, etc., now usually available only through multinational firms.

The direction of foreign assistance policies is clearer. Large amounts of concessional aid are not needed, so style and purpose become much more important. Concessional aid should be pinpointed on the poorest countries, and perhaps provided jointly by the United States and the richer Latin Americans. The form should also be pinpointed; e.g., debt relief may prove superior to new loans, and any needed assistance—perhaps including both U.S. government and IDB guarantees—for Latin access to private capital markets (both in the United States and abroad) might become an important part of the program. The bilateral program must eliminate its bureaucratic strings and political overtones or be jettisoned. The multilateral approach, particularly through the IDB—the institution which Latin America rightly regards as "its own"—should be emphasized. Still better would be steady movement toward developing the SDR link (which, depending on a variety of factors, could provide between a few hundred million and over a billion dollars annually for Latin America) and proceeds from exploitation of the seabeds.

Most of these approaches can only be carried out by the United States in cooperation with other industrial countries, and with other developing countries along with Latin America as beneficiaries. Hence they reinforce the preference for the global as opposed to the hemispheric approach developed in the discussion on trade.

They also highlight the wide array of options available to the

United States and to Latin America. Each has a number of major economic interests in the other: the United States wants assured access to primary products at reasonable prices, more manufactured goods in areas of domestic shortage, markets for its own exports, reasonable treatment for its investments, and cooperative monetary policies. Latin American countries want assurances that their commodity prices do not again collapse, new markets for their manufactures, capital on acceptable terms, technology, assured supplies of food and other needed imports, a greater voice in international decision making and perhaps some concessional aid. At least a few political issues must be considered as well. There are myriad possibilities for specific tradeoffs.

The "special relationship" between the United States and Latin America now needs to be a new kind of special relationship, in which each works together to promote global programs of joint benefit to both. A vision of such expanded and diversified progress together should animate U.S.-Latin American economic relations in the new world economy and polity of the late 1970s and beyond. And since economic issues will almost certainly lie at the heart of overall U.S.-Latin relations for the foreseeable future, the realization of such progress could provide the basis for stability and progress throughout the Western Hemisphere for some time to come.

U.S.-LATIN AMERICAN ECONOMIC RELATIONSHIPS: BILATERAL, REGIONAL OR GLOBAL?

Roger Hansen

The Present International Setting

The international economic framework of the postwar generation has to a considerable degree dissolved, presenting foreign economic policies with an extensive variety of options in a new international economic context. That context is presently characterized by several aspects which defy definitive analysis and make it very difficult to predict major trends over the coming five to ten years.

First, 1973's fourfold increase in the price of petroleum has undermined the usefulness of previous economic projections. While serious efforts are being made in the IBRD, the IMF and within individual governments to determine the domestic and international implications of the price change, little has been learned except that many less developed countries will need increased resource transfers to pay for their petroleum imports (perhaps as much as an additional $10 billion over the years 1974–75). It is not at all clear if and where such financing will come from, even if the $10 billion figure is accurate. Much of it might come from the international capital markets on conventional terms, *provided* that financial intermediation is managed so as to provide continuing access by Third World countries such as Brazil and Mexico to the Eurocurrency markets. Some of it might come from expanded IMF facilities—both the Special Oil facility and a new facility only for less developed countries—*provided* that both are equipped to assist such massive capital transfers more than marginally. Some of it might come from the OPEC nations themselves, *provided* that they undergo a change from the attitude which has characterized most of their efforts thus far. Finally, the developed countries might ensure such capital transfers, *provided* that the United States modifies its present approach which undermines all such efforts in an attempt to keep the pressure on the OPEC countries to lower the price of oil.

In sum, the Commission will have to proceed to policy recommendations with the knowledge that great uncertainty characterizes the implications of the oil crisis for the international economic system in general and its impact on the development prospects for Latin America and all developing areas in particular.

A second difficulty concerns the future of commodity prices, and the fact that approximately eighty percent of Latin America's export earnings represent proceeds from traditional raw material and agricultural commodity sales. Again, there is little if any consensus among the experts. On the one hand, there are those who feel that the world has entered what is now generally referred to as an age of resource scarcity. If so, the price of Latin American raw material exports in general will rise relative to the prices of its imports, and increasingly favorable terms of trade will gradually free the region from those foreign exchange scarcities which prevented more rapid economic growth until the 1970s. The more sophisticated version of this view is based not only upon the presumed scarcity of raw materials, but also upon a changing perception of relative strength on the part of the "South" which will then raise the prices of their raw materials—using cartels or simple patterns of oligopolistic price leadership—even if resources *aren't* all that scarce.

Another school of experts seriously doubts that any watershed has been reached regarding the supply/demand equation for raw materials in general. While there may be exceptions, this group argues, industrial country demand will continue to grow slowly over the next decade, supply will not become a constraint, and therefore conditions favorable to the emergence of cartels, let alone rising prices established by the market mechanism, will not exist. Indeed, many projections for the rest of the 1970s suggest a decline in the present terms of trade for most raw materials, as commodity prices steady or fall, while developed country industrial export prices inflate rapidly. Crucial but uncertain variables in U.S.-Latin American relations and in the development process, therefore, are the evolving North-South terms of trade.

The third major unknown involves the short- and medium-term impact of the changes in petroleum prices on the growth patterns of the developed countries. Even a modest slowing of their growth will have a considerable impact on the export earnings of the less developed countries. And should growth drop below historical rates, the impact on regions like Latin America might be severe. It is the combination of possibilities inherent in all three unknowns cited above that makes any reasonable estimates of the needs of Latin America—needs in this sense defined as *external* contributions to the Latin American growth process, whether in the form of export earnings, borrowing in international capital markets on conventional terms, concessional financing, etc.—so difficult to develop. The present adequate purchasing power of Latin America's exports could increase, remain steady, or sharply decrease. The capacity of Argentina, Brazil and Mexico to cover current account deficits by borrowing in the Eurodollar market may continue indefinitely; it may end rather suddenly. Should the difficulties of one or two OECD countries frighten the international financial community, and should growing numbers of OECD countries move into the Eurodollar market to cover their own huge oil-induced deficits (approximately $40 billion for 1974 alone), the market as a source of funds for even the healthiest of the Latin American economies could disappear just as quickly as it emerged.

Three further unknowns characterize the international economic setting, though they are of lesser, short-term magnitude. *The fourth is symbolized by the suspended state of international monetary negotiations.* For the interim—perhaps several years—the international monetary system, such as it is, will depend on rather fragile "codes of conduct" developed by the Committee of Twenty. The Bretton Woods world of fixed exchange rates is dead; a world of semi-floating exchange rates exists, and emerging codes of conduct among the developed countries seek to avoid beggar-thy-neighbor policies whereby developed countries might be expected to cut back on imports and subsidize exports in order to cover their rapidly expanding oil-related deficits. Whether or not the necessary degree of political will and enlightened self-interest exists to avoid severe financial (and consequently, trade) conflicts is, however, as yet unclear.

The fifth unknown concerns the prospects for major reform in the world's trading system. While the seventh round of GATT negotiations was officially opened in Tokyo in the summer of 1973, that negotiation can and will go nowhere until the President of the United States is given the power to enter into a new series of trade agreements. The bill which would grant him that power, the Trade Reform Act of 1973, is resting quietly in the Senate Finance Committee after passing the House of Representatives last December.

If the bill should become law in anything like its present form, the United States would have a considerable degree of flexibility with which to negotiate the lowering of tariffs, a series of codes on non-tariff barriers, and basic reforms of the GATT itself. Until the bill passes, the Executive Branch has no hope of successfully entering into any such agreements, since all would call for affirmative Congressional endorsement *seriatim.*

The final unknown concerns the future of North-South aid flows in general, and the U.S. aid program in particular. As a percentage of Gross National Product, the official aid flows of the DAC countries have been trending slowly downward for years. For the United States this trend is particularly marked. Given the recent oil price increases and their global income distribution and balance-of-payments implications, the political pressures toward even lesser relative amounts of foreign aid may well be accentuated within the United States and other donor countries.

To these six international economic unknowns might be added a seventh, perhaps more psychological than economic. It is *the degree to which perceived changes in international political and economic power have taken place during the past year or two.* The issue is illustrated best by reference to the "scarcity" problem. The change in developing country psychology may lead raw material products to *act* as if resources were scarce, and their policies of price leadership or cartel arrangements were capable of permanently altering the terms of trade between raw materials and industrial products. If they so act, and if developed countries believe that a "watershed" in raw materials has been reached, then a watershed *will* have been reached regardless of the true nature of the scarcity problem. And this uncertainty regarding a potential shift of economic bargaining strength may prove to be as important a parameter in the international economic picture as any of the others over the next five years. By that time the perception of changing relative power will either have been confirmed by events, or exposed as an inaccurate conclusion overdrawn from one or two "deviant" cases such as oil.

U.S.-Latin American Economic Relations: The View from the South

Turning from the global setting to the more specific details of the U.S.-Latin American economic relationship, Latin America can be seen from two different points of view: first, from the potential impact of the present global uncertainties on Latin American economic development; and second, from the recurring Latin American criticisms of and/or requests for change in U.S. economic policies.

LATIN AMERICA AND THE GLOBAL SETTING

There has been a growing tendency in recent years to consider Latin America as a region which has passed beyond the need for concessional lending. It has been argued that the region's level of economic development (excluding the Caribbean) no longer necessitates access to much by way of grants and soft loans. The region's GNP will surpass $200 billion this year, and the per capita figure will exceed $650.

Such arguments are based on three premises. First, that the *development process* in the region has reached the point where high and rather steady growth rates have been institutionalized—that required levels of savings, investment, infrastructure development, export diversification and other domestic ingredients for sustained economic growth have been attained. *Second,* that Latin America's growth prospects make most countries of the region good risks on the international capital market, thus opening to them new sources of non-concessional finance in the U.S. and the Eurodollar markets. And *third,* that the combination of Latin America's successful efforts at export diversification and the favorable terms of trade for its traditional raw material exports, will assure that foreign debt bottlenecks will not appear in sufficient degree to restrict the present growth process despite the switch from concessional to commercial borrowing.

Regarding the first premise, it does seem indisputable that the institutionalization of the growth process in Latin America—again excluding the Caribbean—is well underway. Evidence for this is reflected in Tables 1 and 2, which summarize both the Latin American growth record and its changing structural components over the past decade.

Further confirmation is provided by Tables 3 and 4, which document the saving and investment patterns of the Latin American countries since the year 1960. Finally, it should be noted with regard to the export diversification issue, that the share of manufactured exports in aggregate Latin American exports rose from 3.1% in 1960 to 9.3% in 1970; this growth took place mostly after 1965.

Nevertheless, several caveats must be entered regarding Latin America's "takeoff" into sustained economic growth. Firstly, as the figures from the accompanying tables suggest, "Latin America" must be disaggregated, and when it is this particular premise loses some of its compellingness. The Caribbean region shares too few economic similarities with the area to be treated in an undifferentiated way. In addition, further distinctions must be made: Bolivia's savings and investment rates are far below the regional average, and its per capita income—$150 in 1973—less than 25% of the Latin American average. The same general picture holds true for Paraguay and Uruguay, the

Table 1. Annual growth rates of the gross domestic product, 1961-72[1]
(percentages)

Country	1961–70	1961–65	1966–70	1970	1971	1972
Argentina	4.2	4.4	4.1	4.4	3.7	3.7
Barbados	4.9	3.9	5.8	7.1	1.5	− 2.4
Bolivia	5.1	3.9	6.3	5.2	3.8	5.1
Brazil	6.0	4.5	7.5	9.5	11.3	10.4
Chile	4.4	5.0	3.9	3.7	8.3	1.6
Colombia	5.2	4.7	5.7	6.7	5.5	7.1
Costa Rica	5.9	4.9	7.0	5.9	7.4	6.4
Dominican Rep.	5.2	2.6	7.8	10.2	9.9	12.5
Ecuador	4.9	4.2	5.7	11.0	7.9	9.9
El Salvador	5.6	6.8	4.4	5.1	4.3	4.4
Guatemala	5.5	5.2	5.8	5.7	5.6	6.5
Haiti	0.8	0.6	1.0	0.7	5.7	5.1
Honduras	4.5	4.1	4.9	3.0	4.3	4.0
Jamaica	5.0	4.7	5.3	9.0	4.5	7.0
Mexico	7.0	7.1	6.9	6.9	3.4	7.5
Nicaragua	7.3	10.2	4.4	5.0	5.5	5.1
Panama	8.0	8.2	7.7	7.0	8.7	7.5
Paraguay	4.8	4.9	4.6	6.1	4.6	5.3
Peru	5.3	6.7	4.0	7.6	5.9	5.8
Trin. and Tobago	3.9	4.4	3.4	2.0	2.5	5.0
Uruguay	1.5	0.8	2.2	5.0	− 0.5	0.0
Venezuela	5.7	7.3	4.1	5.5	4.3	5.5
Latin America	5.5	5.4	5.8	6.8	6.2	6.9

[1] Calculated at 1970 market prices. Local currency figures were converted to dollars at the rates of exchange prevailing in 1970.
Source: IDB, based on official national statistics.

only exception being Uruguay's higher base on per capita income (see Table 5).

Finally, the generally lower level of development of the Central American Common Market countries (indexed by an average per capita GNP of $395 as opposed to the regional average of $635 in 1973, significantly lower than average savings rates, and very limited of export diversification) suggests that the Central American region should also be excepted from most generalizations concerning "Latin America." One might conclude even from this cursory glance that the

Table 2. Structure and growth of the gross domestic product, 1960-72[1]
(percentages)

	Composition		Average annual growth rate			Annual growth rate		
	1960–62	1970–72	1961–70	1961–65	1966–70	1970	1971	1972
Primary sector	23.3	18.2	3.2	3.9	2.5	4.2	3.5	0.5
Agriculture	19.1	14.9	3.1	3.7	2.4	5.0	4.6	0.9
Mining	4.2	3.3	3.7	4.4	3.1	1.0	−1.6	−1.1
Secondary sector	33.2	37.7	6.8	6.1	7.5	8.3	7.5	8.8
Manufacturing	22.2	26.0	7.1	6.5	7.6	7.8	7.8	9.2
Construction	3.6	3.7	5.6	3.0	8.1	8.0	6.9	10.1
Electricity	1.3	2.1	10.9	10.4	11.4	10.8	10.1	6.7
Transportation	6.1	5.9	5.4	5.3	5.5	10.0	5.7	6.8
Tertiary sector	43.3	44.0	5.7	5.6	5.9	6.6	6.6	7.3
Commerce	19.7	19.8	5.5	5.2	5.8	6.4	5.8	7.4
Financial services	7.1	7.7	6.7	6.9	6.4	7.1	6.9	4.6
Other services	9.4	9.4	5.3	5.0	5.6	7.1	7.6	9.7
Government	7.1	7.1	5.9	5.8	5.8	6.0	8.3	6.4
Gross domestic product	100.0	100.0	5.5	5.4	5.8	6.8	6.2	6.9

[1] 1970 market prices.
Source: IDB, based on official country statistics.

Caribbean, the Central American Common Market countries, and Bolivia, Uruguay and Paraguay, should be excluded from most if not all of the economic generalizations and policy prescriptions for Latin America.

Changing oil prices will change the situation of many Latin American countries, but can only enhance the need for policy differentiation. For example, this year's Bolivian oil exports will triple in value; at the same time the oil import bill for Brazil, Uruguay, and Chile will triple. Additional oil import costs to Latin America for 1974—approximately $2.5 billion—will be most harmful to Chile, Uruguay, Central America and many Caribbean countries. Half the increased cost will be paid by Brazil, but her export capacity and her international reserve position will serve to cushion the impact substantially.

Table 3. Gross Investment[a] as a per cent of gross domestic product, 1960, 1969-72, by countries

Country	1960	1969	1970	1971	1972
Argentina	21.6	19.5	20.3	21.2	21.8
Bolivia	15.1	16.1	15.6	15.1	12.0
Brazil	18.4	16.9	17.2	17.4	19.0
Chile	17.4	16.7	17.0	12.6	12.1
Colombia	20.5	20.5	21.5	22.6	20.8
Costa Rica	19.2	26.3	24.3	28.8	27.5
Dominican Republic	11.7	16.8	18.8	19.7	22.1
Ecuador	14.6	17.5	22.1	24.1	21.5
El Salvador	15.4	12.7	13.8	16.7	13.1
Guatemala	10.3	11.4	12.8	14.4	12.9
Haiti	7.4	5.3	5.5	6.1	6.4
Honduras	13.1	19.4	22.0	16.6	16.0
Jamaica	22.0	26.8	25.6	25.3	24.0
Mexico	20.0	20.6	21.7	19.6	20.5
Nicaragua	14.5	18.3	17.2	16.7	16.1
Panama	16.3	23.6	26.4	27.8	30.9
Paraguay	12.4	16.0	14.7	14.6	15.1
Peru	21.6	13.6	12.2	12.7	11.8
Trinidad and Tobago	31.1	20.4	23.7	24.5	23.5
Uruguay	17.6	9.8	9.2	9.5	8.5
Venezuela	20.6	26.0	24.6	24.5	26.6
Latin America[b]	19.4	18.9	19.4	19.0	19.8

[a] Estimated at current prices.

[b] Excludes Barbados.

The second caveat concerns what such statistics obscure. For example, the outstanding Brazilian growth performance skews all of the Latin American aggregate statistics to suggest more strength and flexibility than exists in the Hispanic American economies. If Brazil is not included in the overall regional product, the growth rate for the rest of Latin America has only been 5.4% *per annum* between 1961 and 1970, 4.5% in 1971, and approximately 5.5% in 1972 and 1973 (compared with the figures of 5.5%, 6.2% and 6.6% derived from Table 1).

More importantly, these aggregate growth, savings and investment

figures do not reveal some of the more compelling obstacles to economic development which in many instances are growing rather than receding. Perhaps the two most salient obstacles are the rising rate of unemployment and underemployment, and the lack of any noticeable progress toward more equitable patterns of income distribution.
Rapidly growing manufacturing sectors simply cannot absorb enough of the growing urban work force—increased daily by migrants from the general stagnating rural sectors—to manage the employment

Table 4. Savings' as a per cent of gross domestic product, 1960, 1969-72, by countries

Country	1960	1969	1970	1971	1972
Argentina	20.0	18.7	20.2	20.0	21.0
Bolivia	7.3	10.2	13.2	10.9	7.9
Brazil	16.3	16.0	15.7	14.4	16.0
Chile	12.5	16.0	15.3	9.3	9.1
Colombia	19.5	16.9	17.1	16.4	16.7
Costa Rica	13.5	19.1	15.9	16.3	17.8
Dominican Republic	18.0	9.7	10.5	10.6	17.5
Ecuador	11.8	11.8	13.5	10.7	14.0
El Salvador	10.4	9.3	12.5	12.2	13.6
Guatemala	7.4	9.6	11.4	10.8	10.7
Haiti	9.9	4.8	4.5	2.3	1.4
Honduras	6.8	14.3	12.1	12.9	14.3
Jamaica	16.0	15.8	21.4	12.4	11.4
Mexico	17.7	18.5	18.4	17.3	18.1
Nicaragua	11.6	13.0	11.7	11.5	16.0
Panama	8.1	19.4	20.6	21.2	22.7
Paraguay	8.1	9.2	11.1	10.2	13.0
Peru	21.7	14.2	14.9	12.5	11.0
Trinidad & Tobago	20.3	15.5	13.6	12.2	7.6
Uruguay	11.5	9.2	7.5	6.8	6.6
Venezuela	25.7	24.4	24.4	24.4	26.0
Latin America[b]	17.6	17.2	17.4	16.1	16.9

[a] Estimated at current prices.
[b] Excludes Barbados.
Source: IDB estimates based on official national statistics.

Table 5. Latin America: Per Capita Gross National Product in Constant 1972 Prices (dollar equivalents

	1950	1951	1952	1953	1954	1955	1956	1957	1958	1959	1960
Argentina	738	749	699	723	738	775	762	807	842	773	821
Bolivia									105	101	105
Brazil	224	227	238	237	253	262	262	275	290	296	315
Chile	521	530	549	568	557	539	528	576	584	563	586
Colombia	239	238	244	250	258	260	261	256	253	264	267
Costa Rica											463
Dominican Republic	215	228	248	243	250	258	279	286	295	287	298
Ecuador	203	204	215	217	228	226	226	230	230	233	241
El Salvador											243
Guatemala	220	235	235	236	235	237	253	261	266	273	274
Honduras	201	208	214	221	217	217	218	236	231	236	241
Mexico	397	420	421	428	438	457	467	488	493	496	517
Nicaragua	227	237	265	263	289	293	290	310	300	298	295
Panama	390	375	385	397	393	404	414	446	440	461	481
Paraguay	240	237	229	235	236	245	245	265	264	255	248
Peru	300	324	327	327	351	361	369	364	363	371	395
Uruguay						674	675	672	638	610	625
Venezuela	540	586	610	636	677	707	738	789	819	863	868
Total above countries	348	358	359	365	377	390	393	408	419	415	434
Memorandum Items											
CACM-Total[a]	231	241	251	256	259	262	269	280	280	282	285
LAFTA-Total[b]	357	368	368	373	386	399	403	418	428	425	445

P Preliminary.
[a] Central American Common Market: Costa Rica, El Salvador, Guatemala, Honduras and Nicaragua.

problem. A mixture of four rather obvious domestic policies might alleviate sizable and growing unemployment. One involves efforts to slow some of the world's fastest population growth rates. Excluding the Caribbean, the Latin American population growth rate is presently higher than any other region of the world. Three other policies, whose impact would be felt much more immediately, include a shift in government priorities to development of the traditional rural sector (both to increase food production and provide employment for the rural population); policies of income redistribution which would

961	1962	1963	1964	1965	1966	1967	1968	1969	1970	1971	1972	1973ᴾ
362	835	802	871	938	930	936	964	1,025	1,056	1,076	1,095	1,102
105	109	113	115	117	123	125	133	135	139	141	146	150
338	346	342	343	342	350	357	380	402	426	461	495	536
509	625	644	657	674	701	702	709	719	770	797	795	763
271	276	275	283	284	290	292	299	307	316	324	335	349
455	468	482	461	489	504	528	557	572	589	594	623	653
278	317	334	337	293	320	322	315	344	367	390	426	441
236	240	243	252	251	251	260	256	260	277	290	309	335
244	264	266	282	286	297	303	302	302	302	303	305	307
279	282	302	308	315	321	327	346	353	364	374	387	406
235	236	235	230	240	251	253	267	266	264	267	271	273
522	530	553	596	614	634	649	679	698	722	724	753	787
309	333	355	392	407	403	426	410	432	448	461	463	461
521	550	580	592	614	645	674	699	737	765	809	839	867
257	265	263	268	278	275	285	291	294	303	310	318	327
417	443	448	465	474	487	488	474	470	495	511	525	536
634	610	596	605	604	615	576	577	607	632	621	618	616
873	916	950	1,037	1,062	1,056	1,069	1,089	1,091	1,143	1,144	1,166	1,206
450	456	459	480	492	500	507	525	545	568	586	609	635
287	298	309	316	327	335	344	354	361	368	374	384	393
462	468	469	492	505	512	520	538	558	583	601	625	652

Latin American Free Trade Association: Argentina, Bolivia, Brazil, Chile, Colombia, Ecuador, Mexico, Paraguay, Peru, Uruguay and Venezuela.

increase domestic markets for agricultural and consumer manufactures; and tax and other fiscal reforms to increase Latin America's present savings-investment ratios in order to speed the pace of growth and labor absorption.

All three policies, properly implemented, would ease the problem of increasing unemployment. But all challenge basic domestic interests and pressure groups within Latin American societies, for each involves a shift of resources from the "haves" to the "have-nots" via tax or expenditure policies. Each is, therefore, opposed by a combination of groups at the top of the Latin American socio-economic scale. This opposition, together with the natural impact of industrialization on income distribution in "dual economies," leave Latin America today with a pattern of income inequality *significantly worse* than that of developed countries, centrally planned economies, and even many developing countries of Asia.[1] Given these conditions, the Commission may wish to address itself to the degree to which—if at all—U.S. policies should be targeted to this general set of problems and policies.

To determine whether the process of growth is sufficiently institutionalized to end concessional financing, the following observations seem in order. First, the Caribbean, the five countries of the Central American Common Market, and several South American countries including Bolivia, Paraguay and Uruguay should be excluded from any generalizations. Second, the growth process in the rest of Latin America is still not without its fundamental problems: will growth rates be fast enough, or the changing structure of production rapid enough, to meet the potential demands from growing unemployment, underemployment, and inequitable patterns of income distribution? The authoritarian/corporatist regimes now prevalent in many Latin American countries may, with the help of their *técnico* employees, be able to stabilize the process of continued economic development in the decade ahead. But any such general conclusion is at best a probability, not a certainty.

Those who view Latin America as being "beyond concessional aid" base their argument on the capacity of the region to fill its external resource needs by borrowing on commercial terms in the international capital markets. This may have been accurate prior to the oil crisis, but the real test of its continued accuracy is yet to come. Announced Eurocurrency lendings to non-OPEC developing countries exceeded $2 billion in 1972, and $5 billion in 1973. Recent reports suggest that Latin American borrowing in the Eurocurrency market for the *first half* of 1974 was approximately equal to its borrowings for the entire year of 1973.

---

1. See Economic Commission for Latin America, Income Distribution in Latin America (UN:New York, 1971), pp. 5–6 and *passim.*

Can and will such trends continue? Those with severe doubts note that most of these borrowings took place before the bankers involved considered the medium or long-term creditworthiness of their Third World customers. More important, they fear that as the oil crisis sends the developed countries of the world, especially Europe and Japan, into the same market to cover their huge balance-of-payments deficits, most if not all developing countries will find few commercial lines of credit open to them. The variables—economics, psychological, and political —are immensely complex, permitting a variety of outcomes.

Another aspect of Latin American "access to commercial capital" involves the degree of its export diversification, its supposedly favorable terms of trade on traditional exports, and the resulting view that a growing export capacity (in combination with commercial creditworthiness) has finally carried Latin America beyond the "external resource" bottleneck. Here too, lingering doubts must be expressed. Assume the following (not unreasonable) set of hypotheses: (1) slower than historical growth rates in developed countries as they attempt to cope with the oil price problem, inflation and huge balance-of-payments deficits; (2) consequent falling demand for Latin American raw material exports; and (3) terms-of-trade turning against traditional Latin American exports once again, as after prior booms in the industrialized world.

Should this pattern emerge, Latin America's export boom would tail off at the very moment that the prices of her manufactured imports were growing rapidly, and possibly at the same time that her access to the world's commercial capital markets was being curtailed.

Have Latin American exports in fact diversified enough to withstand such shifts, without being forced to perceptibly slow domestic growth or to find concessional financing to cover another "external resource gap?" Probably not. Firstly, manufactured exports from Latin American countries are still in the range of 10% of total exports, and this includes intra-regional exports. Secondly, three countries alone—Argentina, Brazil and Mexico—produce over 70% of all manufactured exports in the region, and only these three exhibit much diversification within their industrial exports.

The growth rate in the export of Latin American manufactured products has been closer to 20% over the past five or six years, but again the most rapid increases have been registered by the big three. Nevertheless, the growth rates for such middle-tier countries as Venezuela, Chile, Peru and Colombia have also exceeded 15%, indicating that some progress is being made.

What emerges most clearly is the indeterminacy of the present and prospective economic situation. Before the oil price increases and the host of accompanying international uncertainties, "Latin America" seemed like a region moving away from the need for "aid" into the arena of maximum unsubsidized commercial relationships. After the oil price changes, its future is less certain, at least in the short run. Most of the Caribbean and Central America, still closer to the "Fourth World" than the "Third World," have been hit by the oil crisis. So have Chile and Uruguay. And many Latin American countries will be using between 10–25% of their export earnings to cover their additional oil import costs for 1974.

The degree to which "Latin America" (again excluding Central America and the Caribbean) can cope with present international economic uncertainties will depend on four major variables:

1. The degree to which there is a marked slowdown in the economic growth of the developed country economies (which would adversely affect Latin American export prospects);

2. The degree to which developed countries attempt to ease their oil-related balance-of-payments deficits by deliberately cutting back on imports of products which earn foreign exchange for Latin American countries;

3. The degree to which the international financial community—with the crucial support of cooperating governments—is able to manage the financial intermediation problem posed by the oil price rises, in a manner which keeps international financial markets open to borrowings by Latin American countries on terms which do not lead inevitably to severe debt repayment problems; and

4. The degree to which international, regional and in some cases bilateral arrangements improve Latin America's capacity to acquire foreign exchange on reasonable terms during the next 24 months. At

the international level such arrangements will include the two recent initiatives by the IMF to increase its lending capacity to less developed countries in general (the "special facility") and to oil-price balance-of-payments problems in particular (the Special Oil Facility). They may also include joint Fund-IBRD initiatives resulting from efforts to rethink the whole "resource transfer" problem. Finally, they may include new measures in international trade.

Among the steps which could assist the Latin American countries in the trade area would be passage of the U.S. legislation granting generalized tariff preferences to the developing countries and, more importantly, setting the stage for a major trade negotiation in which significant gains might be made by the developing countries in terms of "market access" for their exports. Additional changes of potential benefit to Latin America would certainly include a renewed interest in and acceptance of internationally sanctioned commodity agreements on the part of developed countries.

Regional arrangements can also be of major assistance. Venezuela, with increased earnings on oil of approximately $7 billion in 1974 alone, has already offered $500 million to its Latin American neighbors via the Inter-American Development Bank. Should this be but a first installment, and should ways be found to leverage these contributions in order to increase new sources for lending in Latin America, substantial progress in overcoming some of the problems related to the oil price situation might be developed regionally and in cooperation with the United States.

Regional efforts might include the formation of cartels and/or price leadership arrangements where Latin America controls enough of global production (or develops the capacity to influence extra-regional producers) to retain as much as it can of its recent gains in traditional commodity terms of trade. Needless to say, to the degree that commodity agreements are negotiated at the global level, such regional efforts would eventually become unnecessary.

Finally, some U.S. responsiveness to Latin American demands might also be of marginal-to-major significance, depending upon the *degree* of responsiveness. What are the oft-enunciated Latin American criticisms of U.S. foreign economic policy, and what changes are requested?

LATIN AMERICAN VIEWS OF U.S. ECONOMIC POLICIES: DESIRED
CHANGES

The essence of the U.S.-Latin American economic dialogue from the
Latin American viewpoint consists of the following issues:

1. Far greater access for Latin American exports—manufactured, raw
material, and agricultural—to the U.S. market;

2. U.S. cooperation in support of commodity arrangements which
will raise and stabilize the prices of Latin America's major export
products;

3. U.S. support for increasing the flows of resources—both
concessional and commercial—to Latin American countries;

4. U.S. assistance in Latin American efforts to maximize the gains
and minimize the costs of U.S. foreign direct investment in Latin
America, the minimum form of assistance consisting of a self-denying
ordinance on the use of diplomatic levers (economic or political) to
support U.S. investors in disputes with Latin American governments;
and

5. The closely related request that the U.S. government "cooperate"
in efforts to speed the transfer of technology to Latin America on
cheaper terms than such transfers are now made.

Other analysts would undoubtedly add other issues. I suspect that
U.S.-Latin American relations—at least in the economic arena—will
improve only to the extent that U.S. policy responses to these five
issues provide Latin America with a substantial net gain in a resource
transfer sense, and that even this achievement will not remove the
continuing strains in the "special relationship" in any marked manner.

One final word concerning this agenda. In the eyes of most Latin
Americans, it is *the* agenda for the 1970s and beyond; almost all
non-economic issues are of marginal importance by comparison. Unless
and until several potential intra-Latin American conflicts lead one
country or another to seek U.S. support, or a major shift in the
international political-strategic arena occurs, the major focus of Latin
American governments will be on problems of economic development.

Latin American judgments concerning U.S. interest in and commitment to Latin America and its problems will be made on the basis of
U.S. responses to the five general Latin American requests noted above.

If the response is generous, continuing U.S.-Latin American frictions will be somewhat minimized. If it is less than forthcoming, the "special relationship" will be characterized by a degree of conflict which exceeds that with most other regions of the world as well. The reasons for this are: first, that a lack of U.S. responsiveness at the global policy level will generally intensify the emergent North-South conflict as it involves the United States; and second, that the role of the U.S. market for Latin American manufactured exports and the overwhelming role of U.S. corporations as the major foreign direct investors in Latin America guarantee a far greater potential for conflict than exists elsewhere.

U.S.-Latin American Economic Relations: A View from the North

The view from the North depends upon who is doing the looking. For example, the Department of State, the Department of Commerce, the Department of the Treasury, the U.S. Congress, the AFL-CIO, multinational corporations and the textile industry all see different images, thus creating immeasurable dilemmas for coherent and internally consistent U.S. policy formulation regarding foreign economic policy in general and policies toward Latin America in particular. These dilemmas, with which the Commission must deal as it formulates its own recommendations, can most helpfully be examined in relation to the five sets of Latin American requests for U.S. policy changes outlined in the preceding section. Before proceeding to such an examination, however, a brief statistical picture of U.S.-Latin American economic relations may help set the stage for discussion.

U.S.-LATIN AMERICAN ECONOMIC RELATIONS: BASIC TRENDS

1. Trade: Table 6 presents a highly aggregated view of the trade relations between the two regions. The first point worth noting is that since 1960, both Latin America and the United States have increased their trade with other countries more rapidly than with each other. A

Table 6. Latin American-U.S. Trade in Context of Overall Trade
(percentages)

	L.A. Imports from U.S. Total L.A. Imports	L.A. Exports to U.S. Total L.A. Exports	U.S. Imports from L.A. Total U.S. Imports	U.S. Exports to L.A. Total U.S. Exports
1960	45.2	41.3	21.8	16.7
1965	43.0	33.6	18.4	14.4
1970	41.1	31.2	13.0	13.9
1972	37.1	33.3	11.2	13.8
1973	n.a.	n.a.	12.6	13.1

n.a. Not available.

Source: International Monetary Fund-International Bank for Reconstruction and Development, "Direction of Trade," various issues. Latin America is defined in this table to include the countries of the Caribbean.

second feature is the asymmetrical nature of the trading relationship; the U.S. remains a far more important market to Latin America than vice versa. U.S. exports to Latin America constitute only 13% of total U.S. exports, the figure is slowly diminishing, and by 1973 approximately 52% of the total went to Mexico and Brazil. These two countries aside, Latin America absorbs only 6% of total U.S. exports.

The asymmetry is heightened when one notes that in 1971, the United States absorbed 45% of Latin America's manufactured exports.

To the extent that the world is moving into a period of raw materials shortages (apparent or real), the asymmetry in this area may prove favorable to Latin American efforts to improve their terms of trade with the United States and other industrialized nations. Among the major minerals (in addition to petroleum) that are of strategic importance to the United States, and to Latin America as an exporter, are bauxite and alumina, iron ore, copper, lead, manganese, tin and zinc. Others, like fluorite from Mexico, are of lesser quantitative importance to the region as a whole but of potentially significant bilateral importance.[2]

2. Minerals for which the U.S. relies or may rely significantly on imports and for which one or more Latin American countries are important suppliers includes, in addition to those already mentioned, antimony, barite, bismuth, cadmium, fluorspar, graphite, gypsum, strontium and tungsten.

ROGER HANSEN / 215

Should this lead to a reconsideration of U.S. views on the value of commodity arrangements, Latin America might be in a position to achieve one of the region's major objectives—a substantial resource transfer.

Foreign Direct Investment. The book value of U.S. foreign direct investment in Latin America is presently somewhat in excess of $17 billion. The latest official figures (1972) indicated the following distribution: manufacturing, $5.6 billion, petroleum, $4.3 billion, mining and smelting, $2.1 billion, and other industries, $4.7 billion. For that same year U.S. foreign direct investment in Latin America and the Caribbean constituted two-thirds of all such investment in the less-developed world, and some 17% of the global U.S. foreign direct investment total.

U.S. investment in Latin America accounts for approximately two-thirds of the region's total foreign direct investment. Increasingly it is shifting to the manufacturing sector, where it often controls between 50–100% of ownership in so-called "leading sectors."

Finally, it is interesting to note that U.S. foreign direct investment

Table 7. Latin America: Exports of Manufactured Products
(percentages)

	1967	1968	1969	1970	1971
EEC	8.1	7.3	10.3	11.1	8.6
UK	1.7	1.5	1.9	1.7	1.4
Other Europe	1.9	2.5	1.9	2.3	2.0
Canada	.6	.7	.9	.8	1.1
USA	36.5	42.2	39.8	38.7	44.5
Japan	1.7	1.0	1.2	1.6	1.2
Other Devel.	1.3	.8	.9	.5	.6
Latin America	45.0	41.5	40.6	39.4	37.5
Other Developing	1.1	.9	1.6	2.2	1.7
Centrally Planned Economies	2.1	1.6	.9	1.7	1.4
Total	100.0	100.0	100.0	100.0	100.0

Source: Organization of American States.

Table 8. Principal Latin American Exports: 1968-1973

Product	(in millions of U.S. dollars)					(as percent of total L.A. exports)				
	1968	1970	1971	1972	1973	1968	1970	1971	1972	1973
Petroleum	2126	2539	3037	3091	4521	18	17.4	20.5	18	19.9
Coffee	1609	2053	1786	2091	2844	14	14	12	12	12.5
Copper	971	1132	870	836	1354	8	7.8	6	5	6
Sugar	499	545	625	834	1208	4	3.7	4.2	5	5.3
Meat	297	500	537	856	1045	3	3.4	3.6	5	4.6
Iron Ore	278	493	509	473	638	2	3.4	3.4	2.8	2.8
Cotton	453	435	368	472	597	4	3	2.5	2.8	2.8
Bananas	334	362	370	414	450	3	2.5	2.5	2.4	2
Wheat	139	136	76	116	300	1	.9	.5	.7	1.3
Wool	175	144	119	124	289	1.5	1	.8	.7	1.3
						Top Ten Exports as Percent of Total Latin American Exports				
Total L.A. Exports	11,815	14,570	14,812	17,118	22,689	58.5	57.1	56	54.4	58.5

Source: OAS, IMF, AID

has constituted well over 50% of net U.S. financial flows to Latin America in recent years. As Table 9 demonstrates, during the 1969–71 period, over 60% of such U.S. flows were accounted for by foreign direct investment.

Aid. A word about the trends in U.S. development assistance to Latin America. As indicated in Table 10, bilateral economic aid to Latin America peaked in 1966 and has trended downward since then. Present indications are that the figures for 1974 and 1975 will either confirm that trend or hold steady at a figure near $300 million. While concessional lending has thus decreased substantially over the past eight years, Latin America's access to funds from the Ex-Im Bank, the World Bank Group and the Inter-American Development Bank has increased rapidly. The grant element contained in loans from these three sources has varied, but in general has been much closer to the commercial end of the scale than the long-term, low-interest Alliance for Progress funding. Only loans from the IDB's Fund for Special

Operations have provided Latin America a substantial resource transfer at highly concessional rates.

PRESENT CONSTRAINTS ON U.S. RESPONSIVENESS TO MAJOR LATIN AMERICAN REQUESTS

What are the constraints limiting U.S. responsiveness to the five major Latin American requests for economic policy changes noted at the end of Part II? If the Commission comes to the general conclusion, one held by the author, that very little responsiveness to the five issues raised by Latin America can be expected from the U.S. government over the next 3–5 years, then it would be the height of folly to pretend that a "special relationship" in the positive sense of sharing the burdens of Latin American development exists, or is likely to exist. For the pretense would all too quickly be exposed as yet another phase of U.S. rhetoric, and the consequent frustration and anger in the South which such a recognition would entail could prove very costly to all aspects—economic and non-economic—of U.S. Latin American relationships over the next decade. If the truth of the matter is that a network of domestic constraints severely limits the prospects for U.S responsiveness, then the less said of a "special relationship" the better.

Greater Access to U.S. Markets for Latin American Products. Of all the requests, this one may be the most salient as well as the most unlikely to engender a satisfactory U.S. response. The reason may be summarized very briefly. First, the coalition within the United States

Table 9. Composition of Net Financial Flows to Latin America
(percentage distribution, three-year average)

| | 1969–71 | | |
	DAC	U.S.	DAC minus U.S.
Official development assistance	25.9	32.4	20.18
Other official flows	1.9	0.0	3.56
Private guaranteed export credits	22.0	3.5	38.45
Private direct investment	42.0	60.9	25.16
Other private	8.1	3.1	12.65
Total	100.0	100.0	100.0

Source: OECD.

Table 10. Bilateral and Multilateral Commitments to Latin America
Net Grant Obligations and Loan Authorizations (Gross minus Grant Deobligations and Loan
Cancellations)

PROGRAM	(U.S. Fiscal Years • Millions of Dollars)				
	1961	1962	1963	1964	1965
U.S. OFFICIAL DEVELOPMENT ASSISTANCE:[a]	401.0	947.3	910.3	1,014.3	1,004.3
U.S. BILATERAL ECONOMIC	838.0	1,007.7	971.0	1,180.0	1,148.0
A.I.D.[b]	253.7	478.7	542.0	603.0	523.1
FOOD FOR PEACE (P.L. 480)	145.4	126.4	164.4	286.3	96.3
TRANSFERS TO INTER-AM.DEV.BANK (IDB)					
Subscriptions to IDB/OC funds[c]	–	60.0	60.0	–	–
Callable Capital IDB/OC	–	–	–	–	(205.9)
Contributions to IDB/FSO[c]	–	50.0	–	50.0	250.0
OTHER OFFICIAL DEVELOPMENT ASSISTANCE					
Social Progress Trust Fund—Loans	–	219.9	121.6	38.2	96.2
Peace Corps, Darien Cap, SPTF Grants,					
and Inter-American Highway, etc.	1.9	12.3	22.3	36.8	38.7
OTHER U.S. GOVERNMENT (LOANS)[d]					
Export-Import Bank[e]	437.0	60.4	60.7	165.7	143.7
C.C.C. Export Sales, OPIC, PTA[f]	–	–	–	–	–
INTERNATIONAL ORGANIZATIONS TOTAL	262.7	626.2	373.4	437.7	527.5
World Bank Group Total	160.5	445.8	142.3	266.2	233.7
INND	130.0	408.1	121.0	249.1	205.0
IDA	27.4	30.0	11.3	11.6	18.5
IFC	3.1	7.7	10.0	5.5	10.2
Inter-American Development Bank Tot.	61.3	136.4	183.1	118.2	233.8
Ordinary Capital Fund	33.5	100.7	133.9	109.2	168.9
Fund for Special Operations	27.9	35.8	49.2	9.0	64.8
United Nations Agencies	37.4	38.7	41.5	43.3	51.5
European Economic Community	3.5	5.3	6.5	10.0	8.5
DAC BILATERAL TOTAL[g]	181.7	272.5	332.8	360.8	393.6
To Independent Nations	86.5	156.1	204.6	195.3	231.3
To Dependencies (UK, Fr.Neth.)	95.2	116.4	128.2	165.5	162.3
TOTAL BILATERAL & MULTILATERAL:	1,282.4	1,796.4	1,617.2	1,928.5	1,819.1
(Excluding Transfers to IDB)					

Details may not add to totals due to rounding. ( ) = Non-add.
[a] ODA is official concessional aid for development purposes.
[b] Excludes Alliance for Progress funds used for non-regional programs. Includes capitalized interest.
[c] Transfers include Federal Reserve Letters of Credit in the following amounts for Maintenance of Value (MOV); $4.3 million in FY 1972; $33.3 million and $97.1 million in FY 1973.
[d] Differentiated from Official Development Assistance which is on concessional terms.
[e] FY 1961 through 1968, data refer to loans of five years or more maturity. Excludes participations bought by private banks and other institutions as well as export guarantees and insurance authorized by the bank. Includes U.S. Treasury participations.

1966	1967	1968	1969	1970	1971	1972	1973	13-Year TOTAL
1,091.7	905.3	1,026.0	704.4	863.2	393.0	567.3	841.6	10,669.8
1,219.2	1,335.2	1,325.4	965.4	1,026.4	576.7	1,155.9	1,349.9	14,098.9
638.3	556.9	496.9	290.4	377.7	260.6	324.0	314.4	5,659.7
142.3	62.2	192.6	81.9	159.4	103.5	102.6	88.9	1,752.2
–	–	–	–	–	–	104.3c	33.3c	257.6
(205.9)	(205.9)	(205.9)	(205.9)	(205.9)	(200.0)	(136.8)	(168.4)	(1,740.6)
250.0	250.0	300.0	300.0	300.0	–	–	372.1c	2,122.1
18.2	–	–	–	–	–	–	–	494.2
42.9	36.2	36.5	32.1	26.1	28.9	36.4	32.9	384.0
127.5	429.9	282.6	261.0	163.1	182.2	550.0	426.8	3,290.6
–	–	16.8	–	0.1	1.5	38.6	81.5	138.5
837.8	774.8	833.2	1,035.6	1,467.1	1,428.8	1,583.6	1,600.0	11,788.5
394.6	283.2	393.5	491.0	747.5	745.9	967.1	672.6	5,944.0
364.7	269.7	372.2	451.8	703.0	670.6	915.3	564.8	5,425.3
7.5	2.0	9.1	14.6	11.0	33.6	11.2	46.1	234.0
22.4	11.5	12.2	24.6	33.5	41.7	40.6	61.7	284.7
362.3	437.6	385.4	489.2	668.1	614.5	536.3	864.7	5,090.9
93.2	148.5	113.5	183.1	224.6	238.6	359.0	419.6	2,326.3
269.0	289.1	271.9	306.1	443.6	375.8	177.3	445.1	2,764.6
70.8	47.1	40.0	46.5	42.3	67.9	65.3	55.6	647.9
10.1	6.9	14.3	8.9	9.2	0.5	14.9	7.1	105.7
417.4	407.3	442.7	368.1	453.3	453.3h	504.9	504.9h	5,093.3
211.7	190.1	237.4	169.2	224.3	224.3	190.5	190.5	2,511.8
205.7	217.2	205.3	198.9	229.0	229.0	314.4	314.4	2,581.5
2,224.4	2,267.3	2,301.3	2,069.1	2,646.8	2,458.8	3,140.4	3,049.4	28,601.0

f CCC = Commercial Credit Corporation, OPIC = Overseas Private Investment Corporation, PTA = Private Trade Agreements under Title I of P.L. 480, Food for Peace. Includes $0.1 million for Bi-national Centers, USIS in FY 1973.
g Calendar Year gross disbursements of loans and grants FY 1961–1968 data include concessional and non-concessional, i.e. EXIMBANK, CCC, etc., aid. Data from FY 1969 through FY 1973 include Official Development Assistance only.
h Estimate. FY 1971 to be firm shortly.

which has supported policies of freer trade over the past three decades is moribund. Fearing the increased relative power of the multinationals, disgusted with the misleading promises of a domestic adjustment assistance program, and questioning the normative judgment which places pure economic efficiency above the psychic rewards of steady employment, the U.S. labor movement has moved *en masse* into the protectionist camp. The business community is highly divided, and given the fact that the U.S. is approaching a "service economy" stage of development (at least was until the oil crisis) more and more industrial sectors are, therefore, having trouble competing with products from abroad. Finally, the agricultural sector is split and ambivalent, free trade or protectionist from crop to crop, and increasingly from year to year.

In addition to the slow decay of the necessary Congressional liberal trade majority, the East-West trade investment and technology transfer issue has weakened the free trade cause by equating it to unpopular issues.

Furthermore, the decentralized nature of the U.S. government is most advantageous to those special interest groups wishing to *restrict* rather than *expand* foreign access to U.S. markets. The Agriculture Department, under pressure from tomato growers, blocks access of Mexican tomatoes. The Commerce Department, under orders from a series of Presidents who have made their peace with the textile industry, negotiates internationally sanctioned "orderly marketing schemes" which slow down the importation of products in which most less developed countries have a competitive advantage.

The Treasury Department is beginning to move to enforce the U.S. countervailing duty statute against Latin American export subsidy schemes. Cases involving shoes from Brazil and Argentina, and cut flowers from Colombia, are now under investigation. If duties are imposed, the psychological effect will be enormous. First, it will encourage other U.S. companies to bring action against other Latin American products, most of which now benefit from one or another type (or types) of subsidy. Secondly, since the action is taken by the U.S. *government*, it will obviously appear as an unfriendly act, and a contradiction of all our rhetoric of a new era of "partnership."

The countervailing duty statute has been on the books since 1897. If the Secretary of the Treasury determines that a "bounty or grant" has been received by an imported foreign article, he must order the imposition of a countervailing duty. But the definitional problem is immensely complicated, and Congress has become increasingly exasperated with the Treasury Department for its unwillingness to vigorously enforce the law.

Two recent initiatives threaten to reinvigorate the law, and thus increase the frustration of Latin America with the U.S. government. First, the Senate has threatened to write into the Trade Reform Act of 1973 a clause which will make mandatory a finding by the Secretary of the Treasury within a set period of months after a complaint is filed. In addition, a clause adding judicial review of negative findings will probably be inserted, thus removing the final judgment from the Executive Branch entirely.

Secondly, U.S. companies have decided that they too can overcome the Treasury Department's stalling tactics. In several recent cases they have gone to court seeking writs of mandamus to force the Secretary of the Treasury to take action in accordance with the law. If the courts rule in their favor, one can expect a swift rise in the number of countervailing duty actions facing Latin American exporters.

Even if the Trade Reform Act passes the Congress, there is little in it which provides much increased access to U.S. markets for Latin America. The generalized preference scheme in the bill is so hedged against imports which might "flood the market" from Latin America and other less developed countries that potential impact studies suggest an increase of well under $300 million per year in additional Latin American exports. Admittedly, significant most-favored-nation tariff cuts on certain products would prove more beneficial to Latin America than GSP coverage, in the long run. But opening the developed country markets to manufactured and agricultural products would only come in response to *a comprehensive LDC bargaining strategy which plays on the perceived need for developed country access to the raw materials of the Third World.*

The pessimism which pervades these remarks on "market access" for Latin American products is increased by the fact that "stagflation" may be our major economic problem for some years to come. In a world in which all groups are fighting to hold onto their relative levels of real income and social standing, the pressures on Congress to restrict access to the U.S. market on an increasingly *ad hoc* basis, whenever imports threaten workers or firms, will grow yearly *despite* the fact that lower trade barriers are, in the aggregate, a major weapon in the fight against inflation. As usual, the particular interest in protection vs. the global interest in more goods at lower prices will probably carry the day in the halls of Congress and in the Executive Branch.

Only a major new set of policies—including adjustment assistance, manpower retraining and placement, and a growing degree of industrial planning involving the U.S. government to a much greater extent than before can provide a lasting basis for substantially and rapidly increased access by Latin American and other LDC producers to the U.S. market. Significant adjustment assistance and manpower retraining programs can provide conservative as well as liberal Congressmen with a justification for continued votes for more liberal trade policies. Even organized labor might accept this approach—at least privately—if it believed that the interest of the Executive Branch intended to spread the *costs* as well as the *benefits* of liberal trade, and particularly to provide workers losing jobs in import-impacted industries with adequate adjustment assistance allowances, retraining facilities, and the promise of new employment opportunities.

But the issue of access to the U.S. market goes well beyond labor support or opposition to more liberal trade. If the United States is truly prepared to open its market to the exports of Latin American and other LDC manufacturers, some industries in this country will literally be driven out of business in major product lines. The change must be accompanied by some forethought as to where new U.S. international competitive advantage will lie. The phasing out of some industrial segments should be accompanied by the more-or-less rational develop-ment of other areas where the opportunity exists to benefit from enhanced international comparative advantage.

The first public report of the President's Council on International Economic Policy pointed in this direction. Since the issuance of that report, the rationale for a greatly strengthened adjustment assistance-manpower training program, together with a modest move toward "indicative planning," has become much more compelling. "Operation Independence," the potential for a growing number of resource scarcity situations, and the consequent need to undertake extremely large investment programs which will, over time, substantially alter the structure of the U.S. industrial mix, all support the need for the United States to move toward industrial planning. Such a movement, together with the needed worker assistance programs, can result in a new domestic social contract for a novel era in U.S. economic history.

U.S. Support for Commodity Arrangements. This cluster of issues offers more opportunity for U.S.-Latin American cooperation than any of the other four. The reason is obvious: South America is a resource-rich continent and the United States is the world's greatest consumer of raw materials. In addition, evidence suggests that some of these raw materials will be in increasingly short supply over the next several decades.

Given these circumstances, the U.S. government as well as the private sector appear to be rethinking past resistance to international commodity arrangements. The time is propitious to adopt a much more flexible approach to the subject, and to seek to enter into long-term commodity arrangements in exchange for Latin American and other supplier guarantees concerning access to supplies at "reasonable" prices.

Several issues are worth keeping in mind here. As long as the Latin American countries feel that the short supply situation is permanent, and that their terms of trade will improve, they will be reluctant to enter into commodity arrangements in return for assured access to supply. They may be more interested in trading access to supply for access to markets for their industrial production. And, to the extent that commodity arrangements serve as a proxy for other types of resource transfers, there remains the very serious question of whether or not they are a viable and satisfactory form of transfer. However, to the extent that other transfers are limited and uncertain, this latter question may become rather academic.

U.S. Support for Increasing Flows of Concessional and Commercial Finance to Latin America. Will the United States prove responsive enough to Latin American requests to produce a more cooperative set of North-South relationships within the Western Hemisphere? The evidence suggests that it will not. Indeed, the United States appears to become less responsive with each passing year.

One example is provided by the figures in Table 11. Throughout the latter part of the 1960s and the early 1970s, the amount of U.S. official development assistance has fallen relative to most DAC members. It has also decreased substantially as a percentage of U.S. gross national product. The 1973 figure, not shown, is an estimated 0.24%—another sharp drop which leaves the United States with a worse record than 13 of the other 16 DAC member countries (New Zealand, not included in Table 11, recently joined the DAC).

Behind these figures is a history of Congressional cutting of AID budgets and lengthy delays in fulfilling U.S. pledges on the replenishment of the "soft loan windows" of both the World Bank (the IDA) and the Inter-American Development Bank (the Fund for Special Operations). Congress is now close to two years late in appropriating the final $500 million of a $1 billion pledge to the Fund for Special Operations, and almost as late in the remaining U.S. IDA appropriation. The figures on AID loans to Latin America given in Table 10 confirm that Latin America has not been spared from growing Congressional disillusionment with aid.

Additionally, Executive Branch policies which affect potential resource transfers to Latin America and the Third World in general continue to display a negativism which has come to be characteristic. Among the many examples are little or no support for the IMF's efforts to finance less developed country oil-related balance-of-payments deficits; rhetorical flourishes at the U.N. Special Assembly on raw materials without any positive proposals until the last minute when they were viewed as a maneuver to split the Group of 77; continued refusal to support either a World Bank supplementary finance scheme for the less developed countries or the proposed link between SDR's and development finance, and so on.

Is there any reason to hypothesize that the Congressional attitude will change, and that concessional transfers from the United States to Latin America can be increased? The evidence seems to point in the opposite direction for the region as a whole. First, two other groups of developing countries will be at the head of the concessional lending line. There will be those whose claim is connected to U.S. "security" syndromes. Unless all loopholes in present laws are plugged, the Executive Branch will continue to spend aid money on countries

Table 11. Official Development Assistance Net, in Relation to Gross National Product 1962-1972[1] (percentages)

Countries	1962	1963	1964	1965	1966	1967	1968	1969	1970	1971	1972
Australia	0.43	0.51	0.48	0.53	0.53	0.60	0.57	0.56	0.59	0.53	0.61
Austria	0.03	0.05	0.08	0.11	0.12	0.14	0.14	0.11	0.07	0.07	0.09
Belgium	0.54	0.57	0.46	0.60	0.42	0.45	0.42	0.50	0.46	0.50	0.55
Canada	0.09	0.15	0.17	0.19	0.33	0.32	0.26	0.33	0.42	0.42	0.47
Denmark	0.10	0.11	0.11	0.13	0.19	0.21	0.23	0.38	0.38	0.43	0.45
France	1.27	0.98	0.90	0.76	0.69	0.71	0.67	0.67	0.66	0.66	0.67
Germany	0.45	0.41	0.44	0.40	0.34	0.41	0.41	0.38	0.32	0.34	0.31
Italy	0.18	0.14	0.09	0.10	0.12	0.22	0.19	0.16	0.16	0.18	0.08
Japan	0.14	0.20	0.14	0.27	0.28	0.31	0.25	0.26	0.23	0.23	0.21
Netherlands	0.49	0.26	0.29	0.36	0.45	0.49	0.49	0.50	0.61	0.58	0.67
Norway	0.14	0.17	0.15	0.16	0.18	0.17	0.29	0.30	0.32	0.33	0.41
Portugal	1.26	1.46	1.48	0.59	0.54	0.54	0.54	1.29	0.67	1.42	1.91
Sweden	0.12	0.14	0.18	0.19	0.25	0.25	0.28	0.43	0.38	0.44	0.48
Switzerland	0.05	0.05	0.07	0.09	0.09	0.08	0.14	0.16	0.15	0.12	0.22
United Kingdom	0.52	0.48	0.53	0.47	0.45	0.44	0.40	0.39	0.37	0.41	0.40
United States	0.56	0.59	0.56	0.49	0.44	0.43	0.37	0.33	0.31	0.32	0.29
Total DAC Countries	0.52	0.51	0.48	0.44	0.41	0.42	0.37	0.36	0.34	0.35	0.34

[1] At market prices.

whose support is judged essential for U.S. security reasons. And there will also be those members of the so-called "Fourth World" whose economic plight is so desperate that concessional lending may be the only possible alternative to a realpolitik which would let some states literally starve to death.

Secondly, Latin America for the coming decade is likely to be a region marked by strong authoritarian/corporatist governments, an absence of what most Americans consider basic human rights, increasing arms budgets and potential intra-regional military conflicts, and strong opposition to U.S. special interest groups in the area of oceans policy. To the extent that these governments are stronger than those of the 1960s they will be more willing and able to challenge the U.S. on a broad range of issues, including natural resource policies (which will be easy to characterize as policies aimed at "exporting inflation" to the United States). Each act of Latin American economic self-assertion is likely to produce a "Hickenlooper" or "Gonzales" Amendment of its own. These probable trends do not promise much Congressional support for a "positive" policy toward the Latin American development process.

Additionally, the new foreign aid law expresses a growing Congressional sentiment that aid go to the "forgotten fifty percent" of the population. Given Latin America's extremely inequitable pattern of income distribution and the lack of local government commitment to do much about it, there is some reason to suspect that Congress will regard aid to all of Latin America as "taking from the poor in the rich countries and giving to the rich in the poor countries."

If one adds the conflicts likely to arise over U.S. foreign direct investment in Latin America which will undermine not only U.S. bilateral aid programs, but resource transfers to Latin America via the World Bank and the Inter-American Development Bank as well, the prospects for a strengthened aid program to the region become dim indeed. And finally, foreign investment conflicts may create problems for Latin American borrowing throughout the capital markets of the world.

This picture might change if resource scarcities become acute enough to lead the United States into bilateral deals with individual Latin American countries. In this instance one can be sure that whatever resource transfers required would be made, on the basis of the "aid for security" syndrome, this time the "security" being defined in economic terms. Such policies could probably count on Congressional and public support.

Maximum Latin American Economic Gains from U.S. Multinational Corporations Operating in Latin America; and at a Minimum, an End to "Economic Coercion." To the extent that generalizations are appropriate, it seems valid to hypothesize that Latin America will lead all other developing regions of the world in terms of host country-U.S. foreign direct investment conflict. This follows from (1) the sheer magnitude of U.S. direct investment in Latin America; (2) the growing "defensive" and occasionally "offensive" nationalism of most major governments of the region; (3) a trend toward the employment of Latin American *técnicos* in high places who are suspicious of, if not outright opposed to, foreign direct ownership; (4) the appearance of competition in the form of European and Japanese investors less concerned with majority ownership. These variables seem to be correlated with MNC-host government conflict, and all will be prevalent in Latin America over the coming decade. Add to this list the perceived watershed on the resource scarcity issue and the increasing host government assertiveness, and this picture of potential conflict becomes even more vivid.

It generally takes two to create a quarrel, and if U.S. investors in Latin America were to cut their losses and look for new modes of doing business, perhaps much of the potential for conflict could be dissipated. But the speed with which U.S. corporations will forego the "sanctity of contracts" in favor of a more or less continuous state of bargaining over terms of access to Latin American product and consumer markets is hard to estimate.

Additionally, the U.S. setting involves the Congress and the Executive Branch. With regard to Congress, it is obvious that the "obsolescing bargain" is not yet a coin of the Congressional realm: witness the continued existence of the Hickenlooper and Gonzales Amendments. But the problem is deeper. There is the recurrent theme—sounded in both the Executive and Congressional Branches of our government—that foreign direct investment has a major role to play in the development process, and that U.S. judgment of a country's commitment to development would largely be informed by their attitude toward foreign direct investment. Furthermore, both the

Executive Branch and the Congress have made it quite clear that what is viewed as economic coercion to Latin Americans, e.g., cutting off Latin access to the IDB's Fund for Special Operations or to major debt rollovers, is viewed as sound U.S. policy in instances where the country requesting assistance has expropriated foreign direct investment without making immediate arrangements for adequate compensation.

The only plausible conclusion is that, barring a major reversal of U.S. policy vis-a-vis the freedom of Latin American countries to deal with U.S. investors without governmental and private pressures, little will be accomplished in meeting Latin American wishes regarding multinational corporations. Again, however, one must enter the by now tiresome caveat that if the perceived raw material shortage looms larger, a major reversal is not an impossibility. This is particularly plausible in view of the bad press multinationals have suffered in recent years in various Congressional hearings and as a result of the oil crisis.

The Transfer of Technology. This request generally seems to stand for two distinct but related goals: first, transfer of technology from U.S. firms to their Latin American subsidiaries at cheaper prices; and second, transfer of the *latest* technology together with the capacity to adapt it to the Latin American setting.

Can the U.S. government respond to Latin American wishes in this field with the degree of responsiveness necessary to ease tensions over the issues at stake? I seriously doubt it. Will the U.S. government help Latin Americans to develop guidelines to control the rents now being exacted by U.S. corporations on the transfer of technology to other countries? Will it endorse and support the enforcement of certain limitations in this field in the near future? Will the Congress grant the Executive Branch the powers needed to undertake such cooperation?

With regard to the transfer and operationalization of the latest technology, including changes appropriate to indigenous factors of production, can and will the U.S. government pressure U.S. corporations to meet Latin American specifications? And even if it could—a highly doubtful presumption—should it do so? How would the AFL-CIO judge a U.S. government policy which fostered the export of the most up-to-date U.S. public and private sector technology, and how would it view the foregone U.S. job opportunities at high wage rates implicit in such a policy?

Again we are brought back to the most fundamental issue facing the United States as it begins to cope with growing economic interdependence. The essential goal of the Latin American countries concerning multinational corporations and the transfer of technology is to use the technology, management, skilled manpower, communications and marketing systems to increase Latin America's own employment, production and export base at the lowest possible cost. Even if the U.S. decided that support for such policies were in the "national interest," how could it persuade major sectors of the U.S. population, particularly organized labor, and the Congress? My suspicion is that it couldn't, unless such a policy took into account the domestic welfare implications of an "interdependent" foreign economic policy and distributed the gains and losses from such a policy in a way considered equitable by all major interest groups in this country.

The undertaking would be enormous, and particularly wrenching for many aspects of "the liberal tradition in America." But is there any alternative? A significant move toward some form of indicative planning and other policies seem to be the only options consonant with such an approach. It appears unlikely that a little GSP, a little more "soft loan" money, a few more billions from OPEC and a Venezuelan decision to finance most Latin American oil-related deficits will keep the present system limping along toward a more benign future.

Policy Implications for the United States. What are—or what should be—U.S. goals vis-a-vis Latin America? Does the U.S. perceive any vital security interests in the region? Any vital economic interests? Any "milieu goals" which are particularly salient in a region which, resulting as much from sloppy conceptualization as historical circumstance, is perceived by many to be geographically, historically and culturally "close" to the United States? Anyone who has flown from New York to Buenos Aires will already have begun to suspect the geographical (if not the cultural) affinity argument, but such vapid generalities persist nevertheless. Since my conclusions are in good part conditioned by my own view of the U.S. national interest in Latin America, I will set them forth very briefly.

One prefatory note: I except Mexico and the Caribbean from all my remaining remarks. Regardless of what type of policy one is speaking of, these two areas are in a sense "special": the Caribbean because of its extraordinary economic fragility; and Mexico because of the great degree to which it is already integrated with the U.S. economy and thus—for the present at least—"dependent" upon the United States in a far greater measure than other Latin American States.

For the rest, I see no U.S. security interest in the region at all in a military-strategic sense. Nor do I see any interest based on a democratic political line of argument. Some elements in the United States would be more comfortable living in a world "safe for democracy," but I see no persuasive evidence that this is either very relevant in the present Latin American context or that the United States has the capability to enhance the prospects for democratic government in Latin America or elsewhere in the Third World. Indeed, to the extent that we have intervened in the Third World, the correlation is probably stronger between intervention and emergent authoritarian/dictatorial government than between intervention and emergent democracy.

The issue of U.S. "economic security" interests in Latin America is far more complex to analyze, and far less easy to dismiss. It hinges for the most part on the issue of potential resource scarcity and access to assured supplies of such resources. As Professor W. W. Rostow pointed out recently, mankind has lived through four previous periods in which the resource scarcity problem was of major concern; in each instance a combination of geographical expansion and technological change deflated the fears of the resource pessimists. At the present it is impossible to predict whether or not we are living through another cyclical state of "scarcity" with regard to raw materials, or whether we are actually facing the first stages of a secular trend toward increasing raw material shortages.[3] All that need be said is that the potential problem ought to be given considerable thought, including an examination of how the possibilities of less conflicted U.S.-Latin American relations might contribute to the resolution of problems of resource scarcity.

---

3. See Roger D. Hansen, "The Politics of Scarcity," in *The U.S. and The Developing World: Agenda for Action, 1974.* James W. Howe, ed., published by Praeger Publishers for the Overseas Development Council (New York: 1974).

Beyond the natural resource issue, Latin America does not represent any serious U.S. economic security concerns. It is a dwindling market for U.S. exports as well as for U.S. investment. The latter, to be sure, remains substantial, but the trend is clearly downward. U.S. investment links will probably grow much more rapidly with Europe, Canada, Japan, the Arab countries and even some other Third World areas than they will with Latin America (save Mexico and, for the time being at least, Brazil).

If the *potential* resource scarcity issue is the only serious U.S. national interest concern of the more traditional type, there is also a concern for "a peaceful world order." As the world grows more interdependent, all nations, rich and poor, begin to rub against one another. Can such psychological proximity withstand the pressure for conflict when one-third of the world is very rich while the other two-thirds is, in relative terms, very poor? Does not "a peaceful world order" require continued Western support for the process of economic development in Latin America and elsewhere if we are to avoid a North-South conflict of considerable (even if non-military) magnitude?

From my own perspective, the answer is yes. Therefore, my view of the U.S. national interest regarding Latin America reduces itself to two essentials: develop and pursue policies which sustain the process of Latin American economic development, and within that general framework pay particular attention to measures which will, on balance, increase rather than decrease the global export capacity of Latin American raw materials which *may* prove to be in short supply.

How can the United States best achieve these dual goals? In general, there are four modal approaches.

Policy No. 1—A Policy of Special Relationship. This policy would give primacy to Latin America in the use of U.S. resources to assist in the development process and in the extraction of raw materials. While its ingredients could vary, they would include some if not all of the following:

1. Specialized preferences for Latin American exports to the United States (in other words, an end to the most-favored-nation policy in spirit if not in law, depending upon how such preferences were granted).

2. The targeting of most U.S. foreign aid to the Latin American

republics, leaving it to the European Community and Japan to undertake their own "special relationships" respectively in Africa and Southeast Asia.

3. The development of schemes which guaranteed the republics of Latin America access to U.S. capital markets on conventional terms. The U.S. might, for example, introduce policies whereby some new U.S. development fund guaranteed the interest and principal on Latin American borrowings in U.S. capital markets.

4. A series of long-term contracts on raw materials in which the U.S. promised to buy certain amounts of Latin American products at guaranteed minimum prices in exchange for assured access to such materials.

Policy No. 2—A Policy of Pure Globalism. This policy would *not* seek to favor Latin America in any way. It would treat the issues of development assistance and access to resources on a global basis, and make decisions in a manner in which Latin America was not distinguished from any other area of the world.

Among other ingredients would be the following:

1. A concentration on *global mechanisms* of resource transfer. For example, GSP for all countries without favoritism; sound monetary reform which was most compatible with the needs of all developing countries; a trade negotiation which sought to lower tariffs on products of interest to the great majority of developing countries; aid policies which channeled concessional funds to the most needy and quasi-commercial funds to those countries whose governments seemed the most committed to development *with* gradual income redistribution; and short-term support for the various Bank-Fund and other efforts to finance the "oil deficits" of the less developed countries.

2. No special effort to reach commodity arrangements with the Latin Americans alone, on the assumption that regional arrangements are feasible in the commodity arena and that excessive long-term bilateral contractual arrangements between the U.S. and Latin American countries would simply be replicated by other DC-LDC combinations.

3. An attempt to deal with the raw materials question at the multinational level, prior to or during the course of the (presumably) upcoming GATT-sponsored trade negotiation.

4. An effort to negotiate standardized practices in the use of export subsidy schemes by less developed countries which would be accepted by all developed countries. Such a code, if accepted by Congress, would remove much of the present uncertainty regarding U.S. policy in the countervailing duty area.

5. An effort to negotiate standardized practices for the use of import restraints against the products of developing countries (and developed countries as well) under conditions of "domestic injury." Standardized procedures would be easier to police and would probably benefit the growth of LDC exports of manufacturers.

Policy No. 3—A Policy of Globalism with a Tilt Toward Latin America. This modal policy simply involves following the "globalism" inherent in Policy No. 2, while tilting in the Latin America direction whenever and wherever an opportunity to support a goal desired by Latin America is possible. No good bureaucrat would have any trouble understanding and taking advantage of the nuances of such a policy. Some examples:

1. Be certain that all GSP articles of importance to Latin America are included in the final U.S. list of articles eligible for generalized preferences;

2. Put increasing amounts of U.S. money into the Inter-American Development Bank *relative* to the World Bank and other regional development banks;

3. See that the amount of foreign aid going to Latin America increases relative to other regions of the world;

4. Find reasons to delay if not avoid altogether applications of the Gonzales and Hickenlooper Amendments when Latin American countries are involved;

5. Try to develop common positions as often as possible with the Latin American nations on a broad range of policies from the oceans to the reform of the international monetary system. Each of these policies can be (in some cases, is being) implemented within the context of a presumably "global" approach; no multilateral "rules of the game" are broken even if the spirit of Cordell Hull is somewhat stretched.

Policy No. 4—A Policy of Bilateralism. The entire world is presently sliding into international economic policies which could be characterized as *de facto* bilateralism. It is a world in which many of the shibboleths of the Bretton Woods era of most-favored-nation multilateralism remain, but within and beneath this lofty legal superstructure a series of bilateral deals are being made which may within a few years reduce the concept of multilateralism to an empty phrase. What impact will the $4–5 billion long-term bilateral arrangement between France and Iran have on MEN trade flows, on the negotiating of international rules of access to raw materials, and on "market-oriented" international financial flows? Similarly, what impact on these carefully nurtured multilateral mechanisms will be produced by the U.S.-Saudi Arabian military-economic agreement entered into in June 1974, which has been billed as a model for economic cooperation between the U.S. and the oil-rich Arab countries? In the economic area this agreement calls for the establishment of a Joint Economic Commission and four subcommittees: the first on Saudi Arabian industrialization; the second on manpower and education; the third on technology, research and development; and the fourth on agricultural development.

Agreements of this nature between developed countries and resource-rich developing countries are proliferating rapidly. Some of them may turn out to be compatible with the multilateral international system characteristic of the post-World War II era; many of them may not. *A priori* it is difficult to judge whether or not this trend toward more or less covert types of bilateralism should be a source of pleasure or concern. The arrangements are as yet too novel, and their potential for evoking unrestrained competition to tie up the world's major raw material sources too speculative, to make a firm judgment one way or the other.

In the short term such arrangements may ease fears concerning the financial intermediation problem raised by oil price increases. Furthermore, there has recently been some movement toward cooperation among the OECD countries in the area of energy policies. Finally, such arrangements hold out some possibility of alleviating the developmental problems of the world's least developed countries through rapidly increasing production of low-cost fertilizers, joint OECD-OPEC country concessional resource transfers, and other steps now taking shape.

The less benign potential for competitive scrambles, the dismantling of many of the multilateral rules which have helped to defuse the potential for conflict inherent in international economic competition, and other forces of disintegration which could be brought about by the emergence of a *de facto* bilateral system are too obvious to need spelling out. Whether or not they develop will to a great extent depend upon the degree to which consultation and coordination between the OECD countries accompanies the growth of bilateral arrangements of the Franco-Iranian and U.S.-Saudi Arabian types noted above.

For the sake of symmetry one might list a fifth modal policy approach, a "pure bilateral" approach in which all obeisance to the ghost of Cordell Hull was interred. But in the view of most analysts the costs of that policy would clearly outweigh any gains.

Of the four general approaches among which the United States might choose, which one, or which combination, would seem to maximize the U.S. national interest as defined in this presentation? Let me begin by ruling out general policies No. 1 and No. 4. Regarding the "special relationship" approach, I doubt that Latin America really desires the closer functional linkages with the United States that the successful implementation of such a policy might entail. The diversification of its export markets, access to capital, access to technology and to various forms of foreign direct investment are undoubtedly more preferable to Latin America than an increasing reliance on the United States. Reliance in these areas will only enhance the potential for conflict if and as Latin American *demands* in each of these areas exceeds the U.S. *capacity to respond.*

The probabilities concerning a U.S. response judged to be adequate from the Latin American point of view is the fundamental reason that I would reject any policy which rekindled the myth of a special relationship. Barring those "industrial policy" reforms alluded to, I fear that the promise of a special relationship in the economic realm would be so incapable of implementation that the end product would be deep disillusionment regarding the United States and its motives throughout Latin America.

Without the reforms noted above almost all major Latin American requests from the United States would be rejected: greater market access, technology transfer pressure on the multinationals to export more from Latin America to the United States, and so on. The final blows would be slowing aid contributions and the application of the countervailing duty statute against Latin American manufacturers.

It would take herculean efforts to accomplish within the Executive Branch, the Congress and the relevant interest groups the kinds of reform necessary to put anything positive into the "special relationship" package. Moreover, the obstacles to progress are likely to be greater in a period of inflation than they would be in a period of price stability.

I would also reject Policy No. 4. It seems that the *"de facto* bilateralism" approach is a high-risk policy, even though it is obviously being implemented in any number of ways at the present time. The two major reasons *for* adopting it are (1) the fear of resource scarcity, and (2) the balance-of-payments problems provoked by the oil price rises since late 1973. A third factor supporting it, though generally given less emphasis, is the belief that a host of economic interdependencies between friend and (potential) foe can produce something between livable detente and genuine rapprochement.

To refute point number one, the evidence is not yet in on resource scarcity. Should major shifts in policy, unless they are convincing on other grounds, be made before the fundamental premises of the new policies have been carefully analyzed?

As for point number two, the United States is unlikely to face balance-of-payments emergencies as a result of the oil crisis. Our current account position will deteriorate, but the U.S. will undoubtedly more than cover current account outflows with capital inflows. Admittedly this process cannot go on forever, but the point is whether the U.S. needs to adopt a policy of *de facto* bilateralism *now.* What may be appropriate five years hence is not necessarily appropriate at present. Meanwhile, the United States does have the time and the economic strength to look over all potential policy responses to the oil crisis and other raw material questions carefully, and need not, like France, worry deeply about this year's and next year's fuel bills.

Finally, as for the case that economic entanglement can lead to detente (with Arabs, Soviets, Latin Americans, or anybody else) is a proposition that merits more analysis than approbation. From an international point of view the correlation between economic interchange and peaceful relationships is generally untested and, where tested, often unilluminating or spurious. And from a U.S. domestic point of view, it is unclear what the *general domestic welfare effects* of such foreign packages will be. How will they affect the role of U.S. corporations in American society? How will they affect the relationship between U.S. corporations and the U.S. government? These questions deserve a much closer look before any wholesale adoption of such an approach.

The remaining choice is between general policies two and three—the pure multilateral approach or the multilateral approach with a "tilt" toward Latin America. Of the two, I favor the latter for several reasons.

In the first place, it is too late to be entirely "neutral" with regard to Latin America. The sheer magnitude of U.S. foreign investment in the region and the importance of the United States as a market for Latin American exports have created a "special relationship" in an economic sense that cannot be wished away. It seems clear that many aspects of that relationship carry a strong potential for continued conflict. For this reason alone, a U.S. policy which highlighted a tilt toward Latin America might make some progress toward mutually satisfactory solutions to bilateral and multilateral problems. Such issues as the U.S. GSP list, policy coordination for the upcoming trade negotiation, and joint positions on certain aspects of international monetary reform come immediately to mind.

Secondly, since the late 1800s the foundations have been laid for various forums of U.S.-Latin American cooperation. Regardless of the empty verbiage which has filled those forums, their very existence has created a problem for a policy of absolute neutrality in the international economic policy arena. No matter how well intentioned, given the historical context, a policy of absolute neutrality would inevitably appear negative to Latin Americans. That appearance should not be allowed unless the payoffs elsewhere were considerable.

Thirdly, with specific regard to the raw materials problem, there may well be enough strength in the "economic security" argument to suggest to prudent U.S. statesmen the need to search for a mutually compatible resolution of the "access to resources" question with Latin America. Ideally, this issue should be resolved at the international level. Indeed, it is somewhat difficult to imagine how it can be otherwise resolved in a manner which guarantees increased *global* supplies at prices which give the proper signals to all markets. However, second-best solutions are often the most that can be obtained in international affairs, and in this instance thoughtful consideration should be given to the examination of a contingent second-best approach, especially one which would not preclude eventual globalization of U.S.-Latin American agreements.

Finally, in terms of the goal of "world order," a U.S. tilt toward Latin America within a multilateral framework would serve one further important function. It would involve the United States in a constant and oft-times hostile dialogue with a major area of the developing world. This could serve both parties well. In the first place, it would make it less and less possible for the United States to adopt its increasingly standard position of doctrinaire complacency with regard to the changing positions and desires of the Third World. In the second place, it would remind Latin America that the cost of continued support from the U.S. Congress and other prominent U.S. elites was some movement within Latin America on behalf of the "forgotten fifty percent" in their own countries.

In the long run, the enforced dialogue might prove just as sterile as it has in times past. But that outcome, as long as it was not preceded by promises of a "special relationship" and "a community of interests," would probably be no worse than the absence of any dialogue at all.

The Contributors

C. Fred Bergsten is a Senior Fellow at The Brookings Institution.

Robert G. Cox is presently a Senior Staff Member of the Commission on the Organization of the Government for the Conduct of Foreign Policy. He is on leave from Hennes & Cox Inc., of which he is President.

Jorge I. Dominguez is currently a Research Associate of the Yale Antilles Program. He is on leave from Harvard University where he is an Assistant Professor in the Government Department and a Research Fellow at the Center for International Affairs.

Roger Hansen is a Senior Fellow at the Overseas Development Council.

Stanley Hoffmann is the Chairman of the Center for European Studies at Harvard University.

Riordan Roett is the Director of the Latin American Studies Program at the School of Advanced International Studies, Johns Hopkins University.

David Ronfeldt is an Associate Social Scientist at the Rand Corporation (Santa Monica).

Kalman H. Silvert is Program Advisor for the Social Sciences at The Ford Foundation, and Professor of Politics at New York University.

Index